The Enterprise Resource Planning Decade: Lessons Learned and Issues for the Future

Frédéric Adam
University College Cork, Ireland

David Sammon
University College Cork, Ireland

IDEA GROUP PUBLISHING
Hershey • London • Melbourne • Singapore

Acquisitions Editor:	Mehdi Khosrow-Pour
Senior Managing Editor:	Jan Travers
Managing Editor:	Amanda Appicello
Development Editor:	Michele Rossi
Copy Editor:	Lori Eby
Typesetter:	Jennifer Wetzel
Cover Design:	Lisa Tosheff
Printed at:	Yurchak Printing Inc.

Published in the United States of America by
    Idea Group Publishing (an imprint of Idea Group Inc.)
    701 E. Chocolate Avenue, Suite 200
    Hershey PA 17033
    Tel: 717-533-8845
    Fax: 717-533-8661
    E-mail: cust@idea-group.com
    Web site: http://www.idea-group.com

and in the United Kingdom by
    Idea Group Publishing (an imprint of Idea Group Inc.)
    3 Henrietta Street
    Covent Garden
    London WC2E 8LU
    Tel: 44 20 7240 0856
    Fax: 44 20 7379 3313
    Web site: http://www.eurospan.co.uk

Library of Congress Cataloging-in-Publication Data

Adam, Frédéric.
  The enterprise resource planning decade : lessons learned and issues for the future / Frederic Adam, David Sammon.
     p. cm.
Includes bibliographical references and index.
  ISBN 1-59140-188-7 (h/c) -- ISBN 1-59140-262-X (s/c) -- ISBN 1-59140-189-5 (ebook)
  1. Business logistics--Ireland. 2. Strategic planning--Ireland. 3. Industrial management--Ireland. I. Sammon, David, 1975- II. Title.
  HD38.5.A32 2003
  658.5--dc22
                     2003017923

British Cataloguing in Publication Data
A Cataloguing in Publication record for this book is available from the British Library.

All work contributed to this book is new, previously-unpublished material. The views expressed in this book are those of the authors, but not necessarily of the publisher.

The Enterprise Resource Planning Decade: Lessons Learned and Issues for the Future

Table of Contents

Preface

WHY WE WROTE THIS BOOK

The area of enterprise-wide systems, a recent term used to refer to a broad range of large corporate systems, is now receiving enormous attention from academics and managers from a variety of areas. At its core is the Enterprise Resource Planning (ERP)/Customer Relationship Management (CRM)/ Supply Chain Management (SCM) movement that accounts for most of the latest developments in corporate Information Systems.

As researchers, we have become fascinated by the volume of investment and the amount of managerial and company resources devoted to acquiring and implementing these technologies and systems since the mid-1980s (when these packages were not even called enterprise-wide systems or ERP). As a result, the more we learn about what vendors, systems integrators, consultants, and client organizations are experiencing with ERP, the more we wonder about the rationale for ERP and the managerial validity of how ERP projects are administered.

We are not doubters of the usefulness of ERP, and we are not nonbelievers in the benefits they can yield, but we ask two fundamental questions: (1) is ERP really for everyone, and (2) are organizations, under the guidance of consultants, going about it the right way? Our concerns are tied to one key point that is covered in this book: what happens when generic solutions are applied to the specific problems of an organization? Are there any risks that an organization is led to sacrifice some of the perfectly sound and long-nurtured business processes they are currently using, key elements in their success, in order to force-fit the processes required by the implementation of an

ERP package, with a zero modification objective? Also, could it not be that the difficulties inherent in such a generic approach are compounded by the recourse to an army of consultants already tied to a particular software vendor?

The purchase of corporate information systems has been put forward as an alternative to systems development, but the processes involved in buying ERP packages are removed from the ideal scenario envisaged by the advocates of off-the-shelf (OTS) software purchases. The most striking feature of the process followed by organizations is the absence of proper prior analysis of their needs and the absence of alternatives. Organizations (those we are aware of, at least) are deciding to acquire ERP as a matter of principle, it seems, when not simply instructed to do so by multinational headquarters. No alternatives are considered, little analysis is carried out, no rigorous software selection process is followed, and no negotiation is undertaken in order to decide to what extent the new software is going to replace current business logic or complement it. In one organization we visited, the whole ERP project was stopped when managers realized they just did not know enough to continue with the implementation and awareness-raising seminars were run over a period of several weeks to ensure everyone knew what the ERP software, and the ERP project, entailed. The role played by consultants in ERP projects is not likely to help resolve these problems, as most consultants are already tied into one software vendor and push organizations to go ahead without covering any of the initial steps required for proper preparation in an ERP project.

STRUCTURE OF THE BOOK

This book does not serve as an introduction to ERP. The content does not go into detail in regard to the technical aspects of ERP software. Rather, it concentrates on an investigation of the rationale for ERP by raising key questions that managers should ask themselves prior to considering ERP. Concentration is placed on the process that should be followed in planning to acquire ERP. It concentrates on the impact of ERP on the organization, in particular, on what happens to the core competencies of a firm when it sacrifices most of what it once knew and implements a totally new piece of software covering most, if not all, aspects of its business. Finally, consideration is given to the steps that can be taken to ensure that the ERP package purchased by an organization does not steamroll existing practices, when they are the products of years of learning and just cannot be improved upon. The new target of zero modification in ERP implementation (which was not always a feature of implementation projects in the mid- to late-1990s) makes a lot of sense and reduces the uncertainties involved in applying the ERP rationale to an organization, but that is mostly from a software vendor/system integrator point of view. The interest of the implementing organization and of its managers is clearly the opposite.

These areas are fundamentally important for the future of the ERP market and should be of concern to academic researchers of corporate information systems deployment and of concern to managers who seek to implement ERP and other new frontiers, for example, CRM, SCM, e-business, or ERP III (see Chapter 14).

In this book, we present a collection of chapters written by us or invited from colleagues who share our interest in the ERP movement. Chapter 1 sets the scene and will prove particularly useful to those who are not already familiar with the area of enterprise-wide systems. A number of alternative definitions of ERP are presented, and the reasons why these types of systems have become so important for organizations at this point in time are highlighted.

Chapter 2, written by Bill O'Gorman, retraces the story of ERP to its manufacturing roots and considers the long evolution of MRP/MRPII toward systems that cover the whole firm. Applicable only to manufacturing environments, the birthplace of ERP systems, presented in this chapter is technical knowledge that must be known by researchers and managers who need to understand how ERPs fit in the bigger picture of organizations.

In Chapter 3, a case study of ERP implementation (written in collaboration with Eleanor Doyle) is presented. It is of particular interest, because the project gave rise to the consideration of alternatives and a serious analysis of which product to buy. The case also presents a comprehensive review of the impact of the software from a postimplementation perspective.

In Chapter 4, we consider the weaknesses of the apparent approach to ERP implementation adopted by many firms by comparing it to some of the most famous normative models of decision making put forward since management emerged as a science.

In Chapter 5, our Australian colleagues, Lorraine Staehr, Graeme Shanks and Peter Seddon present a second case study of ERP implementation in which the lack of proper preparation prior to the implementation of the package led to many problems and to the organization not achieving all the benefits it sought. In contrast to our own ideas, they conclude that not enough alignment with the SAP package, rather than too much reliance on it, led to some of the problems.

In Chapter 6, we present a third case study (written in collaboration with David Lawlor), in which concentration is placed on the software selection aspect of the project.

In Chapter 7 (written in collaboration with Peter O'Doherty), we consider whether the concept of ERP is useful to smaller firms as well as to large corporate entities. In particular, we consider whether lower-impact implementations — shorter, cheaper, incremental — are possible, which may make them more acceptable for Small and Medium Enterprises (SMEs).

In Chapter 8 (written in collaboration with Kevin Higgins and Mark Synnoff), we focus on what happens to competitive advantage in an industry where most firms are equipped with ERP and this type of system becomes the *de facto* standard. We put forward key questions that managers must ask themselves before embarking on ERP projects in their firms.

In Chapter 9, Tom Butler and Aidan Pyke illustrates our contention that ERP packages should not be allowed to steamroll existing practices, with a case study of implementation where managers viewed SAP as a means to an end, rather than an end in itself. The research study examines how the organization took tried-and tested organization-specific routines for problem solving, organizational learning, and decision making into account when implementing SAP modules.

In Chapter 10, we put forward a model based on the notion of *organizational prerequisites* that can be used by managers to frame their ERP projects and better prepare in a vendor/consultant independent, methodology-independent, and preimplementation thought process.

In Chapter 11, we put forward a model borrowed from international politics, to illustrate how decision making in relation to ERP implementations in organizations relates more closely to what is termed "nondecision making" than to proper managerial decision making. We also show that ERP projects must be viewed in the context of the interaction between three key actors — the ERP vendor, the ERP consultant, and the implementing organization — if one is to get a full picture of how the ERP market functions.

In the next two chapters, we examine whether the ERP movement brought anything radically new or if it is merely an updated version of previous ideas dating back to the start of Information Technology deployment in organizations. In Chapter 12, the ERP market is studied critically, and it is argued that there is need for stronger influence from the pull side of the market to compensate for the overwhelming push side represented by vendors and consultants. Considered in Chapter 13, written by our Swedish colleagues Sven Carlsson and Jonas Hedman, is the future of ERP and, particularly, the development of enterprise portals.

Finally, in Chapter 14, we conclude with some general ideas on how to progress from here, both from the point of view of people who provide advice about ERP (experts) and from the point of view of people who are considering buying into ERP.

We hope that this collection of chapters will generate much interest and contribute to the development of enterprise-wide systems for the future. We hope to provide true support to organizations and the development of methodologies that are less disruptive to organizational day-to-day business than is the case today. When ERP projects stop being the make-or-break ventures they can be, and when we stop getting these negative reports about failed implementation, the target will have been met, and the ERP market will be less of a jungle than it is today.

Chapter I

Setting the Scene — Defining and Understanding ERP Systems

David Sammon
University College Cork, Ireland

Frédéric Adam
University College Cork, Ireland

ABSTRACT

This introduction chapter briefly retraces the emergence of the concept of enterprise-wide system and provides a complete overview of the definitions that have been proposed for Enterprise Resource Planning (ERP) systems. It then presents the commonly accepted rationale for ERP including the much publicised benefits that organisations can expect from them. Following this, an overview of the ERP market and, in particular, of its leading player SAP is proposed, leading to a conclusion that sets the scene for the other chapters in this book.

INTRODUCTION

In 1996, FoxMeyer Drug, a $5 billion drug distributor, declared bankruptcy after failing to implement an ERP system over a three-year period.

FoxMeyer sued SAP, the world's leading supplier of ERP software, for $500 million, stating that its system was a *"significant factor"* that brought about the company's financial ruin (this despite the fact that FoxMeyer only spent $30 million dollars on the ERP project) (Davenport, 1998). Mobil Europe invested many millions of dollars in an ERP system only to abandon it as a result of objections by its merging partner (Davenport, 1998). Unisource Worldwide Inc. wrote off $168 million in costs when it abandoned its pan-American implementation of SAP software (Bingi et al., 1999). Dell Computers, after months of delay and cost overruns, abandoned their ERP project, because they found that the new system was not appropriate for its decentralized management model (Stefanou, 2000). Hershey Foods Corporation, Whirlpool, Dow Chemical, Boeing, Apple Computers, and Applied Materials all experienced disasters of varying proportions as a result of ERP implementation projects.

Yet, the ERP software market is one of the fastest-growing markets in the software industry, with long-term growth rates of 36% to 40%, with some estimates putting the eventual size of the market by the year 2010 at $1 trillion (Bingi et al., 1999). Since these estimates have been put forward, the ERP market has slowed, but the overall growth of the enterprise-wide application market is still strong, thanks to a number of additional segments, such as Customer Relationship Management (CRM) and Supply Chain Management (SCM).

THE EMERGENCE OF ENTERPRISE RESOURCE PLANNING

The historical origin of ERP is in inventory management and control software packages that dictated system design during the 1960s (Seo, 1999; Kalakota & Robinson, 2001). In the 1970s, we saw the emergence of Material Requirements Planning (MRP) and Distribution Resource Planning (DRP), which focused on automating all aspects of production master scheduling and centralized inventory planning, respectively (Seo, 1999; Kalakota & Robinson, 2001). During the 1980s, the misnamed MRPII (Manufacturing Resource Planning) systems emerged to extend MRP's traditional focus on production processes into other business functions, including order processing, manufacturing, and distribution (Seo, 1999; Kalakota & Robinson, 2001). In the early 1990s, MRPII was further extended to cover areas of engineering, finance, human resources, project management, etc. (Seo, 1999). MRPII is a misnomer, as it provided automated solutions to a wide range of business processes, not just those found within a company's manufacturing and distribution functions (Kalakota & Robinson, 2001), in other words, the complete "gamut" of activities within a business enterprise (Seo, 1999). However, although MRPII systems overcame some of the drawbacks of MRP systems by applying Finite Capacity Scheduling and Manufacturing Execution Systems, in the context of today's modern business environment, MRPII systems have become less relevant because of the following reasons:

1.   Manufacturing is moving away from a *"make to stock"* situation and toward a *"make to order"* ethos, where customization is replacing standardization. This has led to a far more complex planning process.

2.   Quality and cost are only minimum requirements for organizations wishing to compete in the marketplace. Competition moved to a basis of aggressive delivery, drastically reduced lead times, flexibility, and greater integration with suppliers and customers with greater levels of product differentiation.

As a result, MRPII was renamed ERP (Seo, 1999; Kalakota & Robinson, 2001).

An ERP system differs from the MRPII system, not only in system requirements, but also in technical requirements, as it addresses technology aspects, such as graphical user interface, relational database, use of fourth-generation language, and computer-aided software engineering tools in development, client/server architecture, and open-systems portability (Russell & Taylor, 1998; Seo, 1999; Watson & Schneider, 1999). Also, while "MRP II has traditionally focused on the planning and scheduling of *internal* resources, ERP strives to plan and schedule *supplier* resources as well, based on the dynamic *customer* demands and schedules" (Chen, 2001). This brief evolutionary definition of ERP is depicted in Figure 1 and is further discussed in Chapter 2, in which the engineering background of the ERP movement is retraced.

Kalakota and Robinson (2001) position ERP as the second phase in the "technology" and "enterprises internal and external constituencies" integration process, as illustrated in Figure 1. According to Kalakota and Robinson (2001), *Wave 1* of the evolution of ERP addresses the emergence of Manufacturing Integration (MRP), while *Wave 2* relates to Enterprise Integration (ERP). The combined impact of "key business drivers" (replacing legacy

Figure 1. Evolution of ERP Systems

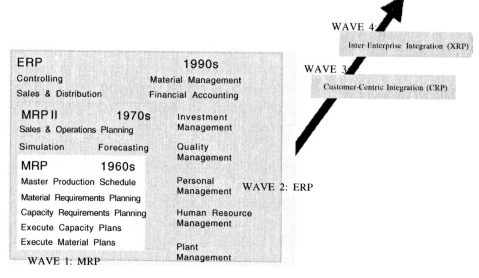

Adapted from Watson and Schneider (1999) and Kalakota and Robinson (2001)

systems, gaining greater control, managing globalization, handling regulatory change, and improving integration of functions across the enterprise) forced the "structural migration" from MRP to ERP (Kalakota & Robinson, 2001). Another significant factor in the second wave of ERP development was Y2K preparation, which was often cited as the major reason for ERP adoption (Kalakota & Robinson, 2001; Themistocleous et al., 2001).

ENTERPRISE RESOURCE PLANNING (ERP) DEFINED

Although there is no agreed upon definition for ERP systems, their characteristics position these systems as integrated, all-encompassing (Markus & Tanis, 2000), complex megapackages (Gable et al., 1997) designed to support the key functional areas of an organization. The American Production and Inventory Control Society (APICS) defines ERP as "an accounting-oriented information system for identifying and planning the enterprise-wide resources needed to take, make, ship, and account for customer orders" (Watson & Schneider, 1999). Therefore, by definition, ERP is an operational-level system. Documented in Table 1 are ERP descriptions extracted from publications dating from 1999-2001. These definitions indicate that an ERP

Table 1. ERP Descriptions

ERP Description	Reference
An ERP system can be thought of as a company-wide Information System that tightly integrates all aspects of a business. It promises one database, one application, and a unified interface across the entire enterprise.	Bingi et al., 1999, p. 8
ERP systems are highly integrated enterprise-wide standard Information Systems (software packages) that automate core corporate activities (business processes) such as finance, human resources, manufacturing, and supply and distribution.	Holland et al., 1999a, p. 289 ; Holland et al., 1999b, p. 273
ERP is an integrated package of software applications designed to automate and integrate a company's business processes throughout its entire supply chain and to provide immediate access to business information. ERP systems can be thought of as wide-ranging, general-purpose management information systems (MIS) for business.	Maher, 1999, p. 36
ERP systems, a form of Enterprise-Wide Information System (EWIS), represent sets of business applications that allow for an organization-wide management of operations. ERP systems are seen as optimization and integration tools of business processes across the supply chain (within and beyond organizational boundaries) implemented through modern information management systems.	Al-Mashari, 2000, p. 3
ERP is known as a large-scale, cross-functionally integrated, packaged system.	Brown et al., 2000, p. 1029
ERP systems are software packages that integrate information across the entire organization. This integration removes inconsistencies and enables the organization to attain consolidated reports.	Shakir, 2000, p. 1033
ERP is an integrated comprehensive Enterprise-Wide Information System.	Milford & Stewart, 2000, p. 951
ERP is a comprehensive Information Technology package built on the promise that all critical information should be totally integrated in a single information database.	Wood & Caldas, 2001, p. 387
ERP links all areas of a company with external suppliers and customers into a tightly integrated system with shared data and visibility.	Chen, 2001, p. 374;
ERP systems are designed to solve the problem of the fragmentation of information over many legacy systems in large business organizations.	Chen, 2001, p. 379
ERP systems are comprehensive, fully integrated software packages that provide automated support for most of the standard business processes within organizations.	Shanks et al., 2000, p. 537
An ERP system is a packaged business software system that enables a company to manage the efficient and effective use of resources (materials, human resources, finance, etc.) by providing a total, integrated solution for the organization's information-processing needs. It supports a process-oriented view of the business as well as business processes standardized across the enterprise.	Nah et al., 2001, p. 285
ERP systems allow a company to share common data and practices across the enterprise and produce and access information in a real-time environment. These systems are designed to solve the fragmentation of information in large business organizations and to integrate information flow within a company.	Themistocleous et al., 2001, p. 195
ERP plays a critical role in improving or reengineering outdated infrastructures, gaining tighter control over internal operations, and driving down costs.	Turban et al., 2001, p. 303
ERP consists of massive computer applications that allow a business to manage all of its operations (finance, requirements planning, human resources, and order fulfillment) on the basis of a single, integrated set of corporate data.	James & Wolf, 2000
ERP systems are large and complex integrated software packages that support standard business activities.	Oliver & Romm, 2000, p. 1039

system is a generic term for an integrated enterprise-wide standard information system (Watson & Schneider, 1999) that impounds deep knowledge of business practices accumulated from vendor implementations throughout organizations (Shang & Seddon, 2000).

ERP can be further defined as a strategic business solution that integrates all business functions, including manufacturing, finance, and distribution (Watson & Schneider, 1999). ERP systems are also being referred to as "enterprise systems" (Davenport, 1998; Chen, 2001) and "enterprise-wide Information Systems" (Al-Mashari, 2000; Milford & Stewart, 2000). They are customized, packaged software-based systems that handle the majority of an enterprise's information systems requirements (Watson & Schneider, 1999). They provide a software architecture that facilitates the flow of information among all functions within an enterprise (Watson & Schneider, 1999). As a result, ERP systems are traditionally thought of as transaction-oriented processing systems (Davenport, 1998; Chen, 2001) or transactional backbones (Kalakota & Robinson, 2001), however, they are continually redefined based on the growing needs of organizations (Davenport, 1998).

These various definitions point to ERP systems as being enterprise-wide information systems that accommodate many features of an organization's business processes. They are highly complex, integrated systems that require careful consideration before selection, implementation, and use. Neglect of any of these areas can lead a company down the path worn by FoxMeyer, Unisource Worldwide Inc., etc.

AN OVERVIEW AND RATIONALE FOR ERP SYSTEMS

ERP systems use a modular structure (i.e., multimodule) to support a broad spectrum of key operational areas of the organization. According to Kalakota and Robinson (2001), the multiple *core* applications comprising an ERP system (a standard ERP framework) are "themselves built from smaller software modules that perform specific business processes within a given functional area. For example, a manufacturing application normally includes modules that permit sales and inventory tracking, forecasting raw-material requirements, and planning plant maintenance" (p. 243). Typically, an ERP system is integrated across the enterprise with a common, relational database, storing data on every function (Watson & Schneider, 1999). They are widely acknowledged as having the potential to radically change existing businesses by bringing improvements in efficiency, effectiveness, and the implementation of optimized business processes (Rowe, 1999). One of the key reasons why managers have sought to proceed with difficult ERP projects is to end the fragmentation of current systems, to allow a process of standardization, to give more visibility on data across the entire corporation, and, in some cases, to obtain competitive advantage (Sammon & Adam, 2000). A seamless integration is essential to provide visibility and consistency across the enterprise.

ERP, in its embryonic stages, catered specifically for manufacturing and production systems, while providing weak support in *"less data-intensive"* areas, such as supply chain planning, customer management, marketing, and sales (Chen, 2001). However, enterprise systems expanded to include *"back-office"* functions (such as operations, logistics, finance, and human resources) and "nontransaction-based systems" (Davenport, 1998) or *"front-office"* functions (such as sales, marketing, and customer service), as integral components of ERP systems (Davenport, 1998; Chen, 2001). These inclusions result from the emergence of Supply Chain Optimization (SCO) (Chen, 2001), or SCM (Turban et al., 2001) and CRM strategies and systems (Chen, 2001), as illustrated in Figure 2. Turban et al. (2001) referred to this "beyond the corporate walls' integration" as *extreme integration* (p. 304). Turban et al. (2001) further commented that in this approach to integration, "SCM can be viewed as the brain and ERP as the strong body" (p. 305).

"While the names and numbers of modules in an ERP system provided by various software vendors may differ, a typical system integrates all these functions by allowing its modules to share and transfer information freely and centralizing all information in a single database accessible by all modules" (Chen, 2001). Provided in Figure 3 is an overview of an ERP system.

Figure 2. ERP Extended

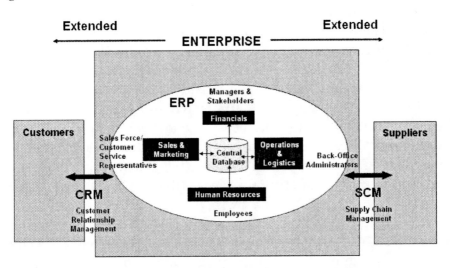

Adapted from Davenport (1998) and Chen (2001)

Figure 3. Module Overview of an ERP System

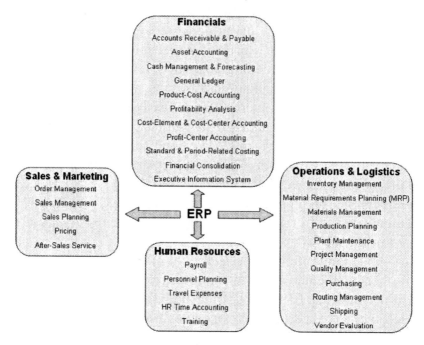

Adapted from Davenport (1998) and Chen (2001)

ERP packages force an organization to implement a proven set of business processes, which means that there is no need for the organization to reinvent the wheel, because ERP packages encapsulate reusable "best practice" business processes. As state-of-the-art technologies and processes move forward, purchasers of packaged software move with them (Weston, 1998; Krumbholz, 2001; Stefanou, 2000). ERP packages give the foundation to the business, and thus, management can concentrate on *"grabbing market share"* (Weston, 1998). Kalakota and Robinson (1999) stressed that the popularity of ERP systems stemmed from the fact that they appear to solve the challenges posed by portfolios of "disconnected, uncoordinated applications that have outlived their usefulness." Holland et al. (1999) agreed, stating that one of the major reasons for the shift toward ERP packages is the need to deal with legacy systems.

These legacy systems provide one of the biggest drags on business productivity and performance, because maintaining many different computer systems leads to enormous costs. These include direct costs, such as rationalization, redundancy, rekeying, reformatting, updating, debugging, deleting, etc., and, more importantly, indirect costs, such as a company's purchasing and sales system that cannot communicate with its production/scheduling systems, so that both its manufacturing productivity and customer service suffer. Management may be left to make vital decisions based on information from incompatible systems, thereby relying on instinct rather than on sound business rationale.

MacVittie (2001) identified three goals behind the implementation of an ERP system:

1. **Integration of financial data:** When managers depend on their function's or unit's perspective of financial data, conflicting interpretations will arise (e.g., Finance will have one set of sales figures, while Marketing will have another). Using an ERP system provides a single version of sales.

2. **Standardization of manufacturing processes:** A manufacturing company that has grown through acquisitions is likely to find that different units use different methods to build the same product. Standardizing processes and using an integrated computer system can save time, increase productivity, and reduce head count. It may also enable collaborating and scheduling production across different units and sites (as in the Vandelay case; Harvard Business School, 1997).

3. **Standardization of human resource information:** This is especially useful in a multisite company. A unified method for tracking employee time and communicating benefits is extremely beneficial, because it promotes a sense of fairness among the workforce as well as streamlines the company as a whole.

BENEFITS OF ERP

Clearly, an ERP system, as defined earlier, and one that is properly implemented, can achieve unprecedented benefits for business computing (Watson & Schneider, 1999). However, some companies have difficulty in identifying any measurable benefits or business process improvements (James & Wolf, 2000; Donovan, 2001). In a recent product brochure titled "Optimize Your ERP Investment" by Cap Gemini Ernst & Young (CGEY), promoting their E³ solution, CGEY revealed the following:

> *...most companies have high expectations of their ERP implementations but some of these fail to deliver on all the*

Figure 4. Myth and Reality of ERPBenefit Realization

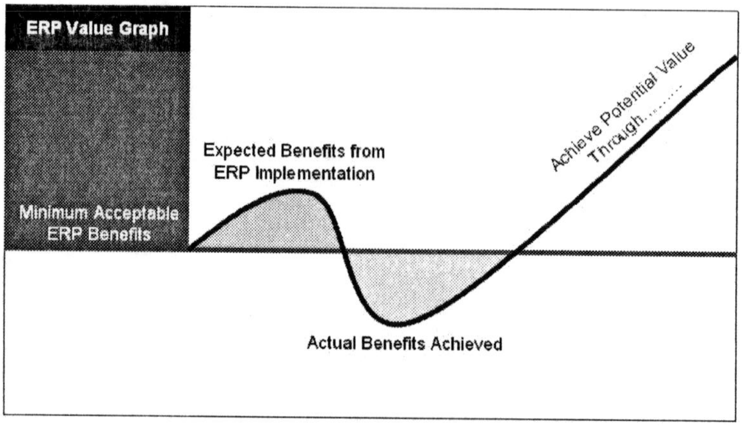

Adapted from Cap Gemini Ernst & Young documentation

benefits that were promised. In fact, these ERP implementations experience high dissatisfaction levels, which is evidenced by many operational glitches and limitations.

Furthermore, they state that:

"in effect, the ERP implementation gives you sight of business potential — but may not deliver much of the expected value."

As a result, they propose that:

"E³ can help you detect and correct ERP-related lost value in your business and deliver those benefits you expected in the first place."

This is illustrated in Figure 4.

Rutherford (2001) observed that only around 10% to 15% of ERP implementations deliver the anticipated benefits. According to James and Wolf (2000), companies that *were* able to identify benefits thought they could have been realized without the implemented ERP system. As stated in James and Wolf (2000): "80 percent of the benefit that we get from our ERP system comes from changes, such as inventory optimization, which we could have achieved without making the IT investment." Therefore, ERP systems can be considered catalysts for radical business change that results in significant performance improvement (i.e., business process reengineering) (Watson & Schneider,

1999). With this in mind, it is clear that ERP systems should have significant impacts on industry. According to James and Wolf (2000), reporting on an instance of an ERP implementation:

> *...many of the benefits that we are able to achieve today could not have been predicted at the time that we started work on ERP. In fact, in hindsight it appears that much of the value of these large systems lay in the infrastructure foundation they created for future growth based on Information Technology.*

Shang and Seddon (2000) posed the question *"what sort of benefits did they* [the organization], *or can they, achieve?"* In answering this question, they presented a comprehensive framework of business benefits that organizations might be able to achieve from their use of ERP systems. They presented 21 ERP benefits consolidated across five benefit dimensions, as illustrated in Table 2. Shang and Seddon (2000) analyzed the features of ERP systems, the literature on IT benefits, Web-based data on 233 ERP-vendor success stories,

Table 2. A Framework of Business Benefits

Dimension	Subdimension	Explanation
[1] Operational	1.1 Cost reduction 1.2 Cycle time reduction 1.3 Productivity improvement 1.4 Quality improvement 1.5 Customer services improvement	Because ERP systems automate business processes and enable process changes, one would expect ERP systems to offer all of these types of benefits.
[2] Managerial	2.1 Better resource management 2.2 Improved decision making and planning 2.3 Performance improvement	With a centralized database and built-in data analysis capabilities, it seems likely that ERP systems will provide informational benefits to management.
[3] Strategic	3.1 Support business growth 3.2 Support business alliance 3.3 Build business innovations 3.4 Build cost leadership 3.5 Generate product differentiation (including customization) 3.6 Build external linkages (customers and suppliers) 3.7 Worldwide expansion 3.8 Enabling e-commerce	ERP systems, with their large-scale business involvement and internal and external integration capabilities, could assist in achieving these strategic benefits.
[4] IT Infrastructure	4.1 Build business flexibility for current and future changes 4.2 IT cost reduction 4.3 Increased IT infrastructure capability	ERP systems, with their integrated and standard application architecture, provide an infrastructure that could support this dimension.
[5] Organizational	5.1 Support organizational changes 5.2 Facilitate business learning 5.3 Empowerment 5.4 Build common visions 5.5 Change employee behavior 5.6 Better employee morale and satisfaction	The integrated information-processing capabilities of ERP systems could affect the establishment of organizational capabilities.

Adapated from Shang and Seddon (2000)

and interviews with 34 ERP cases to provide a comprehensive foundation for planning, justifying, and managing the ERP system. The focus and goal of the Shang and Seddon (2000) framework is "to develop a benefits classification that considers benefits from the point of view of an organization's senior management." Therefore, they addressed the issue raised by Seddon et al. (1999), who argued that it is not meaningful to highlight benefits of IT systems without identifying the stakeholder group of interest. They (Shang & Seddon, 2000) proposed that the framework could be used as a "good communication tool and checklist for consensus-building in within-firm discussions on benefits realization and development" (p. 1005).

Shang and Seddon (2000) focus on the benefits of an ERP system in use and comment that there are few details of ERP-specific benefits in academic literature. They further noted that "trade-press articles" and "vendor-published success stories" were the major sources of data. However, Shang and Seddon (2000) pointed out that "cases provided by vendors may exaggerate product strength and business benefits, and omit shortcomings of the products" (p. 1007). Although Shang and Seddon (2000) highlighted the fact that the purpose of their study was not to evaluate the degree of achievement of benefits of ERP systems, it is an issue that is extremely important as a means of assessing the suitability of the ERP system to the organization's needs. A study conducted by Sammon and Lawlor reiterated this argument, highlighting that a failure to carry out analyses of the mandatory and desirable features required in a system, with an open mind, will lead to blind acceptance of the models underlying the ERP packages currently on sale on the market, with detrimental effects on the organization and its operations. This case is further examined in Chapter 6.

The justification for adopting ERP centers around their business benefits, which, according to Markus and Tanis (2000), can be divided into business and technical. However, Donovan (1998) believes that to receive benefit from implementing ERP, there must be no misunderstanding of what it is about, or underestimation of what is involved in implementing it effectively, and even more importantly, organizational decision makers must have the background and temperament for this type of decision making (Donovan, 2001).

THE ERP MARKET
SAP — The ERP Software Market Leader

The leading software vendor for ERP and collaborative e-business solutions (SAP, 2003) is SAP AG, with its products SAP R/3 (Bhattacherjee,

2000; Turban et al., 2001) and MySAP.com (SAP, 2003). SAP was founded in 1972 in Walldorf, Germany, by five former IBM systems engineers (SAP, 2003), with the goal of producing an integrated suite of applications software that would run all mission-critical corporate operations, from purchasing to manufacturing to order fulfillment and accounting (Bhattacherjee, 2000). A brief history of SAP is presented in Figure 5.

SAP R/3 is composed of four major parts — accounting, manufacturing, sales, and human resources — containing more than 70 smaller modules (Turban et al., 2001). R/3 is packaged as a set of application modules plus the core system called the *Basis System* (Bhattacherjee, 2000). R/3 is a totally integrated system, allowing companies to automate or eliminate many costly and error-prone manual communication procedures (Turban et al., 2001). SAP R/3 can work for multinational corporations due to the fact that it has a strong international appeal, with capabilities to support multiple currencies, automatic handling of country-specific tax laws and regulations, and legal and language needs (Bingi et al., 1999; Turban et al., 2001). The complete suite of SAP R/3 applications is available in 24 languages, including Japanese (Kanji) and other double-byte character languages (Bingi et al., 1999). Furthermore, SAP software is available for 21 comprehensive industry solutions (SAP,

Figure 5. A Brief History of SAP

Brief History	
1972	SAP is founded
1973	SAP R/1 solutions launched
1977	First international customers
1979	SAP R/2 solutions launched
1988	Company goes public (Frankfurt)
1992	SAP R/3 solutions launched
1996	SAP R/3 Release 3.1 is Internet-enabled
1996	Company launches new solutions for customer relationship management and supply chain management; SAP begins developing industry-specific solutions
1998	Company is listed on the New York Stock Exchange
1999	SAP delivers mySAP.com
2000	SAP forms SAPHosting, a subsidiary dedicated to the Internet application service provider and application hosting business
2000	SAP forms strategic alliance with Commerce One to create SAPMarkets, a subsidiary dedicated to creating and powering globally interconnected business-to-business marketplaces on the Internet
2001	SAP acquires Top Tier and forms SAP Portals

Source: SAP (2003)

2003), known as "verticals" (Bhattacherjee, 2000), for all types of industries and for every major market (SAP, 2003).

R/3 is designed as an "open" standard (it can run on a variety of hardware and platforms and software environments), and it uses a thin client and a three-tier architecture, consisting of database, application, and presentation tiers (Bhattacherjee, 2001), as illustrated in Figure 6.

There are more than 8000 data (*configuration*) tables in the SAP database containing user data and system data (Turban et al., 2001; Bhattacherjee, 2000). These complicated tables direct the users through many menus and screens (Turban et al., 2001). Implementing these tables in a multilanguage, multicurrency, multifunction, multiproduct environment can take two to four years (Turban et al., 2001). Accordingly, implementing R/3's basic modules typically takes 18 to 24 months, however, SAP's rapid implementation methodology, Accelerated SAP (ASAP), promises an implementation cycle time of six months (Bhattacherjee, 2000). The ASAP methodology provides a detailed roadmap of the implementation life cycle, organized in five phases (project preparation, business blueprint, realization, final preparation,

Figure 6. R/3's Three-Tier Client/Server Architecture

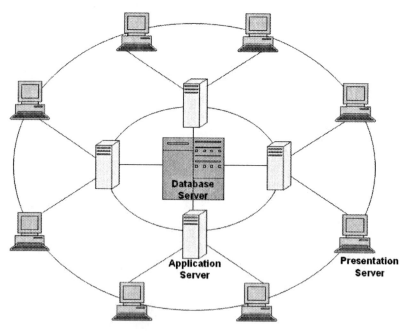

Adapted from: Bhattacherjee (2000)

and go live), with detailed lists of activities to be performed in each phase (Bhattacherjee, 2000).

Although SAP R/3 typically supports 80% to 95% of a large organization's needs and can be implemented as a "standard" application, certain unique functionality or specialized business processes may not be supported to meet customer-specific needs (Bhattacherjee, 2000). However, according to Bhattacherjee (2000), this unique functionality can be obtained in four ways:

1. Interfacing R/3 to existing legacy systems using SAP-supported middleware, which adds to the complexity (Turban et al., 2001).
2. Interfacing R/3 to third-party (SAP partners) solutions.
3. Writing custom software in ASAP/4 to extend R/3's functionality.
4. Modifying R/3 source code directly. (This approach is strongly discouraged by SAP and may lead to loss of after-sales support.)

The broad scope and immense complexity of an R/3 implementation requires hiring a consulting firm for configuring the system based on business specifications, custom-coding additional requirements, and planning and managing company-wide rollout, training, and change management (Bhattacherjee, 2000). As a result, introducing SAP means significant changes in organizational structure, job descriptions, business processes, and organizational strategy (Turban et al., 2001). The R/3 software may cost between $50,000 and $10 million, hardware and related components may cost approximately an equal amount, and consulting typically costs at least twice that of the software costs (Bhattacherjee, 2000).

THE ERP MARKET — TRENDS AND TECHNOLOGIES

The commercial market for ERP systems grew rapidly in the 1990s for a number of reasons, as follows:

1. The client/server environment became a popular enterprise computing platform for many organizations, and ERP systems are designed to take advantage of this platform (Davenport, 1998).
2. ERP systems implementations became the catalyst and enabler for many corporate reengineering activities (Davenport, 1998).
3. ERP systems are Y2K compliant (Davenport, 1998; Kalakota & Robinson, 2001).

4.   Aggressive and powerful ERP providers with research and development organizations are pushing the enterprise systems frontier (Davenport, 1998; Watson & Schneider, 1999).

According to Chen (2001), the popularity of ERP systems started to soar in 1994, when SAP released its "next-generation" (Chen, 2001) client/server-based product, R/3 (Bancroft, 1996; Chen, 2001). As a result, ERP systems dominated the Information Technology (IT) landscape of large and organizations, with ERP strategies representing more than 80% of new large-scale systems development projects (Holland et al., 2000). Therefore, the increasing use of the ERP system, as the infrastructure for all IT systems, made ERP the IT backbone of the modern enterprise (Seo, 1999). This led Davenport (1998) to suggest the following:

> *...while the rise of the Internet has received most of the media attention in recent years, the business world's embrace of enterprise systems may in fact be the most important development in the corporate use of Information Technology in the 1990s.*

The ERP software market is considered one of the fastest-growing markets in the software industry, as illustrated in Table 3. Numerous growth rate and annual revenue figures were presented in trade and academic literature and, in one instance, the eventual size of the market was predicted to reach US$1 trillion (Bingi et al., 1999). Contributing to this phenomenal growth of the ERP market is the estimation that 70% of Fortune 1000 companies (Bingi et al., 1999) and 60% of Fortune 500 companies (Milford & Stewart, 2000) have or

Table 3. ERP Software Market Growth Rates

Growth Rate (%)	Annual Revenue	Reference
32	US$66.6 billion by 2003 (e)	Shakir, 2000
	US$70 billion by 2002 (e)	Shanks et al., 2000
36-40	US$15–50 billion from 1999-2004 (e); eventual size of market to US$1 trillion (e)	Bingi et al., 1999
36	US$15.68 billion in 1997 (a) and US$72.63 billion by 2002 (e)	Holland et al., 1999 Holland & Light, 1999
40	20,000 companies paying US$10 billion in 1997 (a)	Markus & Tanis, 2000
	US$66 billion by 2003 (e)	AMR Research, 1999
	ERP revenue hit $16.6 billion in 1998 (a)	Oliver & Romm, 2000

Note: (e) = expected; (a) = actual

Table 4. ERP Market Tiers

Tier	Definition
Tier 1	Includes the JBOPS (JD Edwards, Baan, Oracle, PeopleSoft, and SAP) -- this group often sells their systems to companies with annual revenues of $250-$500 million and beyond
Tier 2	Includes ERP software vendors that generally sell systems to companies with annual revenues of approximately $10-$500 million
Tier 3	Includes ERP software vendors that generally sell their systems to companies with annual revenues of less than $10 million

will soon install ERP systems. As an example, the sales of the largest vendor, SAP, soared from less than $500 million in 1992 to approximately $3.3 billion in 1997, making it the fastest-growing software company in the world (Davenport, 1998).

The market can be divided into three segments or tiers that identify vendors' target markets (Callaway, 1999), as illustrated in Table 4. The tiers of ERP providers are loosely defined categories that overlap, for example, each of the Tier 1 vendors is aggressively pursuing companies with less than $500 million in annual revenues (Bingi et al., 1999; Callaway, 1999), while many Tier 2 vendors sell their systems to independent divisions of very large companies (Callaway, 1999). Therefore, ERP vendors are "aggressively cutting deals" to make their products more affordable (Bingi et al., 1999), for example, SAP started selling its products to customers in the $150-400 million revenue range (Bingi et al., 1999).

Despite a slowdown of ERP package sales in 1999, continued in 2001 and every year since (Remy, 2003), the trend toward ERP and extended ERP systems is well established (Stefanou, 2000). Although the "high-end of the ERP market is saturated," based on the reality that all of the Y2K problems are resolved (Shakir, 2000), the future growth and new driving force for the ERP market is e-commerce (Bhattacherjee, 2000), Enterprise Application Integration (EAI) (Markus, 2001), and Data Warehousing (DW) (Inmon, 2000; Markus, 2001). Furthermore, Chen (2001) stated that the "environment of ERP systems is constantly shifting with the development of new information technologies and the formation of new partnerships" (p. 375). Also, there is a shift in the distribution of revenues between the sales of licences (in decline) and the provision of additional services, in particular, consultancy aimed at leveraging the ERP investment and obtaining the benefits promised by the vendors (Remy, 2003).

CONCLUSION

Kalakota and Robinson (1999) put forward four reasons why managers are prepared to spend so much money on ERP systems:

1. ERP systems create a framework that will improve customer order-processing systems, which were neglected in recent years.
2. ERP systems consolidate and unify business functions, such as manufacturing, finance, distribution, and human resources.
3. ERP systems integrate a broad range of disparate technologies into a common denominator of overall functionality.
4. ERP systems create a foundation on which next-generation applications can be developed.

This introductory chapter provided a detailed look at what is meant by ERP. The next chapters attempt to bring clarity to the key ERP issues of selection, benefits, risks, and implementation. These chapters should enable readers to answer a broad range of questions: Why do managers commit so many resources to ERP projects? How can the risk factors in ERP projects be reduced? What happens to competitive advantage? And, we aim to provide insight into the complex and confusing area that is an ERP project.

REFERENCES

Al-Mashari, M. (2000). Constructs of process change management in ERP context: A focus on SAP R/3, In *Proceedings of the 6th Americas Conference on Information Systems* (August 10-13). Long Beach, California.

AMR Research. (1999). www.amrresearch.com.

Bancroft, N. (1996). *Implementing SAP/R3: How to Introduce a Large System into a Large Organization*. London: Manning/Prentice Hall.

Bhattacherjee, A. (2000, August). Beginning SAP R/3 implementation at Geneva Pharmaceuticals. *Communications of the AIS, 4*(2), 1-39.

Bingi, P., Sharma, M., & Godla, J. (1999). Critical issues affecting an ERP implementation. *Information Systems Management*, (Summer), 7-14.

Brown, C., Vessey, I., & Powell, A. (2000). The ERP purchase decision: Influential business and IT factors. In *Proceedings of the 6th Americas Conference on Information Systems* (August 10-13). Long Beach, California.

Callaway, E. (1999). *Enterprise Resource Planning: Integrating Applications and Business Processes Across the Enterprise.* Charleston, SC: Computer Technology Research Corporation.

Chen, I. J. (2001). Planning for ERP systems: Analysis and future trend. *Business Process Management Journal, 7*(5), 374-386.

Davenport, T. (1998). Putting the enterprise into the enterprise system. *Harvard Business Review,* (July/August), 131.

Donovan, M. (1998). There is no magic in ERP software: It's in preparation of the process and people. *Midrange ERP,* (September), 8.

Donovan, M. (2001). *Successful ERP implementation the first time.* Retrieved July 25, 2001 from the World Wide Web: www.mdonovan.com/pdf/perfor8.pdf.

Gable, G., van den Heever, R., Scott, J., & Erlank, S. (1997). Large packaged software: The need for research. In *Proceedings of the 3rd Pacific Asia Conference on Information Systems (PACIS).*

Harvard Business School. (1997). Vandelay Industries Inc. Harvard Business School case study reference 9-697-037, revised April 1997.

Holland, C., & Light, B. (1999). A critical success factors model for ERP implementation. *IEEE Software,* (May/June), 30-36.

Holland, C., Light, B., & Beck, P. (2000). An international analysis of the maturity of enterprise resource planning ERP systems use. In *Proceedings of the 6th Americas Conference on Information Systems,* (August 10-13). Long Beach, California.

Holland, C., Light, B., & Kawalek, P. (1999b). Beyond enterprise resource planning projects. In *Proceedings of the 7th European Conference on Information Systems.* Copenhagen, Denmark: Copenhagen Business School.

Holland, C. P., Light, B., & Gibson, N. (1999a). A critical success factors model for enterprise resource planning implementation. In *Proceedings of the 7th European Conference on Information Systems* (pp. 273-287). Copenhagen, Denmark: Copenhagen Business School.

Inmon, W. H. (2000). *ERP and data warehouse: Reading the tea leaves.* Retrieved October 18, 2001 from the World Wide Web: www.billinmon.com/library/articles/arterpfu.asp.

James, D., & Wolf, M. L. (2000). A second wind for ERP. *The McKinsey Quarterly,* 2, 100-107. Retrieved January 10, 2002 from the World Wide Web: www.mckinselyquarterly.com.

Kalatoka, R., & Robinson, M. (1999). *E-business — Roadmap to Success.* Reading, MA: Addison-Wesley.

Kalakota R., & Robinson, M. (2001). *E-business 2.0: Roadmap to Success.* Reading, MA: Addison-Wesley.

Krombholz, M., Galliers, J., Coulianos, N., & Maiden, N. A. M. (2000). Implementing enterprise resource planning packages in different corporate and national cultures. *Journal of Information Technology,* 15, 267-279.

McVittie, L. (2001). *Buckle up: Implementing ERP takes time and patience.* Retrieved March 2001 from the World Wide Web: www.networkcomputing.com.

Maher, J. (1999). ERP in industry: Automate and integrate. *The Engineers' Journal,* (November).

Markus, M. L. (2001). Viewpoint. *Business Process Management Journal,* 7(3), 171-180.

Markus, M. L., & Tanis, C. (2000). The enterprise systems experience — from adoption to success. In R. W. Zmud (Ed.), *Framing the Domains of IT Management: Projecting the Future Through the Past.* Retrieved October 9, 2001 from the World Wide Web: Pinnaflex.com.

Milford, M., & Stewart, G. (2000). Are ERP implementations qualitatively different from other large systems implementations? In *Proceedings of the 6ᵗʰ Americas Conference on Information Systems* (August 10-13, pp. 966-971). Long Beach, California.

Nah, F. F. H., Lau, J. L. S., & Kuang, J. (2001). Critical factors for successful implementation of enterprise systems. *Business Process Management Journal,* 7(3), 285-296.

Oliver, D., & Romm, C. (2000). ERP systems: The route to adoption. In *Proceedings of the 6ᵗʰ Americas Conference on Information Systems* (August 10-13, pp. 1039-1044).. Long Beach, California.

Osterland, A. (2000). Blaming ERP. *CFO,* (January).

Remy, C. (2003). Les PGI nouvelle vague tenus d'apporter intégration et RSI. *Le Monde Informatique,* 985, (June 6).

Rowe, F. (1999). Cohérence, Intégration informationnelle et changement: Esquisse d'un programme de recherche à partir des Progiciels Intégrés de Gestion. *Systèmes d'Information et Management,* 4(4), 3-20.

Russell, R. S., & Taylor, B. W. (1995). *Production and Operations Management: Focusing on Quality and Competitiveness.* Englewood Cliffs, NJ: Prentice Hall.

Rutherford, E. (2001). *ERP's ends justify its means.* CIO Online Quick Poll Report. Retrieved July 18, 2001 from the World Wide Web: http://www.cio.com/poll/042401_erp.html.

Sammon, D., & Adam, F. (2000). Towards a model of ERP software selection — Widening the debate. In *Proceedings of the 10th Annual BIT Conference*, (November 1-2). Manchester, UK.

SAP. (2003). *SAP history*. Retrieved January 22, 2003 from the World Wide Web: http://www.sap.com/company/historytimeline.asp.

Seo, Y. (1999). *MGS614 — Management Information Systems 2: What is ERP?* Retrieved from the World Wide Web: www.acsu.buffalo.edu/~yws.

Shakir, M. (2000). Decision making in the evaluation, selection and implementation of ERP systems. In *Proceedings of the 6th Americas Conference on Information Systems* (August 10-13, pp. 1033-1038). Long Beach, California.

Shang, S., & Seddon, P. (2000). A comprehensive framework for classifying the benefits of ERP systems. In *Proceedings of the 6th Americas Conference on Information Systems* (August 10-13, pp. 1005-1014). Long Beach, California.

Shanks, G., Parr, A., Hu, B., Corbitt, B., Thanasankit, T., & Seddon, P. (2000). Differences in critical success factors in ERP systems implementation in Australia and China: A cultural analysis. In *Proceedings of the 8th European Conference on Information Systems* (July 3-5, pp. 537-544). Vienna, Austria.

Stefanou, C. (2000). The selection process of enterprise resource planning, ERP, systems. In *Proceedings of the 6th Americas Conference on Information Systems* (August 10-13, pp. 988-991). Long Beach, California.

Themistocleous, M., Irani, Z., & O'Keefe, R. M. (2001). ERP and application integration: Exploratory survey. *Business Process Management Journal, 7*(3).

Turban, E., McLean, E., & Wetherbe, J. (2001). *Information Technology for Management: Making Connections for Strategic Advantage* (2nd ed.). New York: John Wiley & Sons.

Watson, E., & Schneider, H. (1999, February). Using ERP systems in education. *Communications of the AIS, 1*(9), 1-47.

Weston, R. (1998). ERP users find competitive advantages. *Computerworld*, (January 19).

Wood, T., & Caldas, M. (2001). Reductionism and complex thinking during ERP implementations. *Business Process Management Journal, 7*(5), 387-393.

Chapter II

The Road to ERP — Has Industry Learned or Revolved Back to the Start?

Bill O'Gorman
University College Cork, Ireland

ABSTRACT

Current thinking and usage of materials management is not to view any individual materials management technique singularly as a panacea in itself, but rather to view the merits of using combinations of these techniques in an effective integrated manner: for example use MRPII at the top level MPS planning stage, JIT at the next level and Kanban (which utilises stock replenishment technique) at the operations level, while at the same time using EOQ and ABC analysis to control the cost of expensive component usage. This chapter traces the development of materials management techniques from the time of the industrial revolution to present day ERP systems. It examines the role and function of the more significant materials and inventory control techniques and explains how each has emerged and has been used as the basis for the development of successive improved techniques. This chapter also comments on the stand-alone nature of each of the techniques. The chapter however concludes with the suggestion that it is only by focusing on an enterprise as a complete system, and not as series of independent sub-systems, and to plan accordingly, that will lead organisations to the next higher level of materials management—Enterprise Resource Planning (ERP).

INTRODUCTION

Explored in this chapter is the evolution of materials and inventory control from the time of the Industrial Revolution to the present-day usage of MRPII and JIT (just in time), as found at the cores of many ERP packages. In this chapter, the need for material and inventory control is examined, and the major developments in this field that provide today's businesses with the basic tools for controlling material and its usage are assessed. Greiner (1998) developed a model of the evolution and revolution of organizations from a management perspective. In this chapter, it is suggested that the same principles apply to the evolution and revolution of materials control within an organization.

Thus, in this chapter, the progression from perceived lack of controls to the reduction of inventory costs and the increase of control over usage, through JIT, is demonstrated. Also, promoted in this chapter is the understanding of a range of issues, including the following:

- The contribution of materials and inventory control to business performance.
- The history of materials and inventory control from the Industrial Revolution to the start of the 21st century.
- The development of materials control techniques from Stock Replenishment to SCM.
- The way the use and development of inventory control techniques leads to SCM and ERP.
- The various inventory control techniques are not mutually exclusive, and some of these techniques complement each other.
- The effective use of these techniques can lead to a more holistic, integrated materials management system for organizations.

BACKGROUND — THE NEED FOR MATERIALS CONTROL

When considering the term "materials control," the narrower term "inventory control" can also be used. The significant importance of material/inventory control is that for most organizations providing products or services to customers, materials account for between 75% to 85% of the total cost of provision of the product or service.

An example of the costs for a typical manufacturing organization is as follows:

Total cost of manufacturing	=	*100*
Material cost of manufacturing	=	*75*
Labor and salaries	=	*15*
Overhead	=	*5*
Profit	=	*5*

This shows the significance of materials in the overall cost of manufacturing. To illustrate the point further, a 1% savings in the cost of materials in the above example leads to a 15% increase in profit. Conversely, an addition of 1% to the cost of materials means a reduction in profits of 15%, and hence, the importance of the contribution of materials and inventory control for business performance is clear.

The cost of materials includes not only the purchase price but also the cost of physical loss of material, scrap, mishandling and overhandling, purchasing too much, paying too far in advance of usage, storage, labor in stores and purchasing departments, loss due to obsolescence, and additional handling charges and transport costs as a result of inefficient scheduling and purchasing management. This complexity, coupled with the scope for significant benefits if improvements can be made in the efficiency of the purchase and use of materials, prompted organizations to acquire computer systems that can support better managerial practices in this domain. This is the source of the movement toward implementation of MRP, MRPII, and, later, ERP systems. More recently, SCM models were also proposed to organizations to help them improve not only the usage of materials but also their circulation within supply chains.

Although materials and inventory are inanimate, the topic of materials and inventory control can arouse completely different emotions in the minds of people in various departments within an organization. Sales and Marketing want to be assured of large levels of finished goods, so that they can meet customers' requests immediately on demand. Financial controllers see materials and inventory as a drain on the capital resources of the organization. They often have difficulty accepting the need to fund working capital (additional money required by a company to maintain a positive cash flow), especially as the cost of working capital is usually high. Production managers see high levels of materials as a means to efficiency in the operation. Their attitude generally is the more material in the process, the more productive the operators — without material (material shortages), operators and machines will be idle.

Thus, the management of material can be charged with emotion. In particular, the mismanagement of materials can be the reason for significant conflict between various departments within an organization. The mismanagement of materials often leads to businesses experiencing financial difficulties, which, in turn, may lead to the downsizing of operations and, sometimes, ultimately to the demise of the organization. These reasons explain the difficulties inherent in the concept of ERP and in its implementation to an organization's operations. In the case of ERP software, political infighting may result from ERP adoption if a dominant coalition attempts to use the ERP package as a means by which to impose its views on other functional areas.

INDUSTRIAL REVOLUTION

The road toward ERP is a long one, and its origins can be traced back to the Industrial Revolution and the initial attempts at optimizing industrial activities. Mantoux (1928) informed us that the object of all industry is the production of goods, "or to be more explicit, of articles of consumption which are not directly provided by nature" (p. 25). Mantoux was writing about the industrialization of England in the latter part of the 18th century — the Industrial Revolution. The Industrial Revolution in England started when producers realized that instead of exporting their wool and grain, there was more to be gained economically by processing these materials into finished products themselves. The impetus of the revolution was augmented by the development of machines and steam-powered engines. The sole object of industrialization was the production of commodities as quickly as possible in substantial quantities. The market was endless. A reduction in prices was more a result of availability as opposed to competition. As prices were reduced, commodities became more affordable to the masses, which spiraled into greater demand for products.

One imagines that the control of inventory prior to the Industrial Revolution was basic and simple. The artisan or producer had a limited amount of supplies and demand and produced to sell, in many cases, only to demand. But the development of mass production techniques changed all that. As McDermott (2001), in his critical commentary on Mokyr's (2001) detailed research and analysis into the rise and fall of the factory system, pointed out, "knowledge about how to produce things began to increase rapidly in the last quarter of the

18th century" (p. 49), and "… no single person, or even household, could know all there was to know about how to produce with the most efficient new techniques" (p. 49). Thus, the factory system, with its "modern" techniques, mass production, and know-how, took over from the artisan cottage-style industry. With this change came the increasing need for systems to support the increasingly complex nature of production facilities and activities.

But with the massing of people together in order to create mass production, another phenomenon, articulated by Smith (1776), arose, namely, the division of labor. Instead of being responsible for and capable of building an entire product from start to finish, the Industrial Revolution spawned the division of work into specific defined tasks. The division of tasks (division of labor) led to greater efficiency, productivity, and output — the ultimate aim of the Industrial Revolution. This, in turn, led to specialization in different areas, such as machine operators, assemblers, supervisors, industrial engineers, and so on. Whether this specialization led to the discipline of inventory and materials control is not clear, but we can assume that certain people were allocated the task of purchasing material for the business, and others were employed to sell the finished product. It is evident from Smith (1776), Mantoux (1928), and Mokyr (2001) that the focus of industry during the latter part of the 18th century and throughout most of the 19th century was on providing as much output as possible, as opposed to controlling inventory. This logic of breaking down the responsibility for production between different functional areas is evident in ERP systems, even though their objective is to integrate all operations and support more efficient sharing of data about business processes.

The Development of Inventory Control Techniques

Gilbert and Schonberger (1983), in their historical analysis of inventory-based production control systems, informed us that "the history of inventory-based production control systems, leading to the development of MRP, dates back to at least 1744" (p. 1). Apparently, in 1744, an advertisement for a Franklin Stove consisted of an illustrated Bill of Material showing the quantity of each component in the product and its assembly location.

In 1804, Whitney popularized the concept of standardized and inter-changeable parts (Heizer, 1998). This standardization of parts and assembly enabled unskilled people to produce a product that would normally have been made by skilled craftsmen. No doubt the assemblers in Whitney's factory had some form of Bills of Materials and assembly instructions to work with in order to manufacture the same type of rifle repeatedly and consistently. Standardization of work practices played a significant role in the development of industrialization worldwide. Nowadays, the same objective of standardization across multinational firms is the motivation for the implementation of ERP systems.

However, having identified the existence of Bills of Materials and standardized assembly and manufacturing practices in the 19th century, the focus was still on output and not on inventory control. It was not until the early 20th century that there was a focus on the impact of material flow and availability on the manufacturing process. In the 1910s and 1920s, the car industry in America became more competitive, and there was an increased focus on costs. But once again, the focus was on reducing the cost of manufacturing through assembly times. How the Ford car company managed this reduction in assembly cost was through the introduction of moving assembly lines. And, as stated in Heizer (1998), "a necessary ingredient for the moving assembly line is timely material movement" (p. 1). Scheduling components and subassemblies to the correct stages of the moving assembly line was now critical to the overall success of the manufacturing operation. As Heizer (1998) noted, "[without] arranging production machinery and cutting supply and inventory costs, the way would not have been paved for economical production of the [product]..." (p. 2). Thus, the Ford organization, in the early 1910s, realized that it was important to have the right material in the right place at the right time.

However, other key factors of management came into sharper focus, as products and markets became more complex, and customer demand became harder to forecast. In particular, Gilbert and Schonberger (1983) noted the following:

> *During the period between 1920 and 1940, forecasting became important. As products became more complex and customer order backlogs dwindled, there was a much greater need for accurate projection of sales. Manufacturers were starting to recognise the need for more flexible production control techniques. (p. 2)*

It was this recognition of the need for more flexible control techniques as well as understanding of the importance of forecasting in relation to manufacturing and the provision of finished product that really started what we accept today as the development of inventory management and control techniques. These techniques are at the core of all ERP and SCM systems.

Inventory/Materials Control or Inventory/Materials Management

A modern-day definition of inventory control (sometimes called materials control) was given in Griffin (2002), "managing the organization's raw materials, work-in-process, finished goods, and products in-transit" (p. 661). However, this is a "catchall" definition for inventory control and is more attune to management than control. There is a difference between "control" and "management." One definition of control was provided in Griffin (2002): "the regulation of organisational activities so that some targeted element of performance remains within acceptable limits" (p. 616). Whereas Henri Fayol's definition of the role of "management" includes "control," and the widely accepted definition of the management process is that it includes four basic activities—planning and decision making, organizing, leading, and controlling.

The first elements of materials management to be used in manufacturing industries were inventory control techniques, such as stock replenishment, economic order quantity (EOQ), reorder point (ROP), periodic ROP, and ABC inventory classification. These techniques, which are mostly in use since the early 20th century, are still used to varying degrees in industry today, almost 100 years later.

These inventory control techniques formed the foundation upon which inventory management techniques and tools such as MRP, MRPII, and JIT/Kanban were developed. Many organizations today use a combination of techniques across the total supply chain. For example, a company may use MRPII at top-level product planning, and when considering JIT deliveries from their suppliers, a company may take EOQ into consideration. At the shop-floor level, the production activity control (PAC) level, where the MRPII plan is executed to schedule production on an hourly or daily basis to provide on-time delivery of finished goods, a combination of MRPII, JIT, and basic stock replenishment is used. In this scenario, MRPII is utilized to plan the finished product level and to schedule orders and receipt of raw material, JIT techniques are used to schedule receipts from the stockroom to the relevant assembly points within the operation, and the control at each stage within the process may be through the simple process of two-bin replenishment (Kanban).

Even though materials control and management were essential parts of economic development for almost 250 years, we are, essentially, still using the same basic principles and techniques that were developed over a century ago. The focus and emphasis on different elements of the techniques changed from time to time. The use of high-speed, high-powered computers enables us to process larger quantities of component numbers, thus affording us the opportunity to focus in more detail on cost reductions through the efficient use of the data generated by computers. This can help us to reduce raw material stocks, work-in-process (WIP), and finished goods levels. In theory, and there are many consultants and practitioners that would concur, the use of computers, the World Wide Web, and materials management techniques such as MRPII and JIT, enables all organizations to shorten their supply chain, which results in massive reductions in inventory costs. These reductions are mainly achieved by only having stock available that is required to meet customer orders. These arguments constitute, for many manufacturing firms, the strongest motivation for purchasing and implementing ERP systems. Typically, managers expect that return on investments will stem from these improvements in the cost structure of the firm.

When events in industry during 2001 and 2002 are considered, especially computer, integrated circuit (IC), and automobile industries, the question has to be asked: If these companies were applying materials management techniques efficiently and only building to customer order, why were so many organizations experiencing difficulties with excessive levels of stocks in raw materials and finished goods?

In the remainder of this chapter, each of the inventory/material control and management techniques will be examined in turn. However, the reader must keep in mind that these techniques are not mutually exclusive, rather, when used properly, they complement each other and can be used together to provide an effective holistic materials management process.

STOCK REPLENISHMENT

This is the simplest, most basic, form of inventory control. As stated by Orlicky (1975), "The term replenishment means restoration to a state of (original) fullness," (p. 5). In other words, when a component is out of stock, or a container is empty, only then is the material replenished. Stock replenishment systems are based on the principle of having inventory items in stock at all times.

Basically, the way this process works is based on a "two-bin" system. Each inventory stock item is held in two bins in the stock room. Each of the two bins allocated to a specific component has an agreed upon number of components. For example, it is agreed between purchasing and production that component Part #12-2468-02 will have a bin quantity of 500 — the agreed-upon quantity is normally based on component usage quantities. Thus, at the start of business for the company, there were two bins in the stockroom, each containing 500 of component Part #12-2468-02, for simplicity, we will call these Bin A and Bin B. As production begins, a quantity of components from Bin A is allocated and issued to the manufacturing process. Over a period of time, more of component 12-2468-02 is allocated and issued to the manufacturing process, from Bin A. It is only when Bin A is empty that an order is placed to replenish the 500 components, and issues are made from Bin B. Therefore, the minimum amount of stock available for this component is between 0 and 500 and depends on the length of time it takes for the next batch of 500 to be delivered. The maximum amount of stock for these components is difficult to define and depends on whether the production facility was cleared of all Part #12-2468-02 before the new order was placed.

There are many difficulties with the stock replenishment system that result in either having too much or too little stock, and a considerable number of times when there is no stock available for several components. These issues arise because organizations are not accurately forecasting demand for their products and services, or they are not updating their forecasts on a sufficiently regular basis. Or it may be that production is consuming material more quickly than predicted or, conversely, slower than predicted. Another major issue with this inventory control system is that the stock-holding levels need to be adjusted on a regular basis in order to compensate for fluctuations in demand. These adjustments are time consuming, even with the use of computers, and are invariably inaccurate. A diagrammatic representation of stock levels using a Stock Replenishment technique is shown in Figure 1.

Figure 1. Example of Stock Levels Using a Stock Replenishment Technique

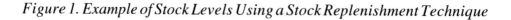
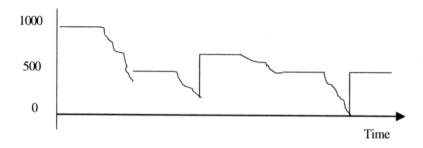

Economic Order Quantity (EOQ)

As stated in Gilbert and Schonberger (1983):

In 1915, F.W. Harris first established the economic order quantity (EOQ) lot sizing technique. This rule stated that the economic run length of lot size should be directly proportional to the square root of the rate of sales and the cost of changing from one run to the next, and inversely proportional to the square root of the cost of stocking. (p. 2)

As can be seen from the above statement, EOQ was originally used to improve the efficiencies of the production process. In the 1940s, after the consultant R.H. Wilson popularized the use of EOQ, it became more associated with the effective purchasing of material.

Schroeder (2000), in analyzing contemporary concepts of operations management, provided us with a relatively simple explanation of the use and construct of EOQ. The derivation of the EOQ model is based on the following assumptions:

1. The demand rate is constant, recurring, and known. There are no random variations, and demand is assumed to continue into the indefinite future.
2. The lead time is constant and known. The lead time, from order placement to order delivery, is therefore always a fixed number of days.
3. No stock-outs are allowed. Because demand and lead time are constant, one can determine exactly when to order material to avoid stock-outs.
4. Material is ordered or produced in a lot or batch, and the lot is placed into inventory all at one time.
5. A specific cost structure is used as follows: The unit cost is constant, and no discounts are given for large purchases. The carrying cost depends linearly on the average inventory level. There is a fixed ordering or setup cost for each lot, which is independent of the number of items in the lot.
6. The item is a single product; there is no interaction with other products.

Under these assumptions, the inventory level over time is as shown in Figure 2. Notice that a perfect sawtooth pattern is shown, because demand has a constant rate, and items are ordered in fixed lot sizes. In choosing the lot size, there is a tradeoff between ordering frequency and inventory level. For example, small lot sizes will lead to a high frequency of orders, delivery times, delivery costs, and processing of incoming material, but, on average, a relatively low level of inventory. On the other hand, large lot sizes mean less

Figure 2. Example of Inventory Levels Using the EOQ Technique Order

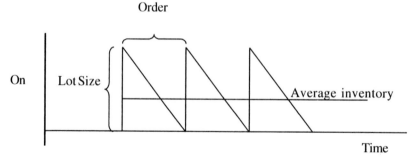

Source: Schroeder, 2000, p. 310

ordering, less order-processing times, and less delivery costs, but the cost of carrying inventory is higher (Schroeder, 2000, p. 310).

There are many issues concerning the use of EOQ. First, a formula needs to be used to calculate the optimum lot size of each batch size for ordering and manufacturing. The equation is straightforward:

$$Q = \sqrt{\frac{2SD}{iC}}$$

where Q is the lot size, S is the cost of order placed (or setup cost), D is the demand rate in units per year, C is the unit cost, and i is the carrying cost or interest rate for the year.

If this formula is used for every component that a company uses to manufacture their products, then it becomes a tedious operation, even when used with computers. For example, an average small- to medium-sized company could have as many as 2,000 components in their manufacturing process.

Some of the more serious negatives associated with this technique are directly linked to the assumptions in creating the model in the first place. As pointed out above, the assumptions are based on constant demand, recurring demand, known and fixed lead times, delivery times and unit cost of production and delivery are constant. Unfortunately, this ideal state does not exist.

It is true to say that there was a time during the 1960s, 1970s, and early 1980s when most industries worked on backlogs. At one time, the measure of success of a company was on the size (number of months) of backlog they had. When working with a fixed "backlog," the use of EOQ may have been useful and effective, but it was still cumbersome and needed constant attention and modification to be effective.

Increases in competition among suppliers and a change in customer attitude from "we will wait for however long it takes" to a more discerning, more demanding, type of customer contributed to the EOQ technique losing favor. Other contributing factors were that, even in the time of "backlogs," demand was rarely constant, suppliers rarely delivered on time, and manufacturing processing times varied.

Another significant factor is that of accuracy. The success of EOQ was dependent on the diligence and accuracy of the person inputing data and his or her persistence in constantly monitoring the industry environment (especially sales demands and forecasts) that may impinge on their business. As stated in Meredith and Shafer (1999):

> *The EOQ is a computed minimum-cost order quantity. As with any model or formula, the GIGO rule (garbage in, garbage out) applies. If the values used in computing EOQ are inaccurate, the EOQ will be inaccurate…EOQ relies heavily on two variables that are subject to considerable misinterpretation. These are the two cost elements: holding cost and order cost. (p. 261)*

Reorder Point (ROP)

As stated in Gilbert and Schonberger (1983), "In 1934, a major step forward in production planning was taken. R.H. Wilson developed the statistical re-order point." The focus of the reorder point (ROP) was to prevent components from running out of stock. Wilson, at this time, introduced the notion of "safety stock." Safety stock is a calculated quantity of each component below which the stockroom level must not go if the production line is to keep operating.

In the 1940s, Wilson combined his technique with that of Harris' EOQ. Wilson popularized the combined technique to such an extent that it became referred to as the Wilson EOQ technique (Schroeder, 2000). The Wilson EOQ became the main inventory control technique for almost 30 years.

The pitfalls for ROP and Wilson EOQ are the same as for Harris' EOQ, detailed above.

Periodic Reorder Point

This is a refinement of Wilson's ROP and EOQ. Under this technique, inventory is reviewed on a fixed-period basis, and a sufficient quantity of items is ordered. This quantity is variable and is influenced by the component usage level within the manufacturing process. The quantity ordered is that which brings stock levels back up to the predefined target level. As in EOQ and ROP, this exercise is performed for each component in stock.

The accuracy of this technique depends on the accuracy and diligence of the people responsible for inputting the data; it also depends on the frequency, accuracy, and timeliness of manufacturing informing the stockroom of the consumption (or nonconsumption) of material.

Even though this technique helps to reduce the amount of stock-outs, of raw material, it does not eliminate them. With this technique, there is also the tendency for having increased stock levels within the operation. In fact, because this technique is based on fixed-period review times, often, it was the case that components were out of stock before the agreed-upon review date. Another limitation of this technique was the lack of accuracy over the amount of components in work in progress (WIP), and as a result, it was often the case that additional components were purchased for products that were not required.

ABC Inventory Classification

ABC inventory classification was a popular method for controlling inventory during the 1960s and 1970s, and it came back in vogue in the late 1980s. It is still used in industry today, to varying degrees. ABC classification is based on Vilfredo Pareto's principles developed during his studies of the population and distribution of wealth in England in 1897. Pareto observed that a large percentage of the total national income was concentrated in a small percentage of the population. As stated in Orlicky (1975):

> *Believing that this reflected a universal principle, he (Pareto) formulated the axiom that the significant items in a given group normally constitute a small portion of the total items in the group and that the majority of the items in the total will, in the aggregate, be of minor significance. Pareto expressed this empirical relationship mathematically, but the rough pattern is 80 percent of the distribution being accounted for by 20 percent of group membership. (p. 9)*

This 80 to 20 rule holds true for most inventories, and it has been relatively consistent in most industries that 20% of the components account for 80% of the cost; the next 30% of the components account for approximately 15% of the cost; and the remaining 50% of the part numbers in stock account for only 5% of the cost. This phenomenon became known as ABC Inventory Classification and was first introduced by H. Ford Dickie in 1951 (Orlicky, 1975, p. 9).

Based on this analysis, the suggestion developed for company owners and materials managers was that instead of focusing time and energy on every stock item, more was to be gained by focusing heavily on the 20% of the components that constituted 80% of the costs. A 10% savings on any one of these high-cost items could yield more savings to the company than a 10% savings on all of the low-cost items (50% of the total part numbers in stock). Thus, what happened over a period of time, was that materials managers, within their respective organizations, concentrated on managing the costs, deliveries and holding stock levels of the high-cost items — the 20%. These managers did not pay as much attention to the medium-cost items — the 30%. They tended to ignore, or at least pay little attention to, the low-cost items.

Industry in general made some handsome gains by focusing on the high-cost items, and significant cost savings were to be made through this detailed focus. However, the downside of the ABC Inventory Classification was that because of the lack of focus on the low-cost items, these were the items that were repeatedly generating stock-outs. It often was, and in many companies today still is, the case that the packing label costing a fraction of a cent, because nobody monitored its stock levels, stopped consignments worth millions of euros/dollars from being shipped.

The above techniques are considered inventory/material control techniques, because they are focused on the narrow control of inventory. The following sections consider the inventory/material management techniques of MRP, MRPII, and JIT.

From MRP to MRPII

During World War II, industry worldwide concentrated on war production. In the United States, this focus on production enabled a number of developments that enhanced the field of production control (Gilbert & Schonberger, 1983). For example, computers facilitated the widespread use of "punched card processing," which made the efficient "bill of material explosion" possible. The making of these punched cards was labor intensive, and many cards were needed for each bill of material (BOM) — even the simplest of bills needed several cards. Overall, the labor and number of cards required made the process inefficient and fraught with errors.

A direct predecessor to MRP was the "quarterly ordering system" developed by George Plossl and Oliver Wight. In America, according to Gilbert and Schonberger (1983):

> *...during the period starting after the conclusion of World War II and ending in the mid-1950s, many manufacturing industries were able to develop production plans based solely on firm customer order backlogs. Americans returning to "normal" life after World War II were clamoring for manufactured goods that were either scarce or unavailable during the war. This strong demand produced order backlogs (12-18 month backlogs were not uncommon) that were longer than most total manufactured products leadtimes. This large pool of demand allowed producer firms to use a tool called the quarterly ordering system. (p. 5)*

This technique was based on knowing the order date for delivery to a customer and utilizing backward scheduling to determine when raw material was required to start the manufacturing process. This backward scheduling and material analysis was performed on a quarterly basis.

The demand for product and luxury items was so great in the 1950s and 1960s that "many industries were changing from post-war manufacture-to-order firms to manufacture-to-stock companies" (Gilbert & Schonberger, 1983, p. 6).

In the early 1960s in the United States, MRP originated as a computerized approach for the planning of materials acquisition and production. According to Browne, Harhen and Shivnan (1996), "The definitive textbook on MRP is by Orlicky (1975)." However, one person that must be remembered in the development, but is often forgotten, is Oliver Wight. Wight's simple understanding and expression of the logic of materials requirements planning — What are we going to make? What does it take to make it? What do we have? and What do we have to get? — forms the basis of MRP development. Wight refers to these, collectively, as the "universal manufacturing question." They apply to everything from the production of jet aircraft, to making dinner (Wallace, 1990).

During the years after World War II, most of material requirements analysis was manual or semiautomatic (punched cards), however, as stated in Browne et al. (1996), "Orlicky realised that a computer enabled humans to apply the technique in more detail and therefore would be more effective in planning and managing material inventories" (p. 95).

The early computerized applications of MRP were Bill of Material Processors (BOMP), which converted a discrete plan of a production for a parent part item into a discrete plan of production or purchasing for component items. Exploding the requirements for the top-level product, through the BOM to generate the component demand did this. The projected gross demand was then compared with available inventory and open orders over the planning time horizon and at each level of the BOM (Browne et al., 1996).

Over time, the technique became more widely used, and various operational functions were added to extend the range of tasks. These extended tasks included master production scheduling (MPS), rough cut capacity planning (RCCP), capacity requirements planning (CRP), purchasing, and production activity control (PAC).

The combination of the planning (MPS, MRP, and RCCP) and the execution modules (PAC and purchasing), with the potential feedback from the execution to the planning cycle, is termed "closed-loop MRP" (see Figure 3).

With the addition of certain financial modules as well as the extension of the master production schedule to deal with the full range of tasks in master planning and the support of business planning in financial terms, it was realized that the resultant system offered an integrated approach to the management of manufacturing operations. This extended MRP was called MRPII (see Figure 4).

Figure 3. Closed-Loop MRP

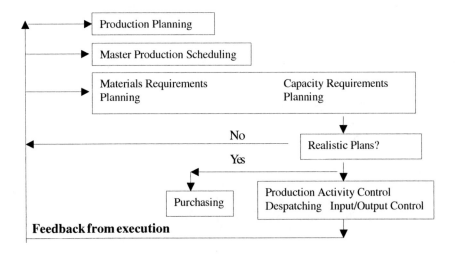

Source: Browne et al., 1996, p. 131

Figure 4. Manufacturing Resource Planning (MRPII)

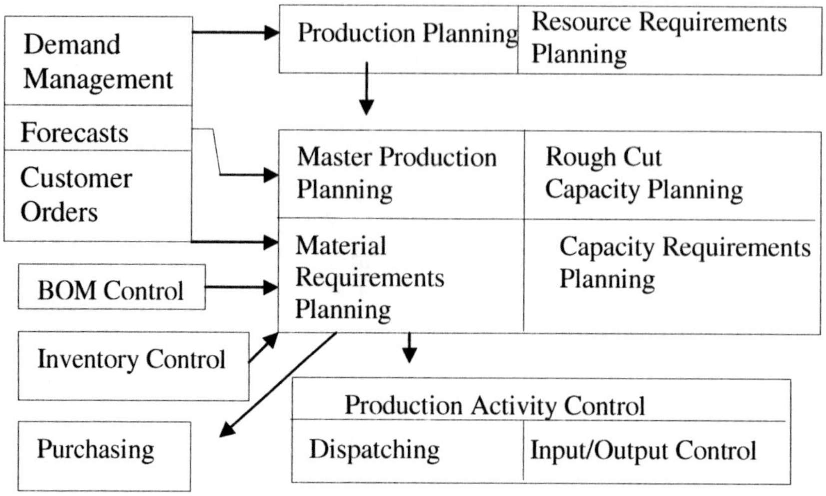

Demand Management	Production Planning	Resource Requirements Planning
Forecasts		
Customer Orders	Master Production Planning	Rough Cut Capacity Planning
BOM Control	Material Requirements Planning	Capacity Requirements Planning
Inventory Control		
Purchasing	Production Activity Control	
	Dispatching	Input/Output Control

Source: Browne et al., 1996, p. 132

Basically, MRPII is a closed-loop MRP system with additional features for business and financial planning. Also included with MRPII are extensive "what if" capabilities.

Some of the main characteristics of MRP are as follows (from Browne et al., 1996, p. 100):

- MRP is *product oriented*, in that it operates on a bill of material to calculate the component and assembly requirements to manufacture and assemble a final product.
- MRP is *future oriented*, in that it uses planning information from the master production schedule to calculate future component requirements, instead of using forecasts based on historical data.
- MRP involves *time-phased requirements*, in that during MRP processing, the requirements for individual components are calculated and offset by their expected lead times to determine the correct requirement date.
- MRP involves *priority planning*, in that it establishes what *needs* to be done to meet the master schedule, as opposed to what *can* be done given capacity, material, and process constraints.
- MRP promotes *control by focusing on orders*, whether production orders or purchase orders.

This appears to be perfect, and in a perfect world, it may be. However, the world of manufacturing and supply and demand is not that clear-cut and simple. Maybe the system is correct and perfect, and that the users are the problem, but this author has not seen a smoothly run, excellently executed MRPII system. MRPII is a push system and, as a result, has a tendency to push inventory into the system and build for stock.

JIT (Just-in-Time) and Kanban

JIT manufacturing techniques were developed in Japan by the Toyota Motor Company in the mid-1970s. JIT manufacturing focuses on having the right component/subassembly/product in the right place, at the right time, and in the right quantity. Another term for JIT is "lean production," meaning that only what is needed should be in the process — in other words, remove buffer stocks and finished goods inventories from the process.

One reason, proposed by Meredith and Shafer (1999), as to why Toyota developed JIT is that:

> *Japan is a small country with minimal resources and a large population. Thus the Japanese have always been careful not to waste resources, including space (especially land), as well as time and labour. Waste is abhorrent because the country has so little space and so few natural resources to begin with. Therefore the Japanese have been motivated to maximise the gain or yield from the few resources available. It has also been necessary for them to maintain respect for each other in order to work and live together smoothly and effectively in such a densely populated space. As a result, their work habits tend to reflect this philosophy of minimising waste and maintaining respect. (pp. 301-302)*

This is a somewhat simplistic view, in the opinion of the author of this chapter, and it more or less "absolves" other nations from implementing JIT successfully.

JIT focuses on the elimination of waste. For example, why have 100 subassemblies ahead of a stage in the process when only one can be worked on at any given point in time? MRP, since the introduction of JIT, was often dubbed JIC, just-in-case, because the philosophy seems to be "let's have the material in stock, and at each stage of the process in case it is needed." The use of JIT identified that buffers hide problems: problems with delivery times from suppliers, quality problems in the process, machine efficiency problems, and so on. The more the buffer stock and inventory levels are reduced in the process, the more problems are identified. Part of JIT's philosophy is to expose these problems, and once exposed to fix them, and to do this cycle of improvement on a continuous basis.

One of the main reasons why JIT has not been as successful in the United States and Europe as it is in Japan could be associated with the lack of "maintaining respect." In order to develop JIT within a supply-chain process, it is necessary to have a considerable amount of trust between supplier and customer.

Kanban is JIT at the operations level within an organization. This focuses on building and providing to the next stage in the process *only* what is required. Material is "pulled" through the process (as opposed to "pushed" by MRP), because it is based on actual customer orders. Each stage in the process pulls what it requires from the previous stage. Trust is equally important at the operations level, as each successive stage depends on the previous stage in the process, providing material on time, the correct quantity, and to the correct quality levels, *every time*.

Materials Management in Today's Environment

The debate continues — which materials management technique is the best? The answer is complex. The choice of system a company uses is dependent on the nature of the industry, the type of product or service being provided, and the relationship between customer and supplier. EOQ might be applicable to a low-value commodity item that has a high turnover and usage rate. Especially when the organization that supplies the commodity to the end customer has adequate financial and storage resources to buy the commodity in bulk. For example, a wholesaler dealing in low-value children's toys may buy in large quantities to minimize purchase and delivery costs per unit. These are nonessential, nonperishable, nonfashion-sensitive items. They can be stored for long periods of time and will eventually sell (e.g., toy guns, dolls). In this particular case, the relationship between the supplier and customer is random and short term. The lead time from customer demand to supply is very short (the product is available on the shelf).

On the other end of the scale, JIT may be applicable where the supplier will not start manufacturing a product until an order is received from a customer. This situation would apply to high-value, capital-intensive equipment, such as aircraft or specialized processing equipment. In this case, the relationship between supplier and customer is long term, and lead times are generally long.

For example, the manufacturer of large aircraft could not resource the holding of finished goods, from a financial point or a storage point, in the hope that a customer may buy an aircraft. Rather, the aircraft manufacturer sources the customers first, agrees to a delivery schedule, and then commences the purchase of materials to manufacture the product. This could be considered a true JIT process, because JIT management implies that nothing is produced if there is no demand for it; the production process is "pulled" by the customer.

As described earlier in this chapter, each of the materials/inventory control and management techniques has its advantages and limitations. The evolution and development of materials management systems suggests that JIT is the ultimate. This claim is based on the fact that the principle of JIT means that all materials and products become available at the moment they are needed, not sooner, not later, but exactly on time and in the right quantity and quality. If organizations adhere to this principle, it means that they will have maximum efficiency and effectivity within their processes — there will be no excess material, no storage of raw material or finished goods, no waste due to misuse of materials, and no waste due to incorrect quality. It means that all the resources of the organization, including people, space, and finances, will be utilized and managed to maximum effect.

In the present economic environment, it is not possible for an organization system to work completely and solely in this way. The reality is that most organizations, if not all, manage a hybrid materials control and management system. Within this hybrid system, there may be one technique that is more dominant than the others; however, as academics, researchers, practitioners, and students, we should not allow ourselves to be confused into thinking that the dominant technique is the only one being utilized by a particular organization.

In the mid-1970s, Toyota introduced JIT techniques into their car assembly plants. Toyota's focus was on minimizing inventory and time waste within their manufacturing organization. The way this was achieved was by taking a holistic view of the entire process and developing an integrated "family" of suppliers that were located (or relocated) close to Toyota assembly facilities. The closeness in distance and working relationships helped Toyota minimize their buffer stocks and manage within the principle of JIT. However, within the extended supply chain, there was a need to hold a certain level of buffer stock at the supplier site in order to guarantee a continuity of supply to the Toyota manufacturing facilities. The external view was that Toyota facilities were operating JIT. The reality was that they were effectively managing an extended supply chain beyond the confines of their own organization.

In the late-1980s and early 1990s, many European and American companies, impressed with the competitive success of Toyota, attempted to introduce JIT techniques into their own organizations. What soon followed was a conflict between MRP and JIT. JIT was not as successful as anticipated in Europe or the United States. The underlying reason for the lack of immediate success was that organizations assumed that JIT could be easily implemented, that it was a company-wide materials management system, and that customers could dictate product requirements, at will, to suppliers. When it was realized that this was not the case, that there was a need to work more closely with suppliers, and that there was a need to integrate the departmental systems, requirements, and processes, then organizations began to make considerable improvements in reducing inventory levels, eliminating waste, and increasing competitiveness.

This more enlightened approach led to the realization that for organizations to improve their competitiveness, there was a need to integrate many materials control and management techniques into one working system—it was realized that there was a need to manage the entire supply chain.

All organizations today operate a hybrid materials control and management system. The techniques used depend on the nature of the product or service and the organization. Different aspects of an organization will be more suited to different techniques, for example, top-level forecasting and scheduling is more suited to MRP, while an assembly cell in a repetitive manufacturing environment is more suited to JIT. One thing, for certain, is that an organization will fail if it does not integrate its techniques and the systems that manage them.

The Supply Chain Management Model in Figure 5 indicates that it is possible for employees in each element to get totally focused on that particular

Figure 5. Supply Chain Management Model

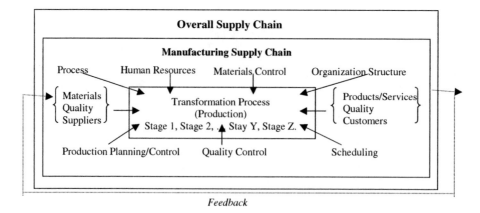

element, to the detriment of other elements. However, a successful organization will integrate these elements. Such an organization will focus on the entire enterprise and ensure that the technique used in one area does not adversely affect other areas. The drive within this organization will be to develop an overall enterprise resource plan, where all techniques and systems are complementary and part of a whole.

HAS INDUSTRY LEARNED OR REVOLVED BACK TO THE START?

Heizer (1998) noted that "…[without] arranging production machinery and cutting supply and inventory costs, the way would not have been paved for economical production of the [product]…" (p. 2), and "…a necessary ingredient for the moving assembly line is timely material movement" (p. 1). These comments were in relation to the Ford automobile assembly plant in 1910. In other words, as far back as the early 1900s, organizations realized it was important to have the right material in the right place at the right time. As Gilbert and Schonberger (1983) put it:

During the period between 1920 and 1940, forecasting became important. As products became more complex and customer order backlogs dwindled, there was a much greater need for accurate projection of sales. Manufacturers were starting to recognise the need for more flexible production control techniques. (p. 2)

These statements indicate that almost 100 years ago, organizations realized the importance of accuracy in forecasting, scheduling, and having the right material in the right place at the right time. This realization became more focused, as trade between Japan, the United States, and Europe became more competitive in the 1970s and 1980s. The new methods of direct selling in the computer industry in the 1990s further increased the focus on accuracy of forecasting, scheduling, and having the right material in the right place at the right time. Many companies in the computer industry in the 1980s and 1990s were considered to be excellent in materials management and, especially, in the utilization of JIT techniques. But yet in the early 1990s, there was an oversupply of integrated circuits (ICs), followed by a closing of many IC manufacturing facilities, which was in turn followed by a serious shortage in memory ICs in

1997-1998. In the early years of the 21st century, the ailing world economy is fueled by manufacturing companies that have excess stocks, and demand for products has declined. If these companies are considered "world class" and excellent at materials management, why are they downsizing, and why are they announcing significant levels of excess material stock?

Another question to be considered is that if such a rich history and deep level of knowledge of materials control and management exists, why are companies still getting it wrong? Maybe the answer is that materials people and general management in organizations still do not fully comprehend the materials function. Maybe it is that sections of organizations are working in isolation of each other. Maybe it is that there is still a lack of openness and trust between supplier and customer, both external and internal to the organization. Maybe it is that people are not adequately trained to manage materials or, more specifically, to understand and manage the entire supply chain — the entire enterprise.

Organizations continue to mismanage material resources because of a combination of these suggestions. A way forward is to select what is good from each materials control and management technique and to integrate them and apply them enterprise wide. Focusing on the enterprise as a complete system, and not as a series of independent subsystems, and to plan accordingly, will lead organizations to the next higher level of materials management — Enterprise Resource Planning (ERP).

CONCLUSION

Explored in this chapter was the development of materials control and management techniques from the time of the Industrial Revolution to the present day. Most of the techniques examined above are still used today. The current thinking and usage of material management is not to view any of the above techniques as a panacea in themselves, but rather to view the merits of using combinations of these techniques in an effective integrated manner. For example, use MRPII at the top-level MPS planning stage, use JIT at the next level, and use Kanban (which utilizes the stock replenishment technique) at the operations level, while at the same time using EOQ and ABC analysis to control the cost of expensive component usage.

No matter what combinations are used, management of an organization must be clear as to what they are using and why. This clarity and reasoning must be understood at all levels of the organization, and everybody from storekeeper, through assembly operator, to managing director must abide by the rules of the systems they are using. Knowledge, discipline, attention to detail, and meticulous accuracy are the keys to success in operating a materials management system. The basic questions that Oliver Wight asked in the early 1960s are valid today and will always be so — What are we going to make? What does it take to make it? What do we have? What do we have to get? ERP systems can provide much quicker and more accurate answers to these questions, but manufacturing excellence cannot stop with a computer application, no matter how complete or complex. Proper collection and processing of data on the factory floor and complete understanding of market behaviors are also critical for implementing excellent manufacturing practices.

REFERENCES

Browne, J., Harhen, J., & Shivnan, J. (1996). *Production Management Systems: An Integrated Perspective* (2nd ed.). Boston, MA: Addison-Wesley.

Gilbert, J. P., & Schonberger, R. J. (1983). Inventory-based production control systems: A historical analysis. *Production and Inventory Management*, 24(2), 1-13.

Greiner, L. E. (1998). Evolution and revolution as organisations grow. *Harvard Business Review*, (May/June), 55-67.

Griffin, R. W. (2002). *Management* (7th ed.). Boston, MA: Houghton Mifflin.

Heizer, J. H. (1998). Determining the responsibility for development of the moving assembly line. *MCB Journal of Management History*, 4(2).

McDermot, J. (2001, December). The rise and fall of the factory system: Technology, firms, and households since the Industrial Revolution — A comment. *Carnegie-Rochester Conference Series on Public Policy*, 55(1), 47-54.

Mantoux, P. (1928). *The Industrial Revolution in the Eighteenth Century: An Outline of the Beginnings of the Modern Factory System in England* (M. Vernon, Trans.). London: Jonathan Cape.

Meredith, J. R., & Shafer, S. M. (1999). *Operations Management for MBAs*. New York: John Wiley & Sons.

Mokyr, J. (2001, December). The rise and fall of the factory system: Technology, firms, and households since the Industrial Revolution, *Carnegie-Rochester Conference Series on Public Policy*, 55(1), 1-45.

Orlicky, J. (1975). *Material Requirements Planning — The New Way of Life in Production and Inventory Management*. New York: McGraw-Hill.

Schroeder, R. G. (2000). *Operations Management Contemporary Concepts and Cases*. New York: McGraw-Hill.

Smith, A. (1776; Reprint 1991). *Wealth of Nations*. New York: Prometheus Books.

Wallace, T. F. (1990). *MRPII: Making it Happen. The Implementers Guide to Success with Manufacturing Resource Planning* (2nd ed.). New York: John Wiley & Sons.

Chapter III

Investigating the Rationale for ERP: A Case Study

Eleanor Doyle
University College Cork, Ireland

Frédéric Adam
University College Cork, Ireland

ABSTRACT

This case illustrates the importance of a reliable information systems infrastructure in supporting the operations and the development of modern businesses. A longitudinal analysis (1995-2001) of Topps Ireland Ltd. is presented. Topps attempted to acquire and implement a state-of-the-art Enterprise Resource Planning (ERP) system in order to increase control over its operations and to develop management information systems to improve decision making in relation to the commercial strategy of the firm. The case shows how the evolution of Topps to an internationally successful competitive situation was enabled and facilitated by the greater control allowed by its ERP system. The case begins with a description of Topps — its line of business and its development over time — and its business strategy in 1995. The reasons that contributed to the decision to select an ERP system for Topps emerge from the case. The "teething troubles" associated with the system are addressed, and latest information from Topps management on the success of the implementation concludes the case.

TOPPS IRELAND LTD., 1995

Topps Ireland Ltd. has operated since 1977 and is a subsidiary of a U.S.-owned multinational company specializing in the confectionary business. Topps is a player in the children's entertainment business on the European market and describes its business as the marketing and distribution of fashion items for the children's market. Hence, Topps is not a typical manufacturing company. Some of the most famous products on which Topps' success was built are the *Bazooka* chewing gums and the *Push-Pops* lollipops that are now household names. More recently, Topps became famous for adding an entertainment component to their confectionary products in the shape of "Casper the Friendly Ghost" toy containers containing gum or sweets. A particular success of Topps comes from their purchase of the rights to make Pokémon™-branded products, including the sale of stickers and catalogs.

The emphasis of their business changed substantially over the years from a manufacturing-focused perspective to an approach based more on the trade of goods imported from the Far East. By 1995, 20% of their products were manufactured locally, the remainder being imported from China, Thailand, and other countries. This represented a significant shift from their position even five years earlier, when less than 20% of products were imported. This switch in business emphasis allowed sales growth to mushroom, with corresponding increases in import/export activities. The product life cycle of some of the products was extremely short, so the company needed to react quickly to change, emphasizing the company's requirement for accurate information that was readily available. This acceleration of the business flows was aggravated by the rapid development of the new trading element of Topps' business.

Topps' products were distributed out of three warehouses — Cork (Ireland), Liverpool (United Kingdom), and Rotterdam (Holland). The Cork plant stored the products manufactured in Cork, while the Rotterdam depot stored imported products, and the Liverpool depot maintained stocks required to serve the UK market. All activities were managed from Cork,[1] with outside companies providing warehousing and distributing facilities at both external locations. The United Kingdom was the biggest market, and a team of sales representatives handled sales to multiple stores and wholesalers. Ireland and the rest of Europe were serviced through distributors in each country. Products were sold mainly on a sale-or-return basis, making it vital that returns be identified quickly and resold within the life cycle where possible. Sales campaigns were not launched simultaneously in all countries and regions, so it was often possible to pass unsold products onto another less-saturated market.

IDENTIFYING THE CRITICAL SUCCESS FACTORS FOR TOPPS IN 1995

Topps' business success revolved around making correct management decisions quickly. Information Technology (IT) supported the vital provision of rapid, accurate information on which to base these decisions. Spreadsheets were used extensively (on a limited number of PCs used in the company) to create mini profit-and-loss accounts representing scenario analyses on specific markets or for specific products and to identify windows of opportunity aimed at maximizing the rotation of stock. The main business tools centered on the official plan and operational plans derived from this approach, which were based on a number of spreadsheet models developed in a PC-based software package. The majority of information was gathered manually, and the non-strategic data-processing services (payroll, invoicing, inventory control, and other nonstrategic transactions processing systems) were provided by software supplied by an external supplier. The software and the computer used to run it were obsolete — Topps was the final customer using these services, which were becoming increasingly expensive and unreliable.

Management at Topps repeatedly complained to its parent company about the failure of their largely manual systems, but each time clearance to purchase a new system was requested, it was refused by headquarters (in New York). Topps management realized that too much replication and duplication was taking place and that a fully integrated financial, manufacturing, and distribution system was required to do the following:

- Support the basic business processes.
- Automate basic flows of information.

A more reliable information basis was required to speed the reporting processes across the organization. A need for the capability of downloading all required information from a central system into existing information systems was identified to improve and make the production of crucial management reports more reliable. Such an approach would require the following: implementation of a network of PCs to enable data collection and screen inquiries throughout the different business functions (new hardware); selection and implementation of appropriate financial, distribution, and manufacturing modules (new software); and staff training.

In March 1995, Topps Ireland Ltd. again attempted to purchase such an integrated software package that would cover the financial, distribution, and manufacturing aspects of their business. The business was growing rapidly across all European markets, and consideration was being given to expanding into a number of South American countries. Topps had mainly been a manufacturing organization, but 75% of their turnover was now coming from trading in goods produced by Far East suppliers.

The most significant problem for Topps was identified as a lack of online stock control for key personnel, as the basic computerized stock system used tracked only goods manufactured in Cork. There were also frequent failures to meet shipping deadlines because of paperwork delays. The robustness of the cash flow was compromised by the lack of control of debtors' balances and invoice due dates. In addition, there were also problems with reporting to the U.S. headquarters due to the unavailability of information on territory and product profitability. Compliance with requirements for regular monthly and quarterly reports on EU movements of goods was slow. As described by the then Financial Controller, the company was vulnerable in the shipping, credit-control, and treasury departments. He concluded that too much information was contained in employees' heads rather than in the company's information systems. Reports written at this time pointed out that hiring extra staff would not solve these problems, and that the availability of a fully integrated system of the ERP type would be required. In addition to this operational data layer, a powerful report generation application would also be required to generate better-quality managerial reporting.

At the time, a number of potential failures were threatening:

- Sales order-processing required attention, as it was feared that Topps might begin to lose a significant portion of the ever-growing business due to orders not being met on time or being forgotten.
- Invoicing procedures needed attention. While this is a crucial element of business, Topps' management sometimes had no clear idea how much

was shipped to a particular customer. In fact, some shipping deadlines were not met due to paperwork delays.

CONVINCING HQ

Over 20 months of time and effort (in tendering and development) were involved in the process that culminated in the selection of the required ERP system and the local information systems (IS) supplier who was to supply the system. Consultants argued that local support would be an important asset during the implementation phase, as people in Topps had little experience with large computer systems (there were no IT personnel in Topps at the time). The next step in the process was to commit the money to this investment of roughly IR£180,000, and the signs were good when the IT Director at HQ responded favorably to the request and agreed with the conclusions of a final report he was sent.

Topps' parent company then purchased Merlin Publishing, a UK-based company similar in size to Topps but operating in the complementary children's entertainment market (i.e., the production of stickers of players in the English premiership and other major European soccer leagues). Due to numerous uncertainties regarding the sharing of business between Topps and Merlin and the relations to be developed between the two companies, HQ decided, again, to block the investment in Topps. Following a number of meetings with equivalent personnel in Merlin, a new strand of reports was sent to HQ to indicate how the systems at both Topps and Merlin could operate and the processes that could be shared between the two companies. A joint report signed by Topps and Merlin was even sent to the United States to emphasize the support that Merlin was ready to give Topps in their implementation of the system selected. A further series of negotiations took place, but the project was put on hold while a global IT strategy for Topps was developed by the IT director at HQ. More than two years after the first reports were written and sent to the United States about the weaknesses of the systems in Topps, nothing had been done, and the manual systems were still holding. A computerized system for Topps Ireland had never seemed so far away.

In a final attempt to demonstrate that there were no managerial grounds for postponing the commitment of Topps to the purchase of a system (software and hardware), another report was sent to HQ. In this report, it was particularly emphasized that a global IT strategy for the company made little sense, as no truly shared processes requiring integration of computer systems were identified, either between Ireland and the United States or between Topps and

Merlin. The computing cultures differed significantly as Merlin had full-time IT personnel and a networked IT infrastructure with its international subsidiaries No common processes existed between Merlin and Topps — no consolidation of financial information was required and a common supplier of systems would lead to significant cost increases in IT provision. Compatibility of each organization's systems would, however, be required to enable the smooth exchange of information and, for example, reports on the performance of various Topps and Merlin products. In addition, the implementation of a global strategy meant that Topps would have to sacrifice the possibility of using local support for the software, an added, and potentially costly, difficulty for a company without full-time resident IT expertise. This report was to change the minds of managers in the parent company. In mid-December 1995, news from HQ indicated that management should start implementing the decision to purchase an integrated computer system covering the financial, manufacturing, and distribution activities. Before the end of January, the cabling was put in place, and system installation began in earnest.

ERP "TEETHING TROUBLES" FOLLOWING IMPLEMENTATION

Topps management found that committing to a solution was not the only important aspect of the decision making in relation to deciding to implement its ERP system. Actual implementation involved enacting the choices made on the basis of management expertise and consultants' advice. And, implementation raised new issues and fresh questions that were overlooked or ignored throughout the previous stages.

More specifically, there were problems with the support provided by the system for the manufacturing operations of Topps' business. ERP systems are an extension of the MRP systems of the 1970s and are all based on some MRP logic. This means that companies should have an MRP-organized factory before they can implement an ERP system that also supports their manufacturing. At the time, Topps reduced its Cork-based manufacturing to a small number of products (most products originating in the Far East), but the factory floor was never MRP oriented. In fact, there had never been any JIT requirement in the factory, and it was not known how useful it would be to switch to MRP at that stage. This issue was increasingly relevant as the manufacturing operations of Topps' activities were being phased out. As a result, "workarounds" had to be implemented at the interface between the ERP and the manufacturing activities. Workarounds were portions of business processes that had to be "invented" in the system to ensure it could be used, even though it did not match the way things were being done. Developing the workarounds was not likely to compromise the success of the ERP implementation, because the products being made in the factory represented a small fraction of Topps turnover (approximately 15%).

There were also problems with Topps' staff's lack of familiarity with the software. These types of problems are common with enterprise-wide software such as ERP, and most companies that implement them find themselves on a steep learning curve from the moment their new system goes live. No amount of training is ever going to give staff members the confidence needed to use their ERP to its full extent. Thus, even though training was extensive, it took a while before staff members became accustomed to the new ways of doing business through the ERP system. Topps' business, like any other business, includes a certain level of idiosyncrasy, and in the ERP area, software providers can never become so familiar with a company that they would be able to anticipate every detail of the business processes. Some are replaced by new processes suggested by the package, but some remain and require workarounds that take a while to establish and to integrate into day-to-day routines. After a few weeks, staff members became more comfortable with their systems, and after a few months, they became experts at exploiting the functionality of their ERP software to develop Topps' business.

Another problem that arose was that of data migration, which is also common with ERP systems. ERP systems are organized around large databases that contain all the data required for the systems to operate properly and to link with other information systems the company may have decided to keep. These data must often be uploaded from the previous system (which is referred to as *migration*). This applies to the more stable data that a business uses, such as Bills of Material (describing the recipe of the company's products — see Chapter 2) and customer data, and also to some much-needed transactional information, such as invoicing data, sales data, and any other accounting-based data. In the case of Topps, the previous system was an obsolete integrated package running on an even more archaic computer. The data proved difficult to extract on account of the lack of flexibility of the old system. Also, the data did not always have the proper level of detail, as modern ERP systems offer far greater depths of information and far more schemes with which to classify and organize data. Thus, a substantial amount of manual data entry was originally required before the system could go live.

After a few months, however, it became clear to the managers at Topps that their ERP system was a sound investment and that the benefits obtained in terms of inventory management and acceleration of business processes would far outweigh these initial "teething troubles."

USING THE ERP SYSTEM —
JANUARY 2001

According to the Financial Controller in 2001, the ERP project was useful and positive from the first year of its implementation, and Topps progressed in leaps and bounds in terms of its information systems. At month's end, half an hour of work was sufficient to produce the group results, including UK operations and all other European branches. This used to take two weeks and, even then, did not allow managers to drill down into products, geographical areas, and activities with any flexibility. The ERP system provided managers with the complete set of information required to analyze the activities of the business. This added flexibility was achieved despite an enormous growth in sales, from IR£20m in 1996 to over IR£50m in 2000. The greatest advantage of the ERP system that was identified was how it allowed managers to control stocks, sales volumes, and quality in a way that was never possible before. Slow-moving lines were exposed, quality problems could be traced to specific consignments, and first-in, first-out stock movements could be strictly enforced. Such is the accuracy of the ERP system, that managers in Ireland could tell operators in the Rotterdam warehouse which cases should be shipped first. In practice, however, they did not need to do so, because the Rotterdam operators had remote access to the ERP system.

This was a significant improvement from a quality control point of view, because the appearance of lollipops disimproves over time (even though they are extremely slow to perish), and they become impossible to sell. Since the implementation of the ERP system, products no longer had to be destroyed on a regular basis.

As far as reporting was concerned, the ERP package was not initially sufficient to cater to Topps' needs. Even though all the required information was available, the report generation capabilities of the system were not sufficiently flexible. This problem was solved in 1998 with the purchase of an additional package (*Daytum*) that used the data contained in the ERP system to provide the drill-down and reporting capabilities required by Topps managers. Reporting could then be written for every single line or item sold by Topps, and customer profitability analyses could be carried out to an extent never possible before.

CONCLUSION
Goals of Information System Implementation for Topps

At the time the ERP system was researched, Topps possessed a combination of up-to-date managerial thinking but rather outdated administration. It was, therefore, certain that the introduction of state-of-the-art computing at Topps would have a significantly positive impact on the performance of the business and create a more reliable administration and management structure in the organization as a whole, especially given the increase in the volume of transactions dealt with by Topps Ireland Ltd. In the end, additional benefits arising from such an introduction include the following:

- An advance toward ISO certification (and the potential resulting benefits).
- A freeing of manpower for higher-level analytical tasks or improved customer service.
- An administrative system less reliant on individuals, thereby providing more permanent and consistent long-run company operations.

Given that Topps' business success revolves around making correct management decisions quickly, it is important that IT be applied efficiently to provide the rapid, accurate information on which to base these decisions. This occurred to a degree with the extensive use of spreadsheets, but these were not centrally available and sometimes were not preserved for use by more than one individual. Consequently, substantial duplication of work arose. Reports took more time to produce than they should, and the standard of presentation suffered as a result. Time better spent in utilizing the information creatively and efficiently to exploit opportunities and be aware of threats was then spent on gathering basic information.

The application of a modern software package substantially improved the quality of managerial reports. The investigations carried out also enabled the reduction of the excessive replication and duplication of work in administering the company. A fully integrated financial and distribution system effectively supported the basic business processes carried out at Topps and automated the basic flows of information within the organization. All modules of the system were not implemented simultaneously. A phased approach to implementation was perferred, once commitment to ultimately implement all modules in the medium term had been established.

ERP systems have inherent strengths and weaknesses and are, therefore, better suited to certain types of organizations and certain circumstances. Management at Topps, therefore, had to understand the inherent tradeoffs of an ERP system before they made any decision regarding the potential appropriateness of the ERP concept for their organization. While many consultants and media reports are prompt to emphasize the benefits of ERP implementations, the key issue resides in understanding the specific needs of an organization and the business model best suited to its operations.

The added difficulty in ERP projects is that few companies, if any, could possibly contemplate developing such vast applications in-house. For the majority of companies, the decision to implement ERP functionalities will mean buying a software package from one of the major suppliers on the ERP market.[2] The software selection phase is not straightforward, and managers must understand what ERP packages are offered, how they differ, and what is at stake in selecting one ERP over another. Each ERP package uses a business model as an underlying framework and can be quite different relative to competitors' products in terms of how they operate or the business processes they support. The problem for Topps management was that not all business models fit all organizations, and the cost of failing to recognize the relationship between the nature of one's business and the ERP system to be purchased could be high. Selecting the right software package, i.e., the right blueprint for one's organization, is a critical failure factor in ERP projects. An analysis of the strengths and weaknesses of ERP systems can help managers facing such decisions. It will reveal a mixed picture of the potential of ERP packages, which may be portrayed as silver bullets as often as villains. The message to be taken from the potential strengths and weaknesses of ERP systems for Topps management, is that they had to conduct a detailed analysis of proposed benefits and costs of their ERP system prior to going down the implementation road to ensure that the system could appropriately meet the organizational requirements. Of vital importance in this process was the consideration of the business strategy needs of Topps and the specific improvements that an enterprise-wide integrated software package would or would not provide.

ENDNOTES

1   While three separate companies existed, all activities were effectively administered through the Cork offices.

2   For example, SAP, Baan, JD Edwards, PeopleSoft, Oracle, or MFG/PRO.

Chapter IV

ERP Software Selection — Widening the Current Debate

David Sammon
University College Cork, Ireland

Frédéric Adam
University College Cork, Ireland

ABSTRACT

This chapter reflects on the nature of managerial decision making in the case of ERP projects. It draws on the increasing volume of organisational ERP literature now being published, but also attempts to draw lessons from the traditional research on decision making processes carried out over the last thirty years. This chapter documents the early stages of a larger research study, which is reported in various chapters in the book. Its main objective is to present a literature-based model, which integrally covers the phases which organisations go through (or should go through) when purchasing ERP packages, from the identification of the problems facing them to the review of the outcomes of the ERP projects. This represents a departure from current ERP literature, which has often focused on the software selection phase as if it were the key to organisational success and neglects the issue of organisational fit – i.e., the extent to which the business model underlying the ERP package selected fits the way an organisation conducts its business. We conclude from our observations that organisations are not well prepared when kicking off their ERP projects and that this may explain why many instances of relative ERP failure have been reported.

INTRODUCTION

ERP systems are integrated, enterprise-wide software packages that use a modular structure to support a broad spectrum of key operational areas of the organization. They are widely acknowledged as having the potential to radically change existing businesses by bringing improvements in efficiency and in the implementation of optimized business processes (Rowe, 1999). One of the key reasons why managers sought to proceed with difficult ERP projects is to end the fragmentation of current systems, to allow a process of standardization, to give more visibility on data across the entire corporation, and, in some cases, to obtain or maintain competitive advantage. Thus, ERP projects have been described as strategic projects with successes or failures that will have great impact on organizations (Rowe, 1999; Shakir, 2000; Wood & Caldas, 2000). Shakir (2000) concluded that ERP projects are expensive and time consuming, with costs typically exceeding US$100,000 and a timeframe for evaluation, selection, and implementation of an ERP system between six months and two years.

One key aspect of ERP projects that was reported by many authors is that failed implementations can be costly for the implementing organization. Foxmeyer (a multibillion dollar firm) paid the ultimate price, as they went bankrupt after failing to implement SAP over a three-year period (Kalakota & Robinson, 1999). Few ERP implementations are entirely successful, with approximately half failing to meet the implementing organization's expectations, due in most part, to an underestimation of the effort involved in change management (Stefanou, 2000; Appleton, 1997). Furthermore, it is estimated that approximately 90% of ERP implementations end up over-time and over-budget, due to poor cost and time estimations (Kelly et al., 1999; Shanks et al., 2000) and changes in project scope (Shanks et al., 2000).

These problems, associated with the high expectations of managers in the beneficial effects of ERP systems, led to a considerable amount of attention being directed to the ERP area. Thus, many leading journals in the IS area released Calls for Papers for special issues on various aspects of ERP projects. However, at this point, it seems that the attention of managers and researchers has focused nearly exclusively on certain stages of ERP projects, while other key points has been neglected. In particular, much of the literature concentrates on the implementation of these systems without paying enough attention to the reasons why organizations go down the ERP route or to the processes whereby managers select one particular ERP package instead of another. In addition, little attention has been paid to what happens after systems are implemented, in an attempt to determine to what extent the benefits that were sought by managers were achieved.

In order to redress the balance in the amount of attention that the different stages of the complex "ERP decision-making process" received, we undertook the study of the earlier and later stages of a number of ERP projects in order to evaluate whether managers follow sound rationales when they embark on the twisty ERP road, and whether their companies truly get value for their money from these risky projects.

DECISION-MAKING PROCESS IN THEORY

The process whereby managers make decisions is one of the most researched topics in the extended management area (Mintzberg et al., 1976; Hickson et al., 1985). Since Dewey (1933) and Simon (1960, 1977), a number of normative models of decision making were put forward that broke down this complex process into a variety of phases. Mintzberg et al. (1976) and Langley et al. (1995) presented excellent syntheses of this literature. Although the models put forward by these researchers have come under some criticism, they are still extremely useful in putting some order into managerial decisions that sometimes remain black boxes. Thus, March (1987) claimed that some decision-making processes appear to be without any order.

One of the most simple normative models — Simon's (1977) four-stage decision-making process — breaks down the decision-making process into (a) intelligence, (b) design, (c) choice, and (d) review. The application of this model to current studies of ERP implementations is interesting, because it reveals how few research projects looked at the first and fourth phases. However, as Pomerol (1994) remarked, the first of these phases is critical in that alternatives not considered initially are unlikely to be brought into the picture at a later stage. In relation to ERP projects, it would be interesting to understand why managers decide to implement ERP packages in the first place and what alternatives they consider. ERP implementations are large and complex projects, and definitive targets must be pursued in the project. Otherwise, the rationale for investing large amounts of capital, along with staff and management time and resources may be unjustified (Adam & O'Doherty, 2000). In terms of Simon's model, this puts sharp emphasis on the review phase, where managers must retrace their steps through the decision-making process and use some predefined metrics to establish what proportion of the objectives they set were achieved. Failure to conduct a review of such large decisions as ERP acquisition can lead to underachievement in terms of return on investment (in a qualitative sense as well as a quantitative sense) and to the sacrifice of valuable managerial and organizational learning.

Each ERP package uses a business model as an underlying framework, and they can differ in terms of how they operate or the business processes they support. The problem for managers is that not all business models fit all organizations, and the cost of failing to recognize the relationship between the nature of one's business and the ERP system to be purchased can be high. As a result, selecting the right software package, i.e., the right blueprint for one's organization, is a critical failure factor in ERP projects (Adam & O'Doherty, 2000; Stefanou, 2000). Managers must be able to put forward a set of specific requirements that correspond to the needs of their organization and not to standard, well-publicized sets of requirements as proposed by magazines and consultants. As always in the IS domain, the finished product, i.e., the implemented ERP system, will only be as good as the analysis that underpinned its selection and implementation.

In addition, Dvorak et al. (1997) and Maher (1999) highlighted that the selection of the system solution is only part of the overall process, and that the implementation of the solution will ultimately determine success and failure. The implementation of ERP systems is seen by researchers as much more effort-intensive than the decision-making process (Bernroider & Koch, 2000). Implementing ERP systems is a complex, lengthy, and expensive process (Shanks et al., 2000). Evidence throughout available literature suggests that many ERP systems implementations fail, to a degree or completely, to meet project constraints due to their complexity. Kelly et al. (1999) said:

The scale of ERP projects has rarely been tackled by most organisations. The reports of project "failures", cost and time

> *difficulties may be due to an inadequate organisational analysis at the beginning of the project.*

This seems to confirm that the initial phases of IS projects (whether they lead to an ERP project or to an alternative) hold the key to ultimate success. These phases broadly correspond to Simon's intelligence stage, where information is gathered about the problems identified by managers, a stage of the decision-making process that is clearly crucial in ERP projects.

A research study conducted by Shanks et al. (2000) presented a synthesis of an ERP systems implementation process model (adapted from Ross, 1998; Markus & Tanis, 1999) and a set of critical success factors for ERP systems implementation from previous empirical studies reported in the literature (extracted from Parr et al., 1999; Holland et al., 1999; Bancroft, 1996). This was undertaken in order to better understand and plan for ERP systems implementations. The four-phase implementation process model proposed by Shanks et al. (2000) is composed of "planning," "implementation," "stabilization," and "improvement." The planning phase, like the Ross (1998) "design" phase and the Markus and Tanis (1999) "chartering" phase, incorporates the selection of the ERP package. According to Ross (1998), most companies stop their evolution at the stabilization stage and never evolve to the improvement stage. In this last stage, organizations should learn enough about their new systems to reap further benefits and improve their business processes in a way not anticipated prior to undertaking the ERP project. Adam and O'Doherty (2000) found some evidence of organizations reaching such a stage in their studies of ERP implementations in Irish SMEs. Their findings indicated that organizations are more likely to achieve significant benefits from ERP implementations when they follow a strong business rationale and monitor the outcomes of their implementations carefully. This indicates that Simon's ideas about a review phase should apply to ERP projects. The review phase is meant to take place after the implementation of a decision and to help managers understand whether the decision unfolded as they planned or whether unanticipated factors intervened. It is our contention that such a phase should exist in ERP projects, and that researchers focusing on such a phase may learn a lot about the critical success factors of ERP projects.

Lucas (1981) defined implementation as the whole process of introducing a system into an organization, from conception of an idea, to analysis, design, installation, and operation. The inclusion of "conception of an idea" is something that seems to be overlooked throughout current research in ERP implementation, highlighting the issue that the decision-making process prior to ERP software selection is not considered within the scope of the implementation process models (Shanks et al., 2000). The analysis step of most ERP projects seems to skip the early stages and to focus on a package evaluation exercise (Kelly et al., 1999). The phase of problem finding (c.f., Pounds, 1969), where organizational actors identify stimuli in the environment that they come to perceive as problems requiring their attention, has not been a feature of many ERP projects. The approach of the year 2000 and the instruction of parent companies were put forward as the most common stimuli in ERP projects, and this does not fit the "silver bullet" image painted by ERP software vendors. If organizations truly went through a complete problem-finding phase in their decisions to purchase ERP packages, they should reach the conclusion that ERP is the way to go in a vendor-independent, methodology-independent, and preimplementation thought process. This is not the case in many projects, as bringing consultants in the company to organize the selection of existing ERP packages is often the first step in reported projects (Wood & Caldas, 2000; Caldas & Wood, 2000).

Furthermore, few companies, if any, contemplate developing such vast applications as ERP systems in-house. This fact translates into some managers taking the acquisition of ERP packages as given, instead of carrying out a feasibility study as is recommended for any IS investment (Ciborra, 1992; Clemons & Row, 1991). For the majority of companies, the decision to implement ERP functionalities will mean buying a software package from one of the major suppliers on the ERP market, e.g., SAP, Baan, JD Edwards (now acquired by PeopleSoft), PeopleSoft, or Oracle. However, the software selection phase is not straightforward, and managers must understand what ERP packages are offered, how they differ, and what is at stake in selecting one ERP over another. Furthermore, they must be able to put forward the key parameters that will be used to judge the success of their ERP projects and to monitor the progress of their organizations after implementation, based on predefined metrics, if their organizations are to benefit from such risky IS ventures.

PURCHASING STRATEGIC
INFORMATION SYSTEMS

The successful selection of a strategic IS begins with an understanding of the external and internal business environments and of the technological environment. Many organizations failed to reap the benefits of their IT investments, because they never achieved the level of integration and cohesiveness required between business and IT. The resultant information systems fail to meet the business requirements of the organization, because system requirements are either ill scoped or the selection process followed is not business driven (Adam & Twomey, 2001). In relation to ERP, the excessive intervention of vendors (through the intermediary of consulting groups) is an additional source of risk, as the needs of the company may not properly be taken into account.

In projects involving the purchase of systems, the relationship between the process followed (the stages) and the product obtained (the system) is particularly complex, because the product only appears at the very end of the process, instead of being delivered in stages (Adam & Twomey, 2001). The ERP area is one in which this is particularly evident, and much research is being devoted to it (Rowe, 1999). This is a major difficulty for organizations, because, at this point in time, the processes and issues associated with the selection and purchase of critical information systems are not as clear as the traditional process of software development (Adam & Cahen, 1998; Marciniak & Rowe, 1998).

Existing literature does not adequately deal with the steps and processes that organizations should follow when buying or selecting strategic IS solutions on the open market. The literature does not answer the question of how and why organizations could or should approach the selection of strategic IS solutions. The literature identifies the importance of IS system solutions to organizations, without providing a process so that the required solutions can be acquired (Adam & Twomey, 2001). Therefore, key questions are not addressed, including how to examine what steps could be followed, how to deal with potential suppliers, and what critical success factors are involved in the selection process.

IMPORTANCE OF THE SOFTWARE SELECTION STAGE IN IS INVESTMENTS

The decision to acquire an ERP system and the selection process leading to it are becoming increasingly complex in a changing and competitive environment (Stefanou, 2000). Within an organization, the ERP selection processes should be undertaken by the usual means of determining the mandatory and desirable features required in a system and then evaluating the various products according to these requirements (Stewart et al., 2000). However, these "usual means" can only be undertaken if the organization has a robust, unambiguous, and complete set of selection criteria. Failure to carry out such analyses with an open mind will lead to blind acceptance of the models underlying the ERP packages currently on sale on the market, with detrimental effects on the company and its operations (Wood & Caldas, 2000). Many organizations use the published specifications of the market-leading ERP vendors, typically SAP, as a framework with which to analyze their own requirements and select the package they want to buy, which is not in keeping with current thinking in IS development and acquisition, insofar as it biases the whole process toward one particular product from the outset.

Information systems have long been thought of as vital business tools (Clemons & Row, 1991). But, when IT (ERP packages in this case) is available to all firms, IS/IT cannot confer long-term competitive advantages over other firms unless they are used in an *inimitable way*, for instance, through a rigorous and specific analysis of organizational needs and capabilities. Furthermore, early adopters of ERP systems might not be in a better position if their followers benefit from their experiences and duplicate the system with newer technology and lower costs or avoid key obstacles to successful implementation. Clemons and Row (1991) put forward the need for managers to create a link between applications of IT and specific complementary resources that could make the difference between temporary successful applications and long-lasting competitive advantages, defined as "the ability to earn returns on investment persistently above the average of the industry." The aim is to avoid a situation in which all competitors access the innovation, and the same equilibrium of competitive forces is restored at a higher level of costs with no real benefits to anyone (see Chapter 8).

It is our contention that the quality of the analysis carried out at the earliest stage of ERP projects, which received little attention from researchers so far, is the primary factor in enabling companies to derive benefits from ERP over and above other firms. As described by Wood and Caldas (2000), too many firms acknowledged having obtained no benefits from these costly ventures, a situation that is not acceptable from a management point of view and that supports Ward and Griffith's (1996) contention that investment justification is "a fiction" in 80% of IS projects.

Thus, the only way to optimize the benefit from an application is to successfully analyze the distinctive competence and the specific needs of the firm. As Lee and Adams (1991) put it:

If all firms could use a cookbook approach to identifying strategic use of IT, then none of these firms would hold an edge over other firms, It is a matter of concern that many existing applications presented as strategic by the literature have quickly turned to a necessity or competitive liability rather than a competitive advantage.

And, as Vitale et al. (1986) pointed out:

Information Technology can shape the firm's strategy only if consideration of information assets and opportunities is incorporated into the firm's strategic planning process in some way. Technological opportunities available in the market place (...) may permit short term strategic gains or catch-up moves. But to achieve defendable, long term strategic benefits, those external opportunities will probably have to be linked to unique assets currently among the company's resources.

This emphasizes the importance of the early stages in the decision-making process of managers concerned that their firm's efficiency should be improved. Failure to identify problems properly and to ensure that purchasing an ERP package is the best solution available will result in the ERP package becoming what Lee and Adams' (1991) call a *competitive liability*—an application that every company feels they need, because all their competitors have one, but that no one can offer an explanation as to why it is needed.

CONCLUSION — TOWARD A FRAMEWORK FOR ERP SYSTEM SELECTION

Research proposed by Stefanou et al. (2000) provides a framework for the selection process of ERP systems. The three-phase ERP selection framework incorporates the "business vision" in Phase 1, the "business requirements vs. constraints and the desire to change" in Phase 2, and the "ERP systems selection/evaluation" in Phase 3. Stefanou (2000) concluded the following:

Careful selection of vendors, products and services provided is necessary but the final decision has to be made considering the amount of organisational change required for the adoption and the implementation of the selected ERP system.

Bernroider and Koch (2000) presented the differences in characteristics of the ERP system selection process between small-, medium-, or large-sized organizations. Their research focused on the different selection criteria, the actors involved in the process, the methods employed, and the implementation characteristics. Bernroider and Koch (2000) also pointed out the following:

The selection of the most appropriate solution is a semi-structured decision problem because only part of the problem can be handled by a definite or accepted procedure such as standard investment calculations and on the other hand the decision maker needs to judge and evaluate all relevant (and intangible) business impact aspects.

Thus, there is no agreed-upon and formal procedure for such critical investments as the purchase of ERP packages (Laudon & Laudon, 1998; Hecht, 1997), while nevertheless, the corresponding decisions strongly influence long-term business success.

In this chapter, we showed that the old-fashioned decision-making models, such as Simon's (1977), which break the process into a number of phases, still have much to offer in terms of the study of ERP implementations. The application of these models to reported cases of ERP implementations clearly shows the failure of both practice and research to follow a complete and independent thinking process, from the identification of organizational problems to the implementation of the purchased package.

These observations lead to a number of interesting conclusions that extend currently proposed models for ERP implementations at both ends. First, managers must take a step back from the media and vendor pounding they are subjected to in relation to ERP and reflect on the nature of the problems facing their organizations. Alternatives must be considered given the large opportunity costs involved in purchasing or not purchasing an ERP package. Second, the requirements of organizations must be analyzed independently of vendor documentation, because the best practice built into market-leading ERP packages may not suit all organizations. Third, the postimplementation phase of ERP packages must be given much more attention, both in terms of preparation (development of metrics to monitor success, reporting channels, etc.) and in terms of managerial attention. Key learning in relation to the ERP software may be obtained that will enable managers to steer their organizations into the improvement phase envisaged by Ross (1998).

Finally, any ERP software selection process used by an organization will have to be based upon a robust, unambiguous, and complete set of selection criteria. These organizational criteria should be identified prior to any discussions with potential suppliers and should be used consistently in the selection of potential suppliers, the evaluation of tenders, and the ultimate selection of the ERP package. Ultimately, such analyses will present decision makers, who are responsible for implementing ERP, with a framework for internally assessing the suitability of the ERP concept and specific ERP packages to their organization, through leveraging their business requirements.

REFERENCES

Adam, F., & Cahen, F. (1998). L'achat des systèmes d'information informatiques comme alternative au développement spécific: le Cas Socrate. *Systèmes d'Information et Management, 3*(4), 79-100.

Adam, F., & O'Doherty, P. (2000). Lessons from enterprise resource planning implementations in Ireland — Towards smaller and shorter ERP projects. *Journal of Information Technology, 15*(4), Special issue on ERP, 305-320.

Adam, F., & Twomey, D. (2001). Purchasing critical information systems — The Bord Gais case study. Forthcoming in *Systèmes d'Information et Management, 6*(3), 75-96.

Appleton, E. (1997). How to survive ERP. *Datamation, 43*(March), 50-53.

Bancroft, N. (1996). *Implementing SAP/R3: How to Introduce a Large System into a Large Organisation.* London: Manning/Prentice Hall.

Bernroider, E., & Koch, S. (2000). Differences in characteristics of the ERP system selection process between small or medium and large organizations. *Proceedings of the 6th Americas Conference on Information Systems* (August 10-13, pp. 1022-1028). Long Beach, California.

Caldas, M., & Wood, T. (2000). *How consultants can help organizations survive the ERP frenzy.* Retrieved from the World Wide Web: http://www.gv.br/prof_alunos/thomaz/ingles/paper6.htm.

Ciborra, C. (1992). From thinking to tinkering: The grassroots of strategic information systems. *Proceedings of the 1992 ICIS Conference* (pp. 283-291).

Clemons, E., & Row, M. (1991). Sustaining IT advantage: The role of structural differences. *MIS Quarterly*, (September).

Dewey, J. (1933). *How We Think*. Boston, MA: Heath.

Dvorak, R. E., Holen, E., Mark, D., & Meehan III, W. F. (1997). Six principles of high-performance IT. *The McKinsey Quarterly*, 3, 164-177.

Hecht, B. (1997). Managing resources — Choose the right ERP software. Plugin *Datamation*.

Hickson, D. J., Butler, R. J., Cray, D., Mallory, D., & Wilson, D. C. (1985). Comparing 150 decision processes. In Pennings et al. (Eds.), *Organisational Strategy and Change*. Hoboken, NJ: Jossey-Bass.

Holland, C. P., Light, B., & Gibson, N. (1999). A critical success factors model for enterprise resource planning implementation. In *Proceedings of the 7th European Conference on Information Systems* (pp. 273-287). Copenhagen, Denmark: Copenhagen Business School.

Kalatoka, R., & Robinson, M. (1999). *E-business — Roadmap to Success*. Reading, MA: Addison-Wesley.

Kelly, S., Holland, P., & Light, B. (2000). A departure from traditional systems development methodologies: Enterprise resource planning, ERP, systems and the use of process modelling tools. In *Proceedings of the 9th Annual Business Information Technology Conference* (November 3-4, 1999). Manchester.

Langley, A., Mintzberg, H., Pitcher, P., Posada, E., & Saint-Macary, J. (1995). Opening up decision making: The view from the black stool. *Organisation Science*, 6(3), 190-205.

Laudon, K. C., & Laudon, J. P. (1998). *Management Information Systems — New Approaches to Organization and Technology* (5th ed.). Englewood Cliffs, NJ: Prentice Hall.

Lee, M., & Adams, D. (1990). A manager's guide to the strategic potential of information systems. *Information and Management*, 19, 105-114.

Lucas Jr., H. (1981). *Implementation: The Key to Successful Information Systems*. New York: Guilford.

Maher, J. K. (1999). ERP in industry: Automate and integrate. *The Engineers Journal*, (November), 36-41.

March, J. P. (1987). Ambiguity and accounting: The elusive link between information and decision making. *Accounting, Organisations and Society*, 12(2), 153-168.

Marciniak, R., & Rowe, F. (1998). Enjeux et complexité des projets de systèmes d'information. *Systemes d'Information et Management*, 43, 3-16.

Markus, M. L., & Tanis, C. (1999). *The enterprise systems experience — From adoption to success*. Working paper. Claremont, CA: Claremont Graduate University.

Mintzberg, H., Raisinghani, D., & Theoret, A. (1976). The structure of "unstructured" decision processes. *Administrative Science Quarterly*, 21, 246-275.

Parr, A., Shanks, G., & Darke, P. (1999). Identification of necessary factors for successful implementation of ERP systems. In O. Ngwenyama, L. D. Introna, M. D. Myers, & J. I. Degross (Eds.), *New Information Technologies in Organizational Processes* (pp. 99-119). Boston, MA: Kluwer Academic Publishers.

Pomerol, J. C. (1994). *Le monde de l'aide à la decision*. LAFORIA — Working Papers Series, 94/20, pp. 1-26.

Pounds, W. (1969). The process of problem finding. *Industrial Management Review*, 10(1), 1-19.

Ross, J. W. (1998). *The ERP revolution: Surviving versus thriving*. Working paper. Cambridge, MA: Center for Information Systems Research, Sloan School of Management, MIT.

Rowe, F. (1999). Cohérence, intégration informationnelle et changement: Esquisse d'un programme de recherche à partir des progiciels intégrés de gestion. *Systèmes d'Information et Management*, 4(4), 3-20.

Shakir, M. (2000). Decision making in the evaluation, selection and implementation of ERP systems. In *Proceedings of the 6th Americas Conference on Information Systems* (August 10-13, pp. 1033-1038). Long Beach, California.

Shanks, G., Parr, A., Hu, B., Corbitt, B., Thanasankit, T., & Seddon, P. (2000). Differences in critical success factors in ERP systems implementation in Australia and China: A cultural analysis. In *Proceedings of the 8th European Conference on Information Systems* (July 3-5, pp. 537-544). Vienna, Austria.

Simon, H. (1977). *The New Science of Management Decision*. Englewood Cliffs, NJ: Prentice Hall.

Simon, H. A. (1960). *The New Science of Management Decision*. Englewood Cliffs, NJ: Prentice-Hall.

Stefanou, C. (2000). The selection process of enterprise resource planning, ERP, systems. In *Proceedings of the 6th Americas Conference on Information Systems* (August 10-13, pp. 988-991). Long Beach, California.

Stewart, G., Milford, M., Jewels, T., Hunter, T., & Hunter, B. (2000). Organisational readiness for ERP implementation. In *Proceedings of the 6th Americas Conference on Information Systems* (August 10-13, pp. 966-971). Long Beach, California.

Vitale, M., Ives, B., & Beath, C. (1986). Linking information technology and corporate strategy: An organisational view. In *Proceedings of the International Conference on Information Systems* (pp. 265-274).

Ward, J., & Griffiths, P. (1996). *Strategic Planning for Information Systems*. New York: John Wiley & Sons.

Wood, T., & Caldas, M. (2000). *Stripping the "Big Brother": Unveiling the backstage of the ERP fad*. Retrieved from the World Wide Web: http://www.gv.br/prof_alunos/thomaz/ingles/paper5.htm.

Chapter V

Understanding the Business Consequences of ERP Systems

Lorraine Staehr
La Trobe University, Australia

Graeme Shanks
Monash University, Australia

Peter B. Seddon
University of Melbourne, Australia

ABSTRACT

This study examines the postimplementation period of an ERP implementation in an Australian manufacturing organization, with the aim of understanding and explaining the business consequences that occurred. The description of the case is followed by an analysis using the structurational model of technology. The radical change in the way users needed to understand the business in terms of the new system, coupled with insufficient training and support postimplementation, and user resistance to change, impacted on the benefits the organization gained from the system.

INTRODUCTION

Enterprise Resource Planning (ERP) systems are large software packages that provide an integrated environment based on an enterprise-wide data model with a set of software applications that allow processing of all the data of the organization (Bancroft et al., 1996). Despite collective investment by organizations worldwide in ERP systems in the order of billions of dollars (Stein, 1999), many organizations do not know if they have achieved a positive return on their investment. Few studies looked at the postimplementation period of ERP systems to determine how and why business benefits evolve over time. Of those that have (Shang & Seddon, 2000; Markus & Tanis, 2000), neither study examined the postimplementation phase of ERP implementation in a manufacturing organization in detail over time to determine its influence on business benefits in the longer term. It is of significant interest to senior management of organizations, IS practitioners, and IS academic researchers to know more about the postimplementation period of ERP systems, the business benefits that result during the period, and how and why these consequences occurred.

ERP systems have been studied from a number of different perspectives. These include project management, outsourcing, organizational knowledge, large packaged software, critical success factors for implementation, and business benefits, to name a few (Esteves & Pastor, 2001). In this study, ERP implementation and use are viewed from the perspective of organizational change (Boudreau & Robey, 1999; Davenport, 2000). The postimplementation period of an ERP implementation in an Australian manufacturing organization is examined with the aim of understanding and explaining the business consequences that occurred. The structurational model of technology is used as the lens through which the postimplementation period is analyzed. A number of researchers used or proposed the use of structuration theory to understand ERP implementation and use (Boudreau & Robey, 1999; Chae, 2001; Pozzebon, 2001; Volkoff, 1999). The structurational model of technology (Orlikowski, 1992) was used by Volkoff (1999) to analyze the implementations of ERP systems in two organizations. The research reported in this chapter is part of a larger study that aims to understand and explain how and why some organizations gain more business benefits from their ERP systems than others. The outcomes from this research are limited, because the structuration model of technology was used to analyze ERP use in only one organization.

The chapter is organized in three main sections. The first section outlines the theoretical background, followed by a description and interpretation of the case using the structurational model of technology, and finally, a discussion and conclusion section.

THEORETICAL BACKGROUND

Structurational theory (Giddens, 1984) provides a lens through which to analyze social systems, but it does not explicitly mention Information Technology. The structurational model of technology (Orlikowski & Robey, 1991; Orlikowski, 1992; Orlikowski, 2000) bridges this gap and provides a model based on Gidden's structurational theory that IS researchers can use to analyze the development, implementation, and use of Information Technology within organizational settings.

In this research, the structurational model of Information Technology is used to understand and explain the business consequences of ERP use in a single organization. Because the structurational model of technology is an emergent process theory (Markus & Robey, 1988; Orlikowski & Robey, 1991; Walsham & Han, 1991), it is a suitable theory to use for an empirical study examining the interactions of context and process over time.

A brief account of structurational theory (Giddens, 1984) is necessary, as it underpins the structurational model of technology. There are three dimensions of institutionalized social structure in organizations: signification, legitimation, and domination. It is important to note that this institutionalized social structure consists of rules and resources that exist only in the human actor's minds. There are also three dimensions of human action: communication, power, and sanctioning of conduct. The dimensions of institutional social structure are produced and reproduced over time by the dimensions of human action. This interaction between structure and human action is called the "duality of structure," and it produces changing interpretive schemes, is affected by resources, and may either establish new norms of behavior or reinforce old ones.

Routinization of social activity is an important aspect of human action in structuration theory and describes the difficulty in getting people to act differently. Walsham and Han (1991) called this "fixity of social conduct." In other words, there is a tendency for humans to exhibit habitual behavior, the behavior they already know and are comfortable with, and consequently, they exhibit a natural resistance to change.

Structuration theory is not without its critics. Jones (1999) provided an overview of these criticisms, discussed the ways structuration theory was used in management and IS research, and outlined two extensions to structuration theory to make it more suitable for IS research. Of the two extensions discussed, Orlikowski's structurational model of technology is "closer to the spirit of structuration theory as Giddens has described it" (Jones, 1999), although the definition of technology as a material artifact presents some problems.

In the structurational model of technology (Orlikowski & Robey, 1991; Orlikowski, 1992; Orlikowski, 2000), shown in Figure 1, the technology plays an intermediary role between the organizational properties in the form of social structure and human action. The development, implementation, and use of technology supports or changes the three modalities: interpretive schemes, resources, and norms. It may enforce new interpretive schemes by producing new ways for human actors to understand their work. It provides specific material resources, and the way it was implemented (its configuration) may change authoritative resources, redistributing power and establishing new norms for human action. Orlikowski (1992) proposed a "duality of technology," because technology is developed and altered by human action, yet it is used by human actors to achieve some purpose. Another important aspect of technology is that it is interpretively flexible in development, implementation, and use. The technology, as a product of human action, is not fixed in a particular configuration from the outset, but there are many choices to be made during the development process with different associated outcomes. Some software (e.g., ERP systems) is also interpretively flexible during implementation, as extensive configuration and customization are possible as part of the implementation process. Likewise, the use of technology is interpretively flexible in that there are different ways that it may be used, influenced by both organizational properties and human actors. Technology, therefore, both enables and constrains human action, and there will be both intended and unintended outcomes from its development, implementation, and use.

THE CASE STUDY

An interpretive case study approach was taken. Full details of the research design can be found in Staehr et al. (2002). Data was collected between February and November 2001. The primary source of data collection was from face-to-face in-depth semistructured interviews with eight key informants, chosen because of their positions within the organization. Interviewees included a member of senior management, the IT manager, two business representatives on the ERP implementation team, three business unit managers, and a business analyst. All interviewees (except one) were employed by the organization for at least two years prior to the ERP implementation. Interviews were tape recorded, transcribed, and returned to interviewees for checking to ensure

Figure 1. The Structurational Model of Technology (Adapted from Orlikowski, 1992)

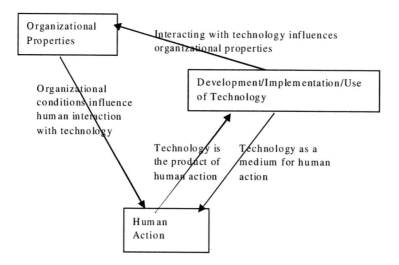

accuracy. To provide triangulation, other sources of data collected were company documentary evidence, for example, annual reports, company news-letters, etc.

A description and an interpretation of the case study using the structurational model of technology (Orlikowski & Robey, 1991; Orlikowski, 1992, 2000) follows. This is organized into three main parts: background information concerning the case study organization, the SAP system planning and implementation, and the use of the SAP system. Although the use of the SAP system is of primary interest, a deeper understanding can be gained by examining the historical and contextual organizational factors that preceded its use.

Background

ManA is a publicly owned Australian company employing around 9,000 staff members across approximately 30 countries and with revenue of $A4 billion annually. It was one of the first companies in Australia to implement an ERP system. In the early 1990s, ManA had legacy systems that needed replacing due to increasing problems with maintenance and the looming year 2000 (Y2K) problem. Some systems, for example, inventory, were 14 years old. At this stage, the company had only a small shared service capability, within IT and finance. A need was seen for an integrated system. Various ERP systems were evaluated, and SAP was the system chosen. ManA intended to ensure that its four divisions were operating at the leading edge of IT and planned to use IT as a basis for improved customer service.

The implementation of SAP throughout the organization was used as an enabler of structural change. The limited IT and finance shared service capability was expanded to include other functional areas, e.g., engineering. However, the shared services are implemented as separate instances of SAP for each division. In ManA, SAP was implemented one division at a time, with the last implementation going live in June 2001. The company is also supporting different versions of SAP, although it is planned to have all divisions on version 4.6 in the next six to eight months (as of August 2001). The organization as a whole spent more than $100 million over time on its SAP implementations. As one of the first Australian companies to implement SAP, its staff members with SAP experience were in high demand. They were offered very high salaries that ManA did not match, and expertise was lost.

This case entity is a consumer products business (BrandX), making up about three-quarters of the Consumer Products (CP) Division in ManA. BrandX consists of a number of different businesses with sites geographically dispersed in Australia and New Zealand. The individual businesses are referred to as A, B, C, etc., in this chapter.

The "go-live" date was four months before the introduction of the Goods and Services Tax (GST) in Australia. As the products were to attract the GST, this meant that there was an unusually high demand immediately prior to the introduction of the GST in July 2000 and a corresponding drop in demand in the six to 12 months after the introduction of the GST. BrandX also had to respond to a changing retail landscape that is moving toward larger retail stores at the expense of small, independently run stores. This had an impact on distribution and the channels used to sell the products. The current state of the IT industry means that CP has only 60% full-time IT staff, and the shortfall is made up with 40% contract staff. This allows some flexibility according to varying needs.

SAP System Planning and Implementation

The influence of the organizational properties of ManA in the form of material resources on the BrandX implementation was evident from the start. BrandX did not evaluate ERP systems for use in its businesses but followed the other divisions within ManA, who were all using SAP (#2 in Figure 2). There is evidence to suggest that SAP was not the best choice from the point of view of manufacturing in BrandX. As the Logistics and Planning Manager, Business B, (BrandX) stated:

> *…early in '97 my team recognised that the software that we had wasn't going to get us to class A in the MRP II project and we looked at five different software alternatives of which SAP was one and I've got to say that it wasn't my preferred option. That was my recommendation to the executive at the time but [ManA] as we were then had previously made the decision to go to SAP…*

The organizational properties of ManA in the form of authoritative resources (#2 in Figure 2) also influenced the composition of the BrandX SAP implementation team. ManA used SAP as an enabler of structural change in its move to expand its shared service capability. This required staff reductions that occurred during the implementation process. The choice of business representatives for the SAP implementation team was used to facilitate some reductions in staff. Instead of using the best business people, second- and third-level staff members were chosen with the knowledge that after implementation, they would no longer have a job within the company. The following quote by the

Figure 2. The Configuration and Customization of SAP R/3 for BrandX

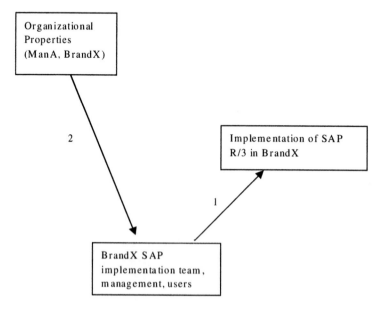

Business Improvement Manager, Financial Shared Services, ManA, outlines the unintended consequences of this course of action:

> *... by taking people from the business and putting them there, yes, you share a bit of knowledge but you also carry across bad practices because if a person is doing a job today and is comfortable with the way they are doing it and you then go and configure your SAP to mirror what you've done, what you've done is you've taken an existing process without reengineering, without doing a BPR, and therefore your bad habits get configured and personally I've actually seen this happen.*

SAP was implemented through the human agency of the BrandX implementation team (#1 in Figure 2). The technology, in this case the SAP software, is the filter through which understanding of the business and its processes must be viewed by users postimplementation. The way the SAP software is configured can shape new structures of signification. Old ways of viewing the business can impact how the SAP system is configured in the implementation process and, therefore, ultimately affect the benefits from its use. The SAP software is interpretively flexible, that is, it is possible to configure the software to suit the existing business processes of the organization or, alternatively, the claimed "best practices" of the software can be used to improve the organization's business processes. For the BrandX implementation, there was no reengineering, and the best practices of the existing businesses within BrandX were implemented. This meant that business processes were standardized across BrandX. However, the consequences of implementing the existing business processes may limit the benefits obtained from the software, as the following quote by the Logistics and Planning Manager, Business A (BrandX) testified:

> *What we did was we said, no, no, no the software has to change to fit the current process. Whether our process is right or not that's what we know so that's what we are going to do. So in essence if the process was wrong all that SAP enabled us to do is do the wrong things more quickly, which was, it's a bit of a cynical view I know, but ideally when you are implementing software you get your processes right before you get the software put in place so that you can take advantage of the software early on.*

The BrandX implementation team was influenced by the organizational properties of ManA in the form of material resources (#2 in Figure 2), that is, by the consultants on the team with experience in other SAP rollouts in the organization. Unfortunately, this experience with previous implementations in ManA involved businesses very different from BrandX. Some of the existing knowledge and norms the consultants had about SAP implementations in ManA (#1 in Figure 2) were not appropriate when it came to the BrandX implementation, because the BrandX businesses were so different from the businesses in the other divisions of ManA. As the Business Improvement Manager, Financial Shared Services, ManA, stated:

> *...the consumer business is very, very different to the rest of [ManA]. It is a totally different business because it's a consumer product business and it's got retail, it's just the sheer size and volume of its customer base, its supplier base and its manufacturing processes are so different to the rest of the organization.*

As indicated in the quote above, the sheer volume of data differentiated BrandX from the other division businesses. For example, the other divisions might deal with 500 large dollar value sales per week, while BrandX dealt with 15,000 smaller dollar value transactions per week. The unusually large number of stock-keeping units (10,000) also proved to be a problem for the SAP software.

The numbers on the project team varied according to need during the various stages of the project, but the core team consisted of 58 people. It was an advantage to have business representatives on the project team who were empowered to make decisions (#2 in Figure 2). This saved time. There was consultation with business management and users who were not on the project team when necessary, especially during the "as-is" phase of the implementation.

The SAP system was implemented on time, within budget, and with the original scope. It was, therefore, considered successful. It was a comprehensive "big bang" implementation (Parr & Shanks, 2000), and the "go-live" date was February 28, 2000. Although it was claimed that the SAP implementation was for business reasons, it is interesting to note that the implementation was approached as a systems replacement. The software was tailored to match existing business processes, that is, there was no reengineering prior to the implementation. The rationale was to take the best practices of the businesses in BrandX and implement those. There is evidence to suggest that this translated into the biggest getting the most say. One small business within the division felt that it did not get the support of the SAP implementation team before implementation due to its small size. It was not a "vanilla" implementation, as the project required extensive customization of SAP (code changes) in the production planning area. This customization was driven by one of the larger businesses within the division (#2 in Figure 2) through the human agency of the BrandX SAP implementation team (#1 in Figure 2). The BrandX SAP implementation team was disbanded three months after the "go-live" date.

The type of training users required varied between the functional units of the businesses. For example, users in finance previously worked with Windows-based systems, and the transition for them was not as great as in other areas. In contrast, in the distribution area, a deliberate effort was made to ease the transition for operators. The SAP input screens were modified to mimic the screens from the legacy system. This was an attempt to bridge the transition from the old interpretive schemes of the legacy system to the new interpretive schemes required by SAP. These customized interfaces were extremely beneficial for users but presented problems when hot packs (software patches) needed to be installed, and will, of course, be a continuing problem with upgrades.

The rules and norms brought by some members of the implementation team from their experience in other ManA SAP rollouts was not helpful, due the vastly different nature of the BrandX businesses (#2 in Figure 2). There was also a perception that the rules and norms of the larger businesses within BrandX were given more say in the implementation of the existing "best practice" business processes.

The decisions made prior to and during the implementation process are important, as they can affect the benefits gained from ERP systems (Markus & Tanis, 2000). When SAP is configured using existing business processes, as is the case in BrandX, this may also limit the benefits gained from its use. The SAP software, configured and customized by the BrandX implementation team (#1 in Figure 2), provided new interpretive schemes that required users to have a new understanding of the business and its processes, and a new way of communicating about their daily tasks.

Use of the SAP System

The first month after "go-live" went relatively smoothly. This was because the old system was used to forecast production for the first month of operation of the new SAP system. It took six months for the old historical data to get loaded onto the new system. Problems with production planning meant that only 30% to 40% of the volume required was manufactured, and it took 12 months to overcome these problems. Insufficient stock was available for the Christmas 2000 period (nine months after "go-live").

There were credit and collection problems due to the financial shared services enabled by SAP. For example, if an invoice was out one item, it had to be sent from the head office, 2000 kilometers away, for verification and adjustment and then sent back before the invoice could be paid. This required high-level communication and explanations between BrandX and its suppliers. These problems persist to some extent.

There were performance problems, and it took nine months and a couple of hardware upgrades before this was resolved. The structures of signification (knowledge of the work being automated) brought by the SAP consultants with experience in other ManA implementations contributed to this problem (#2 in Figure 2). The lack of understanding of how different the BrandX businesses were from the businesses in other ManA divisions contributed to the hardware being unable to cope with the large volume of data.

There were repercussions due to narrowly focused training and to users' lack of understanding of the impact of their mistakes in a highly integrated system. The material resources in the form of change management and training were not adequate in embedding the new structures of signification required by users to do their work effectively. The IT Manager, CP Division, said:

> ...I think the post SAP implementation was where we were lacking. ...what we really didn't do enough of was say how it linked to the job and how the job linked to the wider organization and that if you make a mistake here are the ongoing implications downstream or if there is an issue with your business this is what could have caused it from before...someone before you is actually putting data in.

These new structures of signification affect all users, as comprehension of the new interpretive schemes provided by SAP impacts on how well they are able to interact and communicate with colleagues in the workplace (#5 in Figure 3). As stated by the Materials Manager, Business B (BrandX):

> ...the people who have been around for a while understood, thought they understood how the whole thing worked and now all of a sudden bang they are right back down to kindergarten

level with everyone else and they have got the baggage of having the old system still in their mind while trying to operate an entirely different new system.

The SAP system, with its new rules and resources, threatened the security of employees by the changes required in workplace roles (#6 in Figure 3). As the Materials Manager, Business B (BrandX) said:

I guess our people felt really insecure in their roles. The change was so huge that people felt inadequate in their jobs and they felt threatened by the change.

The training provided prior to implementation apparently did little to allay the anxiety the users experienced in coping with the SAP software.

Organizational conditions influence human interaction with and reactions to technology (#4 in Figure 3). The material resources provided for change management, training, and support had an impact on the benefits BrandX gained from use of the SAP software. Basic training was provided for users before the system went live, but the relevance of this training was questioned in some areas. The information in the training system was not "real" in terms of BrandX's data, and it was not possible to do much with it to see and understand what the new system would be like. Also, it was expected that users would supplement the training sessions by finding time to spend in the training

Figure 3. Use of SAP R/3 in BrandX

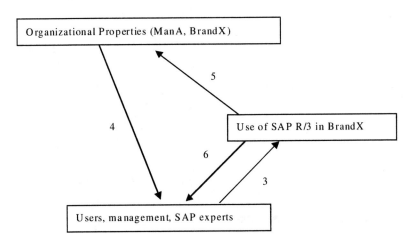

environment during their normal working hours. When the system went live, there was on-site support for only a two-week period at the largest manufacturing site. This was clearly felt to be inadequate, as the following quote by the Materials Manager, Business B (BrandX) indicated:

> *The system support was for the start-up period and it was here on-site. We had a person looking after the purchasing side of things and one from the production scheduling and a couple of support staff from ManA who had already gone live with SAP in previous years. They were on site for about two weeks. They probably needed to be on site for 12 months. ...There was system support through telephones etc. but if you can imagine the amount of phone calls that were going through, etc., etc., etc. We regularly obviously advised that we needed to have support on the shop floor, you know to help people manage through the change. ...So we had support over the phone but that is less than acceptable to be honest.*

It took this site until 18 months after "go-live" before they got a ManA SAP expert on site to help with some major problems that they had with the system. However, it is interesting to note that this need not have been the case. Members of the BrandX SAP implementation team noted early in the implementation process that BrandX would no longer be dependent on internal IT expertise, and that SAP expertise would not only be available within the company but also would be readily available from outside the company. However, organizational properties in the form of existing structures of legitimization influenced this site from going outside the company to acquire SAP expertise, as it was not officially sanctioned conduct (#4 in Figure 3).

In the customer service area, there is evidence of the impact of insufficient training and support postimplementation, i.e., the lack of material resources, on the way the system is used (#4 in Figure 3). As a Customer Service Representative on the SAP implementation team (BrandX) said:

> *...I get very frustrated when you put in manual band-aids when the system will fix an issue...they have put in a manual system where the girls have to key in the plant that they want the order to come from. Not how it should be done. We can exclude that material. ...They don't know they are not using the system*

properly because they do not know how to use it properly. A lot of the benefits from these things is knowing the system.

The quote above illustrates one example of the SAP system being used in an unintended and inefficient way. Previous research showed that these practices quickly become routine and, therefore, difficult to change as time goes by (Tyre & Orlikowski, 1994). This indicates that insufficient training and support postimplementation holds back the realization of benefits from the SAP system for BrandX.

There are examples of decreases in productivity. The input error rate is high, and rework costs are high. A global benchmarking survey of 256 companies showed that ManA's incoming error input rate was very high compared to others around the world. At one site, in BrandX there was an increase of half to one staff member in the warehouse area to ensure data quality (#5 in Figure 3). In the customer service area, the cost of having better information from the system meant that the input time for orders increased slightly, with no change in staff requirements. However, less staff members are required in the production planning area. Both financial and inventory cycle times were reduced, but there was no manufacturing cycle time reduction due to SAP. The most noticeable productivity gains were made in the finance area, but this was largely due to the expansion of financial shared services. The use of the SAP software had an impact on organizational properties by directly influencing the number of staff, i.e., material resources required in different functional areas (#5 in Figure 3).

There has been no IT cost reduction at the CP division level, although there may have been cost reductions at higher levels in ManA. This is due to the high cost of SAP contractors and the dependence of the CP division on them for approximately 40% of IT staff.

The authoritative resources provided by the SAP software brought new visibility and accountability to users of the system at BrandX (#6 in Figure 3). As the Business Improvement Manager, Financial Shared Services, ManA, said:

> *...it forces accountability...with SAP because it's integrated you actually see the impact of your actions almost instantly. ...it's made people more accountable because there's transparency in what happens. ...you have somebody like a warehouse person who'd never worry about dollars before becomes a bit more aware of that.*

Authoritative resources reinforce systems of domination through changes in power relations made possible by the new technology. The integration provided by the SAP software meant that users could no longer hide mistakes, as their work impacted almost immediately in other areas of the business. As a finance business representative on the SAP implementation team remarked, "factory people cannot keep secrets about problems in production." The previous structures of domination in BrandX were extended by SAP, resulting in increased management control. This "informating" aspect of information systems was first observed and defined by Zuboff (1988) and was also reported by Sia et al. (2002) in the study of an ERP system in a hospital.

Although use of an ERP system can be considered mandatory (Pozzebon, 2000), this is not true for all tasks, and one example is management reporting. Although it is acknowledged in BrandX that there is better information available for decision making, it is not generally felt that this is being taken advantage of at this stage. One of the reasons may be the difficulty of overcoming the effects of routinization, which can obstruct the introduction of new ways of doing work. The introduction of financial shared services enabled by and implemented prior to SAP, meant that in many cases, managers and users, although reluctant, were forced to use the system to produce their own reports because the person who had done this for them previously was no longer available. This forced the new norms to come into practice (#6 in Figure 3). The Finance Business Analyst, Retail (BrandX) said the following:

> ...people are used to just picking up the phone to someone and saying can you run this for me and you say well actually you know it's pretty easy for you to do it yourself so I will come up and show you how to run it.

In contrast, the authoritative resources provided by SAP and its enablement of shared services changed workplace norms and, in the process, empowered managers and users (#6 in Figure 3). As Site Manager (BrandX) said:

> I am able to get information I wasn't able to get before and I can get it without having to go to a programmer, without having to put in a request and I can get it immediately and you can download the information to a file and sort it, do whatever you want without any real problem.

However, this is not typical across BrandX. Whereas 95% of the users in the finance area adjusted to the new norms, in other functional areas, the percentage may be as low as 50%.

Increased accountability and visibility of users made possible by the SAP system and its use by management are examples of the way that technology constrains human action. However, users were also empowered by having access to more information and the ability to query the SAP system. This empowerment of users illustrates how the SAP system enabled human action.

Despite the early postimplementation problems, BrandX managed to gradually improve its use of the SAP system. Configuration and customization of SAP continued during the postimplementation period, with SAP experts changing the software to match BrandX's business processes (#3 in Figure 3) and BrandX managers and users taking advantage of SAP capabilities to gradually improve business processes (#5 in Figure 3).

The manufacturing section within BrandX had the most problems with the use of the SAP system. At 21 months post-go-live, one manufacturing site believed that business improvement had only come in the last few months. The staff at the largest manufacturing site did not believe its customer service levels were back where they were before the SAP implementation. The current priority at BrandX is ongoing improvement of business processes and their alignment with SAP. However, it should be noted that 21 months post-go-live is still relatively early in the postimplementation phase. The realization of business benefits can take time to achieve, with some estimates as long as four years (DeLoitte Consulting, 1999).

DISCUSSION AND CONCLUSION

The structurational model of technology was used as a lens in order to gain a deeper understanding of the postimplementation period of an ERP system in a single manufacturing organization. It highlighted the importance of historical and contextual factors in understanding how new organizational properties were shaped through human agency during the implementation and use of the SAP software and how existing organizational properties were reinforced and strengthened. It also facilitated viewing the postimplementation period from multiple levels of analysis, for example, the level of organization (ManA, BrandX), group (SAP implementation team, management), and individual (user).

A number of historical and contextual factors conspired to limit the business benefits that BrandX achieved from its SAP system. Specific factors during the implementation process were as follows:

- SAP may not have been the best ERP software choice (from the BrandX manufacturing perspective).
- The method of selection of members of the BrandX SAP implementation team had an impact.
- The consultants brought assumptions about the BrandX businesses to the implementation team.
- Configuration and customization of SAP to match existing business processes may not coincide with specific needs.
- Training was conducted only prior to "go-live".

During the postimplementation period, they included the following:

- The limited nature of the available support to assist users with SAP
- The lack of ongoing training in SAP
- The limited ongoing support to work on improving business processes
- The lack of a formal business benefits realization process

The implementation of the SAP system in BrandX was viewed as a system replacement (a mainly technical perspective), with limited acknowledgment that SAP would be used within a social system. It is how users interact with a technology in their daily tasks, not the mere fact that the technology is there, that affects the business benefits gained from a technology (Orlikowski, 2000). This highlights the importance of the postimplementation period and the need for ongoing quality training and support, the very resources that were limited in the postimplementation period in BrandX. The fact that there was no benefits realization process during the postimplementation period is not surprising, as the SAP implementation was viewed merely as a system replacement.

This study supports the findings of Ross and Vitale (2000), who reported that inadequately resourcing the postimplementation phase, inadequately addressing resistance to change, and failing to establish metrics can affect the value an organization obtains from its ERP system. A major limitation of the findings from this research is that it is a single case. Future work will involve examining the postimplementation periods of ERP systems in another three manufacturing organizations, with the aim of understanding and explaining why some organizations gain more benefits than others from their ERP implementations.

REFERENCES

Bancroft, N., Seip, H., & Sprengel, A. (1996). *Implementing SAP R/3* (2nd ed.). Greenwich, CT: Manning.

Boudreau, M., & Robey, D. (1999). Organizational transition to enterprise resource planning systems: Theoretical choices for process research. In P. De, & J. DeGross (Eds.), *Proceedings of the Twentieth International Conference on Information Systems*, Association for Information Systems.

Chae, B. (2001). Technology adaptation: The case of large-scale information systems. In *Proceedings of the Twenty-Second International Conference on Information Systems*, (December 16-19). New Orleans, Louisiana.

Davenport, T. H. (2000). *Mission Critical*. Boston, MA: Harvard Business School Press.

Deloitte Consulting. (1999). *ERP's Second Wave: Maximising the Value of ERP-enabled Processes*. New York: Deloitte Consulting.

Esteves, J., & Pastor, J. (2001). Enterprise resource planning systems research: An annotated bibliography. *Communications of AIS*, 7, 1-51.

Giddens, A. (1984). *The Constitution of Society*. Berkeley, CA: University of California Press.

Jones, M. (1999). Structuration theory. In W. Currie, & B. Galliers (Eds.), *Rethinking Management Information Systems: An Interdisciplinary Perspective* (pp. 103-135). Oxford: Oxford University Press.

Markus, L., & Tanis, C. (2000). The enterprise systems experience — From adoption to success. In R. W. Zmud (Ed.), *Framing the Domains of IT Research: Glimpsing the Future Through the Past* (pp. 173-207). Cincinnati, OH: Pinnaflex Educational Resources.

Markus, M. L., & Robey, D. (1988). Information technology and organizational change: Causal structure in theory and research. *Management Science*, 34, 583-598.

Orlikowski, W. (1992). The duality of technology: Rethinking the concept of technology in organisations. *Organisation Science*, 3, 398-427.

Orlikowski, W. (2000). Using technology and constituting structures: A practice lens for studying technology in organisations. *Organisation Science*, 11, 404-428.

Orlikowski, W., & Robey, D. (1991). Information technology and the structuring of organisations. *Information Systems Research*, 2, 143-169.

Parr, A., & Shanks, G. (2000). A taxonomy of ERP implementation approaches. In *Proceedings of the Thirty-Third Hawaii International Conference on System Sciences*, (January 4-7). Maui, Hawaii.

Pozzebon, M. (2000). Combining a structuration approach with a behavioural-based model to investigate ERP usage. In H. M. Chung (Ed.), *Proceedings of the Sixth Americas Conference on Information Systems*, Association for Information Systems.

Pozzebon, M. (2001). Demystifying the rhetorical closure of ERP packages. In *Proceedings of the Twenty-Second International Conference on Information Systems*, (December 16-19). New Orleans, Louisiana.

Ross, J., & Vitale, M. (2000). *Information Systems Frontiers*, 2, 233-241.

Shang, S., & Seddon, P. (2000). A comprehensive framework for classifying the benefits of ERP systems. In M. Chung (Ed.), *Proceedings of the Sixth Americas Conference on Information Systems*, Association for Information Systems.

Sia, S. K., Tang, M., Soh, C., & Boh, W. F. (2002). Enterprise resource planning (ERP) systems as technology of power: Empowerment or panoptic control? *The Database for Advances in Information Systems*, 33, 23-37.

Staehr, L., Shanks, G., & Seddon, P. (2002). Understanding the business benefits of enterprise resource planning (ERP) systems. In *Proceedings of the Eighth Americas Conference on Information Systems*, Association for Information Systems, (August 9-11). Dallas, Texas.

Stein, T. (1999). Making ERP add up. *Information Week*, (May 24), 59.

Tyre, M., & Orlikowski, W. (1994). Windows of opportunity: Temporal patterns of technological adaptation in organizations. *Organizational Science*, 5, 98-118.

Volkoff, O. (1999). Using the structurational model of technology to analyze an ERP implementation. In W. Haseman, & D. Nazareth (Eds.), *Proceedings of the Fifth Americas Conference on Information Systems*, Association for Information Systems.

Walsham, G., & Han, C.-K. (1991). Structuration theory and information systems research. *Journal of Applied Systems Analysis*, 17, 77-85.

Zuboff, S. (1988). *In the Age of the Smart Machine: The Future of Work and Power*. Oxford: Heinemann Professional Publishing.

ENDNOTES

*   An earlier version of this chapter appeared in the Proceedings of the 13th Australasian Conference on Information Systems, 2002.

Chapter VI

An Examination of an ERP Software Selection Process: An Irish Case Study

David Sammon
University College Cork, Ireland

Daivd Lawlor
Stryker Instruments (Cork), Ireland

ABSTRACT

In this chapter a case study of a world-class manufacturing organisation implementing SAP is purposefully used to demonstrate the influence of bias over requirements in the decision making process. Furthermore, this research highlights the difficulties in determining if the ERP package selected by an organisation is in fact the right software package, to fulfil the functional requirements of the organisation.

INTRODUCTION

One of the key reasons why managers have sought to proceed with difficult ERP projects is to end the fragmentation of current systems, to allow a process of standardization, to give more visibility on data across the entire corporation, and, in some cases, to obtain competitive advantage (Sammon & Adam,

2000). Thus, ERP projects have been described as strategic projects with success or failure that will greatly impact the organization (Rowe, 1999; Shakir, 2000; Wood & Caldas, 2000). One key aspect of ERP projects that was reported by many authors is that failed implementations can be costly for the implementing organization (Kalakota & Robinson, 1999). Few ERP implementations are entirely successful, with approximately half failing to meet the implementing organization's expectations. As highlighted by Sammon and Adam (2000), it seems that the attention of managers and researchers focused nearly exclusively on certain stages of ERP projects, while other key points were neglected, notably, why organizations go down the ERP route or on the process whereby managers select one particular ERP package instead of another (as illustrated in Chapter 4). In addition, it seems that little attention has been paid to what happens after systems are implemented, in an attempt to determine to what extent the benefits that were sought by managers were achieved.

Shang and Seddon (2000) posed the question "what sort of benefits did they [the organization], or can they, achieve?" In answering this question, they presented a comprehensive framework of benefits that organizations might be able to achieve from their use of ERP systems, as illustrated in Chapter 1. The SERPS model proposed in this chapter uses the same definition of benefits as Shang and Seddon (2000). However, the preliminary list of benefits illustrated in this model is structured and presented differently. In order to broaden the research focus in the area of ERP decision making and software selection, we have undertaken to formulate the model by expanding on previous research (Sammon & Adam, 2000), and focusing on modeling the "Intended Benefits" associated with ERP offerings. The proposed research model attempts to identify the criticality of an Intended Benefit to the selection of a particular ERP and further examines if the selected offering was, in fact, the most appropriate in relation to the actual benefits being realized. The evolution of the model documented in this chapter and its application to the case study provides an early indication of its usefulness for managers and researchers in the area of ERP software selection and implementation.

ERP SOFTWARE SELECTION AND FOUNDATIONS OF THE RESEARCH MODEL

To be able to define, assess, and classify requirements requires knowledge. One critical success factor in the procurement process of IS is to have adequate knowledge (Robson, 1997). This means that an organization must invest in enough IS competence, internally or externally, to be able to explore its needs and priorities and to rank and judge alternatives (Robson, 1997). The procurement process, of course, inherently carries within it the risk of making poor selections (Robson, 1997). Therefore, to make an effective selection, an organization must know what it wants to do and define its goals clearly (Robson, 1997). Only management time and attention can reduce selection risk, and so, as well as first knowing what to do and second, having access to enough knowledge to do it, the third feature of effective selection is to be prepared to spend the amount of time appropriate to the significance of the acquisition (Robson, 1997).

Those making decisions in companies must consider many variables that are unrelated to software when they research potential ERP packages (Callaway, 1999). The volume of questions to be answered to successfully select the best system for the enterprise can seem overwhelming (Ptak & Schragenheim, 2000). Given the magnitude of the decision, selecting an ERP system can be daunting (Callaway, 1999). Ptak and Schragenheim (2000) posed some interesting questions concerning ERP software selection, as follows:

- Given that there is a magnitude of ERP systems available, how can those at a company be sure they selected the one that is the best fit?
- Does it really matter which software is purchased?
- Why not just purchase the same system that everyone else seems to have?
- There must be a reason why particular software has most of the market, right?

According to Kuiper (1998), this stage of the ERP project is the most difficult and the most critical. Callaway (1999) further commented, "most companies falter at this stage because they lack an effective methodology for sorting and ranking the many options. Vendor hype further complicates the selection process" (p. 32). Kuiper (1998) cited six common mistakes made by those in a company when choosing an ERP package, as illustrated in Table 1.

There are a number of ERP software selection methodologies documented in the literature (Kuiper, 1998; Callaway, 1999), for example, Kuiper's funnel method, Dobrin's three-dimensional (3-D) Web-based decision support tool, and the Clarkston Potomac methodology. All of these methodologies differ in their approaches to ensure successful ERP software selection, and each has unique defining characteristics. However, choosing an ERP system is difficult, and no single method is correct for software selection (Callaway, 1999).

Companies must approach the problem with a plan, either on their own or with the help of an expert — an added challenge (Callaway, 1999). Fortunately, obtaining the services of an expert is nearly effortless, as most consulting firms and research firms offer ERP selection services (Callaway, 1999). As such, an ERP system implementation essentially implies that a large part of the IS function (i.e., standard business application development and source code maintenance) in an organization is outsourced (Watson & Schneider, 1999). Management consulting firms grew practices around this outsourcing opportunity and generated many new career opportunities (Watson & Schneider, 1999).

Brown et al. (2000) commented that despite widespread ERP investments, only a few studies investigated ERP selection criteria (Bernroider & Koch, 1999; Van Everdingen et al., 2000). Brown et al. (2000) posed the following question: "What ERP package capabilities are associated with the purchase of an ERP?" (p. 1029). Brown et al. (2000) reported on one part of a multiyear empirical study of ERP purchase and implementation issues. The overall research objective was an holistic one: assume that multiple organizational and ERP package characteristics are important to understanding an organization's purchase decision. In Brown et al. (2000), the objective was to "identify a full but parsimonious set of factors that reflect the range of business-

Table 1. Common Mistakes in Choosing an ERP Package

Common Mistake	Outcome
They limit their search to the most widely known vendors	As a result, they may overlook software that is more suitable for their needs
They do not formally define their requirements for the software	Companies that arbitrarily choose ERP systems risk disgruntling members of the project team and fostering a climate of conflict throughout the project
They demonstrate software before they define their requirements	Companies that make this mistake are more likely to be influenced by showy demos
They over-specify their requirements	Referred to as the "Candy Store" syndrome — if everyone in a company asks for every feature they want in a new ERP system, the cost, length, and complexity of the project increase
They become too involved in software analysis	Spending too much time studying requirements causes ERP selection to lose momentum; overextending an ERP project for any reason — particularly at the outset of the project — is risky; the longer the project takes, the more likely the employees and implementation team members are to lose their enthusiasm for the effort
They treat ERP selection as a matter of purchasing technology rather than as a major business decision	Companies that fail to see the strategic importance of selecting the appropriate ERP system risk choosing the most inappropriate system

and IT-related capabilities associated with the purchase of ERP systems" (p. 1029). Brown et al. (2000) identified four business factors (data integration, new ways of doing business, global capabilities, flexibility/agility) and four IT factors (IT purchasing, IT cost reduction, IT expertise, IT architecture) and viewed the identification of a set of factors that describe ERP package capabilities as a first step toward better understanding the benefits expected by organizations that choose to adopt an ERP solution. Furthermore, Brown et al. (2000) confirmed that many of the ERP purchases, between 1996 and 1999, were at least partially motivated by the avoidance of Y2K problems, while also by the desire to improve their IS capabilities.

Within this chapter, the SERPS (Successful ERP Selection) research model is based on a set of "Intended Benefits" that are reported to materialize from the implementation of an ERP system. These factors are the result of a synthesis of existing ERP literature, as documented in Table 2. As the model is in its infancy, the factors listed are the most widely cited in the literature reviewed, and this is, therefore, not proposed as an exhaustive list. As an extension of this model, the researchers used the Intended Benefits as a set of generic checks from which an implementing organization documents a corresponding set of Organization-Specific Factors (OSFs). This term is used to define and structure the problems in existence within the context of the implementing organization. Furthermore, the criticality of each of these OSFs can also be identified by the implementing organization. Finally, the model supports the illustration of how successful the selected ERP was in satisfying the requirements and perceived benefits of the implementing organization.

Case Description

The organization studied is a forward-thinking world-class manufacturer. The ERP implementation was within a division of the organization, which consisted of five sites worldwide. Throughout this chapter we refer to this division as the 'Business Unit'. The first site to implement ERP, to support production, was based in Ireland. This project was known as the single instance project. The cost account manager within the organization pointed out that this "ERP instance will be used as the starting point for the 'Global Core' and will be the de-facto standard" across the five divisional sites. Due to the nature of the organizational division, a high-volume repetitive manufacturing environment, selecting the right manufacturing system for such a start-up was important. The system would have to be flexible enough to meet the changing demands of a start-up organization as well as to fit in with the enterprise strategy, which is the global ERP single-instance initiative.

All five of the divisional sites ran on separate materials management systems. The multiplicity and complexity of the existing system's setup was high, with a multitude of system inefficiencies existing. The first phase of the materials management systems replacement exercise was known as the "Holy Grail" project. The project consisted of a six-month analysis of the Irish site. Within the analysis phase, a Request for Information (RFI) document was sent to eight vendors. The RFI document contained the requirements identified by the organization. Based on the responses to the RFI from each vendor, a further short list was selected, presentations of the software and site visits then followed, and as a result, SAP was chosen. Furthermore, a total of 50% of project time was assigned for business process analysis and documentation. This gave a detailed knowledge of their business as well as what they required from a system. The first phase, as indicated by the cost account manager, involved "a detailed requirements analysis of the business, based on which, off-the-shelf third party software solutions were evaluated and SAP selected based on a number of criteria, primarily functionality." The second phase was the SAP implementation.

Singapore was the second site to go live with SAP. Corvallis and San Diego went live together in November 2000, as they are in the same time zone and so have a shared system. According to the cost account manager, the Irish site was regarded as the test site for future ERP implementations. Singapore came to the Irish site prior to their implementation for advice on how to implement SAP and the whole process they should follow. Corvallis and San Diego came to Singapore and the Irish site for similar help. Once all five sites went live with SAP, the next step was single-instance or global SAP. The cost account manager pointed out, "why not single instance, it's complex (i.e., different time zones), but the benefits are there." The Irish site and the site in Puerto Rico were the first two sites to go live on the same instance, and this occurred on March 17, 2001. However, even though the initial implementation of SAP began in 1998, the organization would not know if the benefits of having global integration and a SAP global single instance would materialize until 2002.

THE ORGANIZATION-SPECIFIC FACTORS FOR SOFTWARE SELECTION

Within the organization studied, an exhaustive list of selection criteria was generated in the form of the RFI document. For the purposes of this research, these selection criteria are grouped into 16 organizational requirements. Each requirement relates to an Intended Benefit, presented in Table 2. These organizational requirements were viewed as the necessary areas that the chosen ERP must address and facilitate. Therefore, the organization seems to have undertaken the selection process by the "usual means." However, the organization can also be found guilty of "blind acceptance of models underlying the ERP," in this case, SAP. There is evidence within the case to suggest that organization members made the decision to choose SAP by being influenced by factors other than the 16 organizational requirements. These factors seem to introduce an element of bias into the selection decision. The criticality and significance of addressing the organizational requirements to the software selection process seems questionable; for example, is it in the best interest of the organization to "Replace Existing Systems" with the best ERP offering or with SAP? According to the SAP IT Systems Analyst, members of the organization did the following:

> *...asked themselves certain questions relating to the software when deciding what ERP system to purchase and SAP addressed all of these issues. The software was seen to be very appropriate to their line of business as it is an integrated system on a site-by-site basis (everyone can see what everyone else is doing) and globally it is totally integrated (single instance).*

Replace Existing Systems

The Business Unit had to replace its old legacy systems at each site, as they no longer met the organization's needs. These systems were never designed to connect to one another. They were not very functional by today's standards and did not enable globalization to occur. The Business Unit had to move from a centralized, mainframe-based architecture to a client-server architecture. This is a more modern enterprise-wide infrastructure that would result in a more scalable, flexible infrastructure. With five sites around the world on four different continents, the Business Unit needed a more integrated system to integrate these five sites. The legacy systems were fragmented, obsolete, and prevented them from timely response to their ever-changing business needs. According to the cost account manager, "the best thing to do was replace all systems at each site with an integrated ERP system."

Reduce IS Costs

Having one integrated system throughout the Business Unit is a lot more efficient than having five decentralized systems. The Business Unit was facing

Table 2. Organizational Requirements for ERP Software Selection

Intended Benefits	References
Replace existing systems	Norris et al., 1998; Doane, 1998; Oliver & Romm, 2000; Brown et al., 2000; Holland et al., 1999; Wagle, 1998; Stefanou, 2000; Levis & Von Schilling, 1994
Reduce IS costs	Wagle, 1998; Kelly et al., 1999; Lozinsky, 1998; Bancroft et al., 1998
Y2K	Oliver & Romm, 2000; Bancroft, 1998; Fryer, 1999; Markus & Tanis, 2000; Slater, 1999; Norris et al., 1998
Increased system flexibility	Bernroider & Koch, 2000; Brown et al., 2000; Bancroft et al., 1998; Oliver & Romm, 2000
Single instance	Norris et al., 1998; Fryer, 1999; Keller & Teufel, 1998; Holland et al., 1999
Real-time data availability	Baatz, 1996; Bancroft et al., 1998; Doane, 1997; Fryer, 1999
Stronger system to cope with increasing business complexity	Bernroider & Koch, 2000; Holland et al., 1999; Oliver & Romm, 2000; Stefanou, 2000; Taylor, 1999
Integration	Brown et al., 2000; Oliver & Romm, 2000; Stefanou, 2000; Taylor, 1999
Increase organizational flexibility	Bancroft et al., 1998; Welti, 1999; Brown et al., 2000; Doane, 1997; Levis & Von Schilling, 1994; Holland et al., 1999
Improve value chain	Baatz, 1996; Doane, 1997; Fryer, 1999; Taylor, 1999
Strategic capabilities	Baatz, 1996; Stefanou, 2000; Brown et al., 2000
Business process reengineering	Doane, 1998; Brown et al., 2000; Holland et al., 2000; Norris et al., 1998; Stefanou, 2000
Meet competitive goals	Brown et al., 2000; Holland et al., 1999; Stefanou, 2000
Globalization	Baatz, 1996; Bancroft et al., 1998; Doane, 1997; Fryer, 1999; Welti, 1999
Improve decision making	Al-Mashari, 2000; Bancroft et al., 1998; Doane, 1997; Fryer, 1999; Parr et al., 1999
Standardization/common processes	Baatz, 1996; Bancroft et al., 1998; Fryer, 1999

ever rising IS costs at each site and had to address this problem. Purchasing packaged solutions and their upgrades would result in time and cost savings in the long run, when compared with developing and maintaining in-house customized solutions.

Y2K

The Y2K problem was not an issue for the Business Unit. They previously addressed their Y2K problems and all systems in place prior to the SAP implementation were Y2K compliant.

Increased System Flexibility

As stated by the cost account manager, "the system set-up at each site was inflexible prior to SAP implementation." Having each site running on a separate system with zero integration was inefficient and did not enable the Business Unit to respond to its changing business environment. With today's world-class manufacturing business environment constantly changing, especially in the IT sector, organizations need to be able to adapt to changing business circumstances. The system prior to the SAP implementation was not flexible enough.

Single Instance

According to the SAP IT systems analyst:

> ...the single instance concept where all sites will be set-up on a single central database running on one server could only be made possible if the same system was installed and implemented across the five Business Unit sites.

Only then could a single instance eventually occur, and the benefits of a single instance be provided. It would facilitate the Business Unit to become more competitive and respond more efficiently to its changing business environment. While also aiding in the globalization effort in connecting the five sites.

Real-Time Data Availability

The Business Unit needed a system that could provide up-to-date, real-time data to all who needed it at any given time for effective analysis and decision making. The previous systems across the Business Unit could not provide this. Prior to the SAP implementation, the Business Unit was faced with a reduced ability to make effective decisions across its value chain. Implementing a fully integrated system like SAP, where data is updated in real time, provides effective information for decision making and operations. With the implementation of SAP, it was noticed that there is common information, and more information, and it is available to more people. Departmental boundaries are dissolving as a result, i.e., all of final assembly manufacturing are working off the same reports. Some of the benefits to having real-time data available everywhere include improved visibility of the actual user performing transactions; improved visibility of increased accountability, standard costs, BOM, or flow problems; and improved control and elimination of lost transactions.

Stronger System to Cope with Increasing Business Complexity

As stated by the cost account manager, "the Business Unit needed a stronger system to cope with the increase in production levels across the five-sites." With the increasing demand for their products, the Business Unit had to ramp-up production and introduce more production lines. The Business Unit needed to address the increasing complexity of its business in the face of increasing competition. The current system was not capable of handling this increase in production, especially within the site researched, which, because of its start-up status, had huge production ramp-ups for the coming years. A globally integrated system had to be introduced to cope with the rising level of production and transactions. When SAP was introduced, productivity increased. The time to issue raw materials to all lines was taking two and a half hours by the end of two weeks, which was more than a 50% productivity improvement. People from Phase 1 could be assigned to assist with Phase 2 operations due to productivity improvements.

The Business Unit also had to cope with its increasing business complexity and increasing competition. This increasing business complexity led to rising inventory levels and inventory write-offs. This then led to reduced customer service levels and a loss in market share. The Business Unit is in a competitive marketplace, and one way to deal with competition is to reduce your costs. With the implementation of SAP, the Business Unit could reduce costs through improving decision making and reducing errors. For example, according to the cost account manager:

>...when SAP was implemented price errors on purchase orders were weeded out. Financial analysts were no longer misled by inaccurate information, which gave a distorted view of how much the organization is spending on materials. With the implementation of SAP the risks of errors occurring are seen and proper steps can be taken such as monitoring transactions and taking immediate steps to solve problems if they occur.

This also improves the global value chain.

Integration

The system at the Business Unit prior to SAP implementation were not integrated, and this reduced efficiency and increased the amount of errors occurring in the business. Standardization of data and processes is a prerequisite for effective integration and integration provides the foundation for extending the supply chain. Some of the benefits that integration provides include global inventory reports, aggregated statistics and information on other aspects of the supply chain, integrated product data management, global spares management, global suppliers management, etc. Also, cross-site information sharing will be enabled. All of these features can, in theory, be delivered without standardization and integration but not without severely limiting speed, flexibility, people productivity, system responsiveness, and increasing costs. Other benefits provided by the integrated system, according to the SAP Finance Business Analyst, were as follows: procurement and accounts payable are now on the same system; there is visibility of vendor payment position for buyers; certain reports are generated in 30 minutes, where it used to take four hours; the month-end close around accounts payable and the general ledger took two hours instead of the usual three days.

Increase Organizational Flexibility

Flexibility is one of the requirements of a world-class manufacturer. Flexibility was considered in terms of a system being able to meet the requirements of the business as these requirements change. As stated by the cost account manager,

> ...more was demanded from the existing system as the business was growing. The system did initially have the flexibility to meet the start-up schedule but as the business grew, more was demanded from the system and it was too simplistic to provide these requirements.

This problem was occurring across the Business Unit, because the business as a whole was growing. As an example, the site operates a JIT system. For this to work effectively, the supplier should have responsibility for inventory availability and quality. The system should allow integration with the supplier so that the supplier will manage the sites' inventory. This is what flexibility is about, the ability of a system to meet the business requirements as they occur. The supplier should have the visibility of the system to see actual and planned data, to ensure inventory is available. However, the existing system could not provide this function and so was clearly lacking in the flexibility to meet business requirements as they occurred.

Improve Value Chain

As stated by the SAP Finance Business Analyst, "the Business Unit wants to improve the value chains at each site as well as the global value chain." The first site to implement SAP must eliminate any nonvalue-added activities with the new system to achieve this. An example of a nonvalue-adding activity identified was the Business Unit maintaining the same information on two different systems. With an integrated and highly automated system like SAP, a lot of the administrative and processing work at the Business Unit was reduced. Eliminating waste removes nonvalue-added activities and so improves the value chain. Another example of the benefits SAP provided to the value chain was when implementation occurred, the delivery performance improved from 65% on time to nearly 100%. Also, work in progress inventory dropped over 50%.

Strategic Capabilities

A system like SAP provides many strategic capabilities, such as faster integration of new acquisitions, as well as e-commerce initiatives, however, these were not critical factors in the Business Unit's decision to implement SAP.

Business Process Reengineering

Implementing SAP gave the opportunity to reengineer and improve business processes. The first system evaluation process undertaken for the existing systems was purely to find a system that could be implemented quickly enough to meet the start-up schedule. No business process reengineering was called for, because obviously, it was a start-up situation, and new processes as well as new systems had to be put in place. What resulted from this according to the cost account manager "was the growing need of the business to expand the system. It then became overloaded and extremely inefficient and it was necessary to redesign the inventory system in light of current and future needs."

Meet Competitive Goals

The Business Unit must meet its competitive goals as a world-class manufacturer. Goals such as the ability to make fast responses to business changes, reduced cycle times, employee empowerment, and reduced global cost structures. As stated by the cost account manager, "the systems in place throughout the Business Unit prior to SAP implementation did not enable them to meet their competitive goals." The systems in place had many drawbacks, which included a limited management of inventory across the five sites, an inability to manage suppliers as if the Business Unit were a single customer, difficulty in linking planning functions across sites, and finally, there was a total lack of integration between systems, and they were not well supported.

As stated by the cost account manager, "the Business Unit maintains an environment where the activities of each factory are dependent upon the activities of other factories." For example, Dublin depends on Singapore for some components, while Singapore may depend on Corvallis for another component. If a change in output occurs in one factory, that change will have to be communicated to the planning systems of all other involved factories. As stated by the cost account manager, "more and more, we had been experiencing significant failure to perform their job." There was no effective way for factories to tie together their plans electronically with the old system. To summarize, the Business Unit is a global business that had a need to share high-level information, but it did not have a global information system. The result of not having a centralized system means that the Business Units ability to access and exchange information, to communicate efficiently, and to coordinate operations is limited. The Business Units competition is growing dramatically, putting downward pressure on product pricing. Failure to address their global cost structure would lead to reduced profitability and erosion of market share. In addition, the legacy systems were fragmented and obsolete and prevented them from timely response to their ever-changing business needs. The longer the Business Unit delayed in moving to a worldwide integrated systems transaction platform, the more the system's complexity, cost, and cycle time increased, while information performance, reliability, and availability decreased. According to the cost account manager, "the Business Unit needs to move to an integrated enterprise resource planning platform as soon as possible to develop and maintain a competitive supply chain."

Globalization

The Business Unit is a global business in need of a globally integrated system. The decentralized system in place prior to SAP implementation, according to the cost account manager, "was clearly not sufficient." What was needed was an ERP solution to facilitate globalization. ERP packages like SAP use a single database, which provides access to enterprise-wide data across geographic and business unit boundaries. The system is fully integrated, so the data is updated in real time, providing effective information for decision making. As stated previously, the Business Unit maintains an environment where the activities of each site are dependent upon the activities of other sites. Each site is tightly linked to each other. It is a global business that needs to share high-level information but did not have a global information system to enable this, until now.

Improve Decision Making

The systems in place across the Business Unit prior to the SAP implementation created information and data that were insufficient and inaccurate. This meant that the Business Unit was facing a reduced ability to make effective decisions across its value chain. This clearly did not improve the Business Unit's competitive position in the marketplace. With an integrated system like SAP, decision making can be greatly improved, reducing the amount of errors occurring. The company immediately recognized improved information quality and accessibility with the implementation of SAP. Improved reporting also eliminated one person spending eight hours per month manually generating the monthly reports, which in turn, improved the value chain.

Standardization/Common Processes

The Business Unit needed to standardize business processes, data, and systems across the five sites to make the global business more efficient and to improve the global value chain. Standardization would provide multiple benefits, such as the following: improve global reporting capabilities, which would enable comparisons across the five sites; ensure simplification of processes; simplify product transfers between sites; and make cost roll ups comparable across sites. Not standardizing reduces the Business Unit's ability to move to a single instance. The cost of not standardizing means that information exchange across sites is limited, and the lack of availability and inconsistency of data could cripple decision making; that the use of global processes, such as engineering change management, planning, shipping, global vendor management, etc., will be limited; and that the cross-site management of manufacturing and inventory by business teams will be limited without accurate, reliable, and consistent information being readily available and accessible. As stated by the SAP IT Systems Analyst, "it was seen that bringing in a system like SAP across the five-sites could provide standardization and realize the benefits of standardization."

ANALYZING THE ORGANIZATIONAL REQUIREMENTS: WHY SAP?

The organization had a vision of a global system and a single instance across the five sites. SAP was seen to be the software system of choice because of its ability to provide what the organization required with such a high level of functionality. From an analysis of the organizational requirements, the ability of SAP to fulfill the organizational requirements seems obvious. Apart from "Y2K" and "Strategic Capabilities," which were not critical factors to selection, all of the remaining requirements were, it seemed, adequately addressed with the introduction of SAP. However, if attention is focused on the perceived successfulness or aptness of the chosen ERP, SAP, to the organization, it can be identified that five out of the 16 requirements (31%) could have been fulfilled by any of the ERP offerings short listed, not just SAP, as illustrated in Table 3. Although 11 out of the 16 requirements (69%) are specifically addressed by the SAP offering in this organization, it cannot be determined until 2002 if the selected ERP (SAP) was, in fact, the best offering. The organization's vision and strategy to have a global ERP single-instance system operate across the five sites means that there is no guarantee that the requirements will be fulfilled in the longer term. This may be considered a limitation of the study, in that single instance had not occurred across the five sites at the time of undertaking the research. Bearing this in mind, however, if the researchers cannot determine if the selection is a success based on the research data collected, then the organization must be at least faced with the same doubt. Short-term benefits (on a site-by-site basis) were realized from the introduction of SAP, but no benefits can be realized for global single instance until 2002, and after all, this is the underlying rationale of the organization in selecting SAP. Business circumstances may change by then, causing some of the expected benefits not to be realized, a problem existing with all ERP systems offering a single instance. According to Rutherford (2001), only around 10% to 15% of ERP implementations deliver the anticipated benefits. So why SAP, really?

This was the first time SAP would be used to support production throughout the organization. SAP was seen to fit the business the best and was also seen to be highly functional when compared to the other ERP offerings out there. According to the cost account manager, the six-month analysis stage showed that SAP was the best solution. Furthermore, the cost account manager stated that, "if SAP was seen not to be the best solution for the organization then a good argument would have to be put forward so as to prove this but this did not come about." Therefore, the organization seemed to have already decided on choosing SAP as the system of choice prior to the six-month analysis. It appears to the researchers that the biasing factors influenced the organization's software selection process more so than fulfilling the organizational requirements. According to the cost account manager, "SAP was always going to come up as the system of choice unless a very good argument

Table 3. Analysis of Fulfillment of Organizational Requirements, through SAP

Organizational Requirements	This was a Successful ERP Selection, However, any ERP System...	Cannot be Determined until 2002
Replace existing systems	Can replace an organization's legacy systems, not just SAP	
Reduce IS costs	Will reduce IS costs, not just SAP	
Y2K	Is Y2K compliant, not just SAP	
Increased system flexibility		If global SAP is a success and if a global, flexible system is implemented
Single instance		If single instance, supported by SAP, will be a success
Real-time data availability		If true real-time data will become available across the five sites
Stronger system to cope with increasing business complexity		If the ability to cope with increasing business complexity will be realized throughout the organization
Integration		If the benefits of a globally integrated system will be realized, with single instance, even though integration is occurring on a site-by-site basis
Increase organizational flexibility		If true organizational flexibility will occur, even while flexibility is improving on a site-by-site basis
Improve value chain		If the global value chain will improve, even while value chains are improving on a site-by-site basis
Strategic capabilities	Can provide strategic capabilities, not just SAP	
Business process reengineering	Gives the opportunity to reengineer and improve business processes, not just SAP	
Meet competitive goals		If competitive goals can be realized globally, even though they are evident on a site-by-site basis
Globalization		If globalization can be achieved
Improve decision making		If decision making will be improved across the five sites
Standardization/common processes		If true standardization occurs across the five sites

was put forward to decide otherwise." Therefore, SAP may not be the *most* suitable choice, merely a suitable option. However, despite these biasing factors influencing the organization's decision, SAP seems to be a success so far, in the short term, on a site-by-site basis.

From an analysis of the SERPS model (Table 4), it is clear that a successful ERP selection was made from the point of view of each OSF. However, there are OSFs marked as UNSURE, which addresses the issue that the global single instance will not materialize until 2002. Therefore, the OSFs marked as UNSURE mean that while most of these factors are realized on a site-by-site basis, the benefits may or may not be realized on a global single-instance level throughout the organization. The Business Unit does not know if the global value chain will improve or if organizational flexibility will improve throughout the organization. It is worth reemphasizing that one of the main reasons for implementing SAP was for global integration and global single instance, however, this was not yet realized.

The Irish site found the implementation of SAP complex, organizationally disruptive, and resource intensive, but it was expected and they prepared for it, which is the most important thing. As stated by the cost account manager, "all deadlines were met on schedule." They kept under the budget, which was allocated to the project and had excellent project manager support. Nine months after SAP implementation, the benefits were evident in many areas. It was not possible to do a quantifiable cost-benefit analysis after the system was introduced, but there were evident improvements in most areas. For example, when SAP was introduced, productivity increased. The time to issue raw materials to all lines saw a productivity improvement of more than 50%, and the delivery performance improved from 65% on time to nearly 100%. Also, price errors on purchase orders were weeded out. Financial analysts were no longer

Table 4. The SERPS Research Model

Intended Benefits	Organization-Specific Factors	Critical (Yes/No)	Successful ERP Selection
Replace existing systems	No longer met the IJBU's needs; the Business Unit needed a client–server architecture, as this is a more modern enterprise-wide infrastructure suited to its business	Yes	Yes
Reduce IS costs	The Business Unit had to deal with ever-rising IS costs	Yes	Yes
Y2K	This was not an issue	No	n/a
Increased system flexibility	The current system across the five sites was decentralized, with a total lack of integration and flexibility	Yes	Unsure
Single instance	Globalization effort	Yes	Unsure
Real-time data availability	Must improve decision-making quality at the Business Unit	Yes	Unsure
Stronger system to cope with increasing business complexity	The volume and complexity of transactions is increasing at the Business Unit; production is also increasing	Yes	Unsure
Integration	The Business Unit needs to reduce the domino effect of errors within the business	Yes	Unsure
Increase organizational flexibility	The Business Unit must respond to its changing business environment	Yes	Unsure
Improve value chain	The Business Unit needed to reduce waste in its value chain	Yes	Unsure
Strategic capabilities	This was not an issue	No	n/a
Business process reengineering	The Business Unit wanted to reengineer and improve business processes across the five sites	Yes	Yes
Meet competitive goals	The Business Unit needed a system to achieve its competitive goals not possible with their legacy systems	Yes	Unsure
Globalization	The Business Unit is a global business that needs a globally integrated information system	Yes	Unsure
Improve decision making	Data and information prior to SAP implementation was insufficient, inaccurate, and difficult to capture across the Business Unit, causing poor decisions to be made	Yes	Unsure
Standardization/common processes	This will provide multiple benefits for the IJBU across the five sites	Yes	Unsure

misled by inaccurate information, which gave a distorted view of how much the organization spends on materials. The organization immediately recognized the improvement in information quality and accessibility with the implementation of SAP. Improved reporting eliminated one person spending eight hours per month manually generating the monthly reports. Certain reports are generated in 30 minutes, where it used to take four hours. The month-end close around Accounts Payable and the General Ledger took two hours instead of the usual three days. Therefore, the benefits included increased profitability, increased customer satisfaction, increased efficiency, lower cost structures, increased productivity, competitive advantage, execution excellence, etc.

As highlighted earlier, SAP was the ERP system of choice at the end of the analysis stage. However, SAP had an advantage over other ERP offerings analyzed, and this is where the bias element comes in to the software selection process. First, SAP was already used in different areas of the organization. It was used in distribution centers when Ireland distributed goods to Europe. It was also used in financial services centers, such as Accounts Payable for the Irish site, based in Scotland, and for R&D in Puerto Rico (a nonproduction site). As a result, there was a certain familiarity with the system. According to the cost account manager, "they could actually see SAP in action, i.e., Puerto Rico, as opposed to only seeing presentations of other systems." Second, a document was composed entitled "Why not SAP?" as opposed to "Why SAP?" and made available throughout the organization. This literature highlighted the fact that SAP was supported and pushed from the executive level. Finally, most multinational companies implementing SAP are migrating toward a single global instance, unless there is a compelling business barrier, i.e., 3COM, Microsoft, and CK Witco. Therefore, this organization wanted to follow in these companies' footsteps, especially when these companies are competitive forces in similar markets. The six-month analysis went ahead, despite the fact that SAP was the favorite choice. This was because the six-month analysis was essentially a detailed analysis of the business. It gave the site a detailed knowledge of its business and business processes, and this is essential for any ERP implementation. It identified what the organization required from a system, and the organization made sure that SAP was the right choice.

Another point of interest is that there was minimal resistance to change within the organization when SAP was introduced. The main reason for this was simply that it was a start-up site. As stated by the cost account manager, "employees didn't have enough time to become comfortable with the existing system, to create too much resistance to change." Furthermore, the role of the management-of-change (MOC) team as well as substantial training classes for operators and other relevant personnel reduced the disruption levels when SAP went live. However, the cost account manager further added that, "one of the biggest apprehensions was around how easy the ERP system would be to use by the operators and technicians." As a result, the going-live of SAP was communicated effectively throughout the organization, and when "going-live time" arrived, there was little or no resistance. To stimulate employee awareness, prior to actual training, posters were displayed throughout the site captioned, "Are you ready for SAP?" and "SAP going live soon." As stated by the SAP IT Systems Analyst, the start-up status of the site allowed for "minimal customization of the system, but maximum change of the business." This is necessary for SAP implementation due to the high level of integration and complexity of the system. The start-up status meant that the business was not yet too complex for reengineering to cause too many critical problems. Current business processes could be reengineered and improved to conform to the SAP architecture. However, as stated by the cost account manager, "the organization had the flexibility and resources to handle the implementation of such a system because of its start-up status."

The researchers believe that if a start-up operation did not exist in the Business Unit, then SAP may never have been chosen as the system of choice, because it may have been seen as too complex and too risky to implement, causing too much change for the business. High resistance to change and too much business process reengineering could cause implementation failure and even organizational downfall. The Irish site was capable of adapting to new business processes as well as of changing the old business processes to conform to the SAP architecture. The business was not too complex or established yet for change to cause too many problems. If single instance proves to be a failure, it could cause the downfall of the IJBU. The systems are already in place, investment was made, and the business was changed. Business circumstances may change by then, causing some of the OSFs documented in the SERPS model not to be realized. This problem exists with all ERP systems offering a single instance.

SUMMARY

The organization studied in this chapter was motivated by biased factors as opposed to the fulfillment of organizational requirements when choosing an ERP system, which influenced the decision to implement SAP. The software selection process undertaken may be seen as a necessary evil to support investment decisions already made by the management of the organization. From the researcher's point of view, this snapshot of a software selection process increases the level of confusion existing around understanding ERP decision making. This study further highlights the presence of somewhat irrational and political decision making within the organization, in relation to ERP software selection. Further research within this organization is required, post-2002 and the "global single-instance" initiative, to identify if the requirements of the organization are fulfilled, long term, with the introduction of SAP.

REFERENCES

Al-Mashari, M. (2000). Enterprise-wide information systems: The case of SAP R/3 Application. *Proceedings of the International Conference on Enterprise Information Systems (ICEIS),* (pp. 3-6).

Baatz, E. B. (1996). Ready of not. *CIO,* (June), 36-42.

Bancroft, N., Seip, H., & Sprengel, L. (1998). *Implementing SAP/R3.* Greenwich, CT: Manning.

Bernroider, E. & Koch, S. (2000). Differences in characteristics of the ERP system selection process between small or medium and large organizations. *Proceedings of the Americas Conference on Information Systems,* USA.

Brown, C.V., Vessey, I., & Powell, A. (2000). The ERP Purchase Decision: Influential Business and IT Factors. *Proceedings of the 6th Americas Conference on Information Systems,* Long Beach, California (August 10-13, pp. 1029-1032).

Callaway (1999). Enterprise Resource Planning: Integrating applications and business processes across the enterprise. *Computer Technology Research Corporation,* 1st ed.

Doane, M. (1997). *In the Path of the Whirlwind.* Sioux Falls, SD: The Consulting Alliance.

Doane, M. (1998). *The SAP Blue Book.* DA Press.

Fryer, B. (1999). The ROI challenge: Can you produce a positive return on investment from ERP? *CFO Magazine,* (September).

Holland, C., Light, B., & Beck, P. (2000). An international analysis of the maturity of enterprise resource planning ERP systems use. In *Proceedings of the 6th Americas Conference on Information Systems*, (August 10-13). Long Beach, California.

Holland, C. P., Light, B., & Gibson, N. (1999). A critical success factors model for enterprise resource planning implementation. In *Proceedings of the Seventh European Conference on Information Systems* (pp. 273-287). Copenhagen, Denmark: Copenhagen Business School.

Kalatoka, R., & Robinson, M. (1999). *E-business — Roadmap to Success.* Reading, MA: Addison-Wesley.

Keller, G. & Teufel, T. (1998). *SAP R/3 Process Oriented Implementation.* Reading, MA: Addison-Wesley Longman.

Kelly, S., Gibson, N., Holland, C., & Light, B. (1999). A business perspective on legacy information systems. *Communications of the Association for Information Systems, 2*(7). July.

Kuiper, D. (1998). The key to custom fit. *Evolving Enterprise,* (Spring).

Levis, J. & von Schilling, P. (1994). Lessons learned from 3 implementations: Knocking down barriers to client-server. *Information Systems Management,* 15-22.

Lozinsky, S. (1998). *Enterprise-Wide Software Solutions: Integration Strategies and Practices.* Reading, MA: Addison-Wesley Longman.

Markus, M. L., & Tanis, C. (2000). The enterprise systems experience — from adoption to success. In R. W. Zmud (Ed.), *Framing the Domains of IT Management: Projecting the Future Through the Past.* Retrieved October 9, 2001 from the World Wide Web: Pinnaflex.com.

Norris, G., Wright, I., Hurley, J.R., Dunleavy, J., & Gibson, A. (1998). *SAP: An Executives Comprehensive Guide.* New York: John Wiley & Sons.

Oliver, D. & Romm, C. (2000). ERP systems: The route to adoption. *Proceedings of the Americas Conference on Information Systems (AMCIS),* (August 10-13, pp. 1039-1044).

Parr, A., Shanks, G., & Darke, P. (1999). Identification of necessary factors for successful implementation of ERP systems. In O. Ngwenyama, L. D. Introna, M. D. Myers, & J. I. Degross (Eds.), *New Information Technologies in Organizational Pro.*

Ptak, C.A. & Schragenheim, E. (2000). *ERP Tools, Techniques, and Applications for Integrating the Supply Chain.* St. Lucie Press/APICS Series on Resource Management.

Robson, W. (1997). *Strategic Management and Information Systems.* London: Pitman Publishing.

Rowe, F. (1999). Coherence, intégration informationnelle et changement: Esquisse d'un programme de recherche à partir des progiciels intégrés de gestion. *Systèmes d'Information et Management, 4*(4), 3-20.

Rutherford, E. (2001). *ERP's ends justify its means.* CIO online Quick Poll Report: http://www.cio.com/poll/042401_erp.html. 18/07/2001.

Sammon, D., & Adam, F. (2000). Towards a model of ERP software selection — Widening the debate. In *Proceedings of the 10th Annual BIT Conference*, (November 1-2). Manchester, UK.

Shakir, M. (2000). Decision making in the evaluation, selection and implementation of ERP systems. In *Proceedings of the Sixth Americas Conference on Information Systems* (August 10-13, pp. 1033-1038). Long Beach, California.

Shang, S., & Seddon, P. B. (2000). A comprehensive framework for classifying the benefits of ERP systems. In *Proceedings of the Sixth Americas Conference on Information Systems* (August 10-13, pp. 1033-1038). Long Beach, California.

Slater, D. (1999). An ERP package for you ... and you ... and you ... and even you. *CIO,* (February). www.cio.com.

Stefanou, C. (2000). The selection process of enterprise resource planning, ERP, systems. In *Proceedings of the 6th Americas Conference on Information Systems* (August 10-13, pp. 988-991). Long Beach, California.

Taylor, J. (1999). Fitting enterprise software in smaller companies. *Management Accounting,* (February), 36-39.

Van Everdingen, Y., Van Hillegersberg, J., & Waarts, E. (2000, April). ERP adoption by European midsize companies. *Communications of the ACM, 43*(3), 27-32.

Wagle, D. (1998). Making the case for an R/3 system. *Corporate Finance,* (December), 6-8.

Watson, E. & Schneider, H. (1999, Febraury). Using ERP systems in education. *Communications of the AIS, 1*(9), 1-47.

Welti, N. (1999). *Successful SAP R/3 Implementation: Practical Management of ERP Projects.* Reading, MA: Addison-Wesley Longman.

Wood, T., & Caldas, M. (2000). Stripping the "Big Brother": Unveiling the backstage of the ERP fad. Retrieved from the World Wide Web: http://www.gv.br/prof_alunos/thomaz/ingles/paper5.htm.

Chapter VII

Do ERP Implementations Have to be Lengthy? Lessons from Irish SMEs

Frédéric Adam
University College Cork, Ireland

Peter O'Doherty
Seabrook Research Limited, Ireland

ABSTRACT

The ERP software market has been growing at a very fast pace over recent years and has been predicted to keep growing rapidly in the long term. However, there is now clear evidence of a slow down in this market and some suppliers of ERP packages have reported poor results. Nevertheless, the abundance of media reports on the subject of ERP has led many managers to wonder whether their companies should implement ERP systems. In order to separate the reality of the ERP phenomenon from the hype that surrounds it, we studied 14 ERP implementation projects in Irish organizations and focused on the key relationships between organizations that attempt to implement ERP systems and their implementing partner. We found that the ERP implementations in Ireland at the moment are different to the projects that have been reported elsewhere in two key respects. Firstly, the organizations interested in ERP software are, on average, far smaller than the case studies reported in the literature and the majority of the cases we reviewed were small and medium enterprises (SMEs). Secondly, the durations of implementation were far shorter than reported elsewhere. These results are not surprising if one considers the smaller average size of Irish organizations, but they indicate that the ERP movement is truly ready for an extension towards the SME market. They also indicate that the duration of the implementation of ERP software may be related to the size and complexity of the client organization and that SMEs can expect to have an easier time implementing ERPs than the current literature suggests. We also found that software implementers play a key role not only in technical terms, but also in managerial and political terms because they can help their clients to correct their expectations and perceptions of ERP systems and ERP implementations.

INTRODUCTION

The abundance of media reports on the subject of ERP led many managers to wonder whether their companies should implement ERP systems. In order to separate the reality of the ERP phenomenon from the hype that surrounds it, we studied 14 ERP implementation projects in Irish organizations and focused on the key relationships between organizations that attempt to implement ERP systems and their implementing partners.

We found that the ERP implementations in Ireland at the moment are different than the projects reported elsewhere in two key aspects. First, the organizations interested in ERP software are, on average, far smaller than the case studies reported in the literature, and the majority of the cases we reviewed were small and medium enterprises (SMEs). Second, the durations of implementation were far shorter than those reported elsewhere. These results are not surprising if one considers the smaller average size of Irish organizations, but they indicate that the ERP movement is ready for an extension toward the SME market. They also indicate that the duration of the implementation of ERP software may be related to the size and complexity of the client organization and that SMEs can expect to have an easier time implementing ERPs than the current literature suggests. We also found that software implementers play key roles, not only in technical terms, but also in managerial and political terms, because they can help their clients to correct their expectations and perceptions of ERP systems and ERP implementations.

The ERP software market has been growing at a very fast pace over recent years and was predicted to grow by 35% to 40% per year in the long term

(Bingi, Sharma, & Godla, 1999). However, there is now ample evidence that these predictions are not accurate, as many leading suppliers of ERP software reported bad results in 1999. Initially destined for larger organizations, ERP software is now also thought to be of some benefit in equipping smaller firms with smaller user populations and more limited financial resources. Different models are being proposed to broaden the market, including the Application Service Provider (ASP) model, whereby organizations no longer purchase the software but access the ERP functionalities across the Internet (Jeanne, 1999).

In the general case, organizations acquire one of the ERP software packages available on the market and seek the assistance of a local implementer (typically a consultancy firm or software distributor) in order to carry out the complex process of preparing the company for the migration of processes and systems to the ERP solution selected. Thus, it was reported that for every Euro spent on ERP software licences, companies must spend a further five to seven Euro on related services, mainly consultancy (Berger, 1998). This means that ERP projects are large, costly, and difficult, and that they require large investment in capital and in staff and management time (Rowe, 1999). However, the extent of the benefits reported in the literature and claimed by vendors and consultants is proving a strong attraction for managers, and there is great interest in methodologies that may be used to decrease the risks inherent in ERP projects.

In order to study the reality of ERP projects in Ireland, we carried out a field study of 14 firms that implemented ERP software in the period 1997-2000. After a review of current reports on the subject of ERP, in this chapter we describe the methodology that was followed in this investigation and present the findings of the study. Finally, conclusions that pertain to the reality of today's ERP projects and guidelines for the relationships between clients and their implementing partners are put forward.

ERP SYSTEMS — FROM MYTH TO REALITY

As Rowe (1999) aptly described, ERP systems represent the implementation of the old managerial dream of unifying and centralizing in one single system (or at least under one name) all the information systems required by the firm. ERP systems provide organizational actors with a common language and a common pool of data. At a practical level, ERP have beneficial effects that remove the need for often disparate and unreliable end-user applications; standardize operating procedures and reporting; and optimize some of the key processes of the firm (e.g., order acquisition and processing, inventory control). At the same time, these systems offer high levels of portability and reasonable flexibility in adapting to the requirements of specific organizations (Rowe, 1999; Forest, 1999).

These beneficial effects are matched by the high level of risk associated with ERP projects. ERP projects are complex and require reliance on many different types of expertise, often sourced outside the organization. Consultants often advise managers to undertake some degree of reengineering of key processes before acquiring ERP systems (Bancroft, 1996), and this adds to the complexity and political character of the projects. There is empirical evidence of the dangers inherent in such vast projects. The case of Foxmeyer (see previous chapter) is illustrative of what can happen to the largest organizations when implementations go wrong (Kalakota & Robinson, 1999).

These difficulties led to some researchers taking a negative view on ERP systems, with Wood and Caldas (2000) using an Orwellian analogy to characterize the goals of ERP systems and question whether the current interest in ERP in the business community is justified more by political reasons than by sound managerial reasoning. Indeed, low levels of satisfaction with consultants were reported by firms that implemented ERP systems (see previous chapter).

Trading Off Benefits and Risks with ERP

The high level of risk inherent in ERP implementations is illustrated by claims that organizations implementing ERP systems should typically only hold on to 20% of their previous applications (Rowe, 1999). But this extensive replacement of previous systems may be a requirement if the major benefits of ERP implementation — greater integration of functional areas and, in the case of multinational firms, greater coordination between entities and between sites — are to be obtained. The case of Vandelay Industries Corp. (Harvard Business School, 1997) shows that one of the key reasons why managers want to proceed with difficult ERP projects is to end the fragmentation of current systems, to allow a process of standardization, to give more visibility of data across the entire corporation and, in some cases, to obtain competitive advantage. Another consequence of this "clean-slate" approach is that organizations find it virtually impossible to revert to their pre-ERP situation, and, in any case, their investment either cannot be recouped or generates very low returns. Unisource Worldwide Ltd. and Dell Computer Corp. both wrote off significant amounts invested in aborted SAP implementations and associated consultant fees (Bingi, Sharma & Godla, 1999). The role played by consultants in ERP implementation has also been questioned and may constitute another source of risk. Only 47% of the respondents to Wood and Caldas' (2000) survey felt that consultants were influential in their implementation of ERP, and only 23% felt that their consultants had the necessary knowledge and experience with ERP.[1]

However, the case for ERP systems seems compelling at this point in time, and the development of more powerful and user-friendly platforms now makes it possible to integrate many large systems in a way that was not possible a few years ago (Wood & Caldas, 2000). Thus, Microsoft spent 10 months and $25 million replacing 33 existing systems in 26 sites with SAP. Managers in this company claim to save $18 million annually as a result, and Gates reportedly expressed great satisfaction with the SAP software (White, Clark & Ascarely, 1997). According to Kalakota and Robinson (1999), Microsoft had grown so fast that it could not keep up with itself, and the number of applications developed to support the company's operation and their lack of integration meant that IS staff lost control over the complexity of the systems they administered. Thus, as many as 90% of the 20,000 batch programs retrieving data and passing it between systems may have been redundant. The move to a single architecture enabled better linkages between business areas as well as with suppliers and customers.

However, there is anecdotal evidence that many companies were pushed into ERP projects by the much-publicized fears of what may happen to legacy systems during the year 2000 change. The increasing proximity of this key deadline may also have helped the emergence of the ASP model, because it was reported to allow a much shorter implementation. This is a less positive rationale for implementing ERP systems, but it certainly aided the cause of the vendors of ERP software.

Broadening the Scope of ERP: Relationship with Current Managerial Thinking

The Microsoft example illustrates that ERP systems can help managers leverage two other key aspects of the management of organizations: Supply Chain Management (SCM) and Customer Relationship Management (CRM). Terrand (1998) described how SCM applications can be bolted on top of ERP systems in order to obtain additional benefits. KPMG (quoted in Terrand, 1998) reported that SCM can provide the following benefits:

- Reduction of planning cycle (95%)
- Reduction of delivery times (10% to 40%)
- Reduction of production times (10% to 50%)
- Lower stock levels (10% to 25%)
- Reduction of late deliveries (25% to 50%)
- Increase in productivity (2% to 5%)

But the area of CRM, which concentrates on a better management of customers and on providing a unified vision of customers' needs and status to all organizational actors, has also become a major focus for the key players on the ERP market. SAP, JD Edwards, QAD, Oracle, and Baan are all proposing CRM modules as part of their offerings (Gros, 1999). Thus, the CRM market which, up to now, was dominated by specialized software houses (95% of the software purchased), is being taken over by ERP vendors (Terrand, 1999).

These two developments are significant, because they give ERP systems an outward-looking orientation that earlier offerings did not provide. ERP products are now also EDI compliant, in an effort to boost the possibility of integrating them with state-of-art software solutions.

*MIS*conceptions About ERP

Major concerns of managers with ERP remain in the perception that ERP implementations take a lot of time and are best suited to large organizations that can afford to spend time redesigning their most important processes. Besson (1999) reported how quick managers have been to point the finger at ERP software packages and their excessive complexity as a reason why projects failed. But he questioned whether the required paradigms and managerial skills exist for such projects, and whether the failures he investigated were not due to failure to plan for and organize the implementation of the new system. He also made the case that the perception that "political" conflicts between ERP implementers and users is the major cause of failure of ERP implementations may be misleading. While it is evident that ERP projects often generate conflicts in organizations, it is questionable whether the debates are solely about a group of organizational actors refusing the benefits of modernity and progress (Besson, 1999). In some cases, managers' underestimation and mismanagement of the scale of change required in implementing ERP systems coupled with their low level of awareness are sources of great difficulty (Harvard Business School, 1997). Such misconceptions may be the result of the strength of the promotional push behind ERP (Lampel, 1995) and the abundance of media reports about ERP (Caldas & Wood, 2000).

GOALS OF THE STUDY

In this study, our sample consisted of 14 organizations, all customers of Ireland's sole distributor for MFG/PRO, a mid-range ERP software package. We specifically focused on the profile and size of these organizations and on the key parameters in their relationships with their supplier of ERP software.

As a primer, we carried out a pilot study of one of these organizations that had just implemented its ERP package and that possessed interesting characteristics with regards to our study (as in Patton, 1990, p. 180). Based on our observations that the full implementation of the package had taken only five months at this site, we proceeded to confirm that ERP implementations are not always the very large and dangerous projects described in the current literature by way of a survey of 14 organizations.

Analyses of the findings and the conclusions of the research were undertaken in collaboration between the academic researcher and the most senior project leader in the software distributor (the coauthors of this chapter) in order to give equal importance to the opinions of all parties involved and reduce the possibility of bias.

The organizations that took part in the survey were those that were happy to let us investigate all aspects of their ERP projects and where staff could find the time to talk to us about their experiences in detail. They covered a broad range of activities (from telecom system suppliers to distributors of medical supplies for animals) and degree of expertise with the deployment of IT (from 10 to 500 employees), but 64% of them were SMEs according to European standards (SMEs are defined as having less than 250 employees and a turnover inferior to 40m Euro).[2] Thus, they constituted a good sample of the variety of organizations implementing ERP solutions in Ireland at this point in time. The selection mechanism employed, whereby the clients of one ERP supplier were studied, was opportunistic, but it enabled us to access a significant number of organizations without having to deal with common problems in breaking barriers and identifying knowledgeable respondents. Also, the fact that all organizations were dealing with the same supplier of software and the same software package guaranteed the comparability of their experience with ERP implementations and helped us concentrate on the key factors that remain true across organizational settings and those that only appear in specific circumstances.

The Pilot Study at ABC Communication

ABC Communication Ltd. is a global supplier of communication software. At the time this study took place, it had a turnover of IR£30 million and 200 employees. The company established a strong global position in Europe and Australia in integrated network products. As the company continued to expand rapidly and acquired another company supplying complementary products, the directors decided that an ERP package should be purchased to rationalize internal operations and help the increasingly complex management of inventory. The company initiated the selection process in November 1998 on the basis of a number of specific management targets, i.e., the following:

- Support of the launch of new products in European and UK markets
- Implementation of "Business Excellence" strategy
- Integration of operations with DEF Ltd. (the newly acquired company)
- Full Y2K compliance well in advance of the new millennium
- ISO 9000 certification

The goals of the ERP implementation also included better data access and better visibility on order completion and delivery, reduced operating costs, ability to cope with the increased volume of data, and further extension toward the company's future e-business strategy.

The key constrain in the project was that the ERP package had to go live before the end of May 1999 in the headquarters of the company and before the end of September 1999 in all the other sites. Because a number of essential (and nonreplaceable) applications had to be integrated with the ERP package, this project presented additional difficulties, which is why we selected this case for our pilot study, following Patton's ideas on intensity sampling.

To make the tight deadline achievable, ABC and the supplier of the software agree on a zero-modification strategy. As a result, the selection process was primarily aimed at finding a "best-fit" solution, i.e., one that would immediately offer functionalities able to support the current business processes or that would suggest business processes that could immediately be implemented in ABC. The project was hoped to provide the opportunity, whenever possible, to implement redesigned processes, but the maintenance of the ISO 9000 accreditation was an overriding objective, given how long it had taken ABC to obtain this certification.

After one month of negotiations and a thorough demonstration of how this ERP package worked, the actual implementation took four months from the time hardware was purchased to the time the 32 users were able to use the system. One more month was required before all the functionalities of the systems were in full use, mainly because of training issues. This illustrates one key problem with tight implementation schedules: they leave no time for training because staff cannot help the implementation team and train at the same time. The targets initially set by top management were, therefore, easily achieved, and the schedule suggested by the local implementer was actually improved upon during the execution of the project (training excluded).

The evaluation interviews carried out with management and staff at the end of the project revealed the high level of satisfaction of users and managers with the system. In particular, a number of tangible benefits were identified, including the following:

- Greater flexibility in work practices
- Better business approach vis-à-vis customers
- Increase in staff efficiency, meaning that similar numbers are able to cope with an increased volume of business
- Better linkages with vendors and suppliers
- Reduction in the number of errors
- Improved inventory control
- Better access to information
- Better sales support

The interviews with managers provided other insights into the kind of benefits that can accrue to organizations that implement ERP systems. The ability of the software package to automatically generate high-level reporting on the key performance indicators of the company was particularly noted and resulted in much higher-quality reporting across the board. Interestingly, ABC is the only case study where direct improvements in high level reporting were reported straight after ERP implementation, that we are aware of. This may be due to the lack of proper reporting procedures prior to the introduction of the ERP software. The improved response time to customer inquiries, while not quantifiable in financial terms, was also put forward as a major source of satisfaction for top management.

Another interesting facet of this project was that the accountant of the company was assigned the leadership of the project. This manager had no specific responsibilities in terms of information systems at ABC, but he was a champion for the ERP projects from the start. This indicated that the push for ERP projects does not always come from the IS functional area and that sound business reasons can be used to justify such projects. As a result of this project, the accountant gained significant status and was largely credited with the success of the project.

Discussion

With a turnover of IR£30 million and a workforce of 200, ABC is not the typical target of ERP vendors. Cases of ERP implementations previously reported routinely involve companies worth several billion dollars and multiple sites. In this respect, this project seems to be ahead of the evolution of the ERP market toward smaller organizations.

The short duration of the implementation is another key aspect of this case. Five months (including training) makes this ERP project short in comparison to other cases reported in the media. Based on our observations, this ERP project was a full-scale project that involved major modifications in the business processes of the firm and yielded a broad range of benefits, in keeping with the theory behind the ERP concept. Therefore, it cannot be said that this project was shorter because of the incomplete nature of the implementation or of the restriction to a small number of targets. Our analysis of the case leads us conclude that the smaller size of the company and the zero-modification stance of top managers are likely explanations for the duration of the project. Smaller companies deal with smaller numbers of customers and suppliers, and their inventories are less complex. They also have fewer staff members and require less training. As a result of the smaller number of people involved, their IS projects are easier to coordinate and manage, which enables project managers to adopt and stick to a more aggressive schedule.

The zero-modification stance taken by top management is certainly a key factor in explaining the duration of the project. The SOCRATE case study of the French railway company (SNCF) that also involved the purchase of a software package (Adam & Cahen, 1998) is interesting, because this IS project nearly failed (or even failed outright according to some authors such as Eglizeau et al., 1996) due to the scope of customization that was required. In particular, the development team came under unbearable time pressures, because they failed to realize the number and extent of the changes required. In relation to the ERP project at ABC, it is evident that the decision made by top managers limited the risks brought by the project and shortened its duration.

Beyond these commentaries, there still is no certainty that the case at ABC is representative of the ERP projects taking place in Ireland at this point. The low generalization value of case studies was noted by previous authors (Lee, 1989). In order to strengthen our beliefs in the findings of this case, we carried out a survey of ERP implementations. This survey is described in the next section.

SURVEY OF ERP IMPLEMENTATIONS
Profiles of the Organizations Studied

The survey focused on 14 companies at various stages of maturity with the ERP software. As in Wood and Caldas's (2000) survey, some of the companies were subsidiaries of foreign multinational firms and could benefit from specific implementation guidelines and from the past experience of staff at their headquarters. This enabled them to implement the software more quickly than other companies. Presented in Table 1 are the key characteristics of all the companies studied.

The average size of the companies we studied was 150 employees, with a turnover of IR£115m, which is smaller than most of the instances reported in the current literature (nine out of 14 could be categorized as SMEs). For instance, the respondents in Wood and Caldas (2000) were described as

Table 1. Profiles of Organizations Studied

Company	Industry	Size: Employees and Turnover (IR? p.a)		Status of Project
Co. A	Medical packaging supplier	50	2m	Postimplementation
Co. B	Animal medical products	100	25m	Postimplementation
Co. C	Telecom network products	200	30m	Postimplementation
Co. D	Mining and industrial products	600	250m	Postimplementation
Co. E	Sheet plastic producer	30	2m	Ongoing (Phase 1 completed)*
Co. F	Procurement specialist	100	20m	Ongoing (Phase 1 completed)
Co. G	Plant protection	40	15m	Ongoing (Phase 1 completed + Phase 2 started)
Co. H	Fitters: oil/gas installations	50	4m	Close to completion
Co. I	Medical supplies	10	n/a	Postimplementation
Co. J	Tobacco products	n/a	160m	Close to completion
Co. K	Food products	50	n/a	Ongoing (Phase 1 completed + Phase 2 started)
Co. L	Lens coloring	500	n/a	Postimplementation
Co. M	Electric connectors	180	500m	Postimplementation
Co. N	Entertainment products	25	250m	Postimplementation

* Note: Phase 1 completed means that the organization is already using the software but is expected to further develop its usage of ERP functionality (e.g., by acquiring more modules).

large- or medium-sized organizations, and case studies commonly cited in textbooks involve very large implementation projects such as the Microsoft case ($25 m) or the Foxmeyer case ($30 m).

The domination of SME-type firms in our sample reflects the small average size of organizations in Ireland (roughly two-thirds of Irish organizations have less than 250 employees), but they come as a surprise, because the current wisdom in relation to ERP systems (as abundantly reported in the media, e.g., Jeanne, 1999) is that ERP systems are only for large organizations because of the costs and implementation times involved. One of the questions being asked at this point in time, is whether the ERP market can now be redirected toward SMEs and whether new methodologies for quicker implementation can be found. Our data indicate that SMEs are already involved in the ERP phenomenon to a large extent, as most of the organizations we studied undertook their implementation projects in 1998 or 1999. The new ASP model for distribution of ERP functionality (which has been said to be targeted at sub-£120m firms) may, therefore, not be the only route to ERP for smaller companies.

Profile of the Projects and Impact on the Organization

The 14 projects we looked at ranged from one to 24 months and averaged eight and a half (8.5) months in duration, with just above a third of the companies taking nine or 10 months. Even though these projects appear to be shorter than those reported in the media or in other similar studies, these figures confirm that ERP implementation projects are large IS projects. A comparison with Fitzgerald's (1998) survey of IS development is appropriate, because it was also carried out in Ireland. This survey found that the average duration of in-house development, outsourced, and purchased software projects was only five point seven (5.7) months, which means that 65% of the projects we studied are above the average reported by Fitzgerald and 14% are four times as long. The projects studied in the five larger companies of the sample (those that could not be classified as SMEs) had an average duration of nine point four (9.4) months, which is somewhat above the overall average, but in fact, only three of these five companies were above the eight and a half (8.5) overall average (and only company N was substantially above, with an 18-month project), which does not suggest that the larger companies take longer to implement ERP software. Clearly, these results must be viewed in the light of the small size of the sample and the absence of a large organization in the sample. It is also interesting to analyze the number of users of the software in each of the sites.

The cases studied had, on average, between 21 and 22 users initially and between 27 and 28 at the time this study took place (i.e., postimplementation). Significantly, only four companies increased their numbers of users after the software went live (less than 30%), even though many sites implemented their software as far back as 1998 or 1999.

Finally, we focused on the effects of these projects on the inhouse IS staff organizations employed. As can be seen in Table 2, 10 companies (70% of the cases studied) had no resident IS expertise prior to their implementing ERP, and five (35%) maintained this situation at the end of the project. In total, only five companies hired IS staff as a result of the ERP implementation, three of

Table 2. Key Characteristics of the ERP Projects Studied

Company	Start Date	End Date	Number of Users (Start/End)	In-House IS Capability (Start/End)
Co. A	November 1997	August 1998	5/10	None/limited
Co. B	November 1997	July 1998	16/32	None/2 staff
Co. C	December 1998	March 1999	32/32	2 staff/3 staff
Co. D	March 1999	November 1999	100/150	8 staff/8 staff
Co. E	November 1998	July 1999	5/5	None/none
Co. F: Phase 1; Phase 2	March 2000; April 2000	April 2000; August 2000	50/50	None/contractors
Co. G: Phase 1; Phase 2	November 1997; April 2000	January 1998; May 2000	8/8	1 staff/2 staff
Co. H	Early 1998	End 1999	10/10	None/none
Co. I	March 1998	April 1998	5/5	None/none
Co. J	March 2000	May 2000	10/10	None in Ireland
Co. K: Phase 1; Phase 2	Early 1997; April 2000	Mid 1997; June 2000	8/8	None/none
Co. L	January 1998	November 1998	32/32	2/2
Co. M	May 1997	October 1997	16/30	None/1 staff
Co. N	Early 1997	Mid 1998*	5/5	None/none

*Note: *The exceptional duration of the project in company N was due to slow decision making at the choice stage and does not mean that the software implementation took longer than other cases in the sample.*

these being "green field sites," where there had been no IS department before (four if the hiring of contract IS staff is equated with hiring full-time staff). In cases where IS staff members were hired, the increase was measured, as no company hired more than two staff members as a result of the project. These figures are significant in that they indicate that ERP software may not have a great impact on the IT staff requirements of organizations. Table 2 also indicates that many companies are still able to rely totally on IS service providers for all their IS needs, even after implementing ERP software. These figures also suggest that a large proportion of Irish SMEs do not have full-time resident IS expertise. Unfortunately, it is not possible to compare this result to Fitzgerald's (1998) study (although its results include average-size IS departments), because the sample used in his study was biased toward firms that had an identifiable IS manager. More research would be required to ascertain whether the sample used in this study is biased toward companies that are weak in their deployment of IT. However, it must be noted that the presence of four subsidiaries of international groups (with IT support from headquarters) influences this result. Alternatively, it could be suggested that companies that have not developed any IT capability see in ERP projects the opportunity to catch up in a rapid and robust manner by acquiring a total system that can easily be installed and maintained by an experienced outside implementing partner. Managers may think that such acquisitions can bring them back in contact with the best practice in their industry without having to experience the usual growing pains of incremental IS development. This must be considered in the general context of IT outsourcing, which is coming back at the forefront in many firms around the world.

GOALS OF THE PROJECTS
AND PROJECT LEADERSHIP

One of the key issues with ERP is whether the benefits commonly associated with ERP implementations actually materialize or whether they are exaggerated by media hype (Caldas & Wood, 2000). In order to ascertain how successful the organizations we studied were with their projects, it was therefore necessary to establish, as a first step, the goals pursued by managers when they purchased ERP software. The data pertaining to these issues are presented in Table 3.

From these data, it is clear that most organizations in the sample are pursuing specific goals in their ERP projects. The most common goals pursued were the implementation of a robust transaction processing system (nine companies)—a "world-class system" for two companies. For nine companies, the traditional benefits of ERP systems, in particular cost reduction benefits, were also sought, while for 28% of our respondents, Y2K was a major incentive to buy an ERP system, although in no case had it been the only rationale. Three companies also sought improvements in the visibility of their transactions, while four companies bought ERP software under instruction from their foreign headquarters and put forward no specific goals for the implementation.

Finally, e-business was a long-term objective for six companies. It was a key finding that, in three cases, actually implementing the ERP software developed the perception of the managers and led to additional goals being pursued. In two of these cases, the availability of a solid platform for order acquisition and processing gave managers confidence that their company should experiment with e-business. In the third case, the ERP system was intended to boost the value of the company prior to its sale, but again, the availability of the ERP software led to managers attempting to capitalize on the good work done and reap additional benefits.

There were also encouraging signs, in three of the four subsidiaries, that local managers had taken ownership of the ERP project and were eager to see it succeed. This meant that even in the absence of clear "local" managerial rationale initially, the ERP implementation was being taken seriously, and the potential of the system that was being implemented was understood by organizational actors. These findings are divergent from those of Caldas and Wood (2000), who found that "following the trend" was the motivation of 77% of their respondents. They also found that 41% of companies implemented ERP systems under pressure from their IT departments. This contrasts strikingly with our finding that in only two companies (14%) had the IT department been the champion or even the origin of the manager of the project.

Only 35% of the companies we investigated had an IS department prior to the implementation of the ERP software, which indicates that the motivation behind the ERP movement often comes from other areas. Thus, the accounting/finance area championed the ERP project in 57% of the companies, while 21% of projects were led by Operations Managers on the client's side. It is difficult to assess why these results diverge so markedly from those reported in Caldas and Wood's study, but the fact that 85% of their companies were subsidiaries of multinational groups (and therefore were asked to implement ERP systems by their headquarters) may have had a negative influence on the perception of managers regarding their ERP projects. Also, the fact that most companies in

Table 3. Goals Pursued and Project Leadership

Company	Goals Pursued		Project Champion	ERP Manager
A	**Initially:** **Now:**	• "A" system • To be able to show the big boys • E-business • Stock reduction	Finance Director	Finance Director
B	**Initially:** **Now:**	• Replace old systems (Y2K) • Common ERP benefits • E-business • Euro transactions	Operations Manager	Operations Manager
C		• E-business • Replace old systems (Y2K) • Data access/visibility • Reduce costs • Cope with volume of data	Accountant	Accountant (gained much status after project)
D		• Y2K • Integration of systems • Visibility • Supply chain improvements • Center of excellence • E-business	Finance Controller	Financial Controller
E	**Initially:** **Now:**	• Boost company value • Stock right-sizing • Visibility • Accountability • Process improvements	Production Manager	Accountant (after change of owner)
F	**Phase 1:** **Phase 2:**	• Replace old systems (Y2K) • E-business • CRM • Expansion • Executive Information System • MRP and inventory control	Operations Director (hands-off) + Contract IT Lack of true champion, as project leader for the implementer feels must act as champion	Operations Director
G	**Phase 1:** **Phase 2:**	• World-class system • E-business • Euro transactions • Manufacturing processes	IT Manager	IT Manager
H		• Group decision • "Flair"	Finance Manager	Finance Manager
I		• Bought by large group (worldwide user of ERP)	Operations Manager	Operations manager
J		• Instruction from group	European IS Manager	
K	**Phase 1:** **Phase 2:**	• World-class system • ERP functionality • Manufacturing • MRP • Costs tracking	Accountant	Accountant
L		• Worldwide implementation	Financial Controller	Financial Controller
M		• A system required • Common ERP functionalities	Financial Controller	Financial Controller
N		• Replace existing systems • MRP • Cope with growth in volumes	Financial Controller	Financial Controller

our study were SMEs means that coordination and consensus about such projects were easier to achieve for these organizations.

Benefits Gained from ERP Implementations

Following from the question discussed in the previous section, we then looked at whether the ERP system was widely adopted by staff in the organization and whether staff were convinced by the benefits brought by the software. We asked project leaders in the client organizations whether they were satisfied with the implementation of the software and also to what extent the goals pursued (as outlined in Table 3) were achieved. All sites were satisfied with their ERP software and its implementation, apart from a certain amount of anxiety which staff experienced as they began to realize the extent of change that the ERP system required. This included concerns about trying to replicate existing functionality rather than meeting business requirements with the new system, migrating data, and designing workarounds. Although migrating data was simplified by emerging common standards, the lack of data integrity from legacy systems can still prove to be a big problem. In addition, in some cases, no workaround is available for a specific requirement, which gives rise to tough negotiations between the implementer seeking zero-modifications and the client seeking "100% functionality."

By and large, all of these problems had solutions, and the implementer and the client collaborated in designing them. Surprisingly, not all of the organizations in our sample attempted to specifically measure the outcome of their ERP projects. Company C was an interesting site, because managers carried out a specific analysis of the consequences of the ERP implementation. They reported a broad range of improvements in business efficiency, including: the ability to handle an increased volume of transactions with the same staff, easier linkage with customers and suppliers, less errors and reruns, better access to information, and easier after-sales support. They also reported additional benefits such as improved quality of business reporting and easier access to Key Performance Indicator analyses for top management. Managers were particularly impressed with the improvements relating to the speed and accuracy of enquiry responses in general, which they perceived as a key factor in their business. The manager interviewed concluded that the ERP system had enabled top management to implement major growth plans for the company.

Other companies reported problems that occurred after the implementation was completed and the ERP team was disbanded. One of the main concerns of managers was that, in the short term, their organization was more vulnerable to any staff member involved in the ERP project leaving the company too soon. If transfers of key knowledge about the ERP system have not had time to occur, then the company stood to waste time in achieving the objectives pursued. However, some interviewees put forward the introduction of proper incentive schemes as a solution to this problem. The shortage of experienced staff in the area of ERP in Ireland is such at this point in time that staff members who took part in a successful ERP implementation come under pressure to capitalize on their newly gained experience and to seek higher salaries.

Management must acknowledge this fact and update the status and reward level of staff involved to reflect the additional skills gained in the ERP project and the resulting modifications in their job content.

Managers also referred to the *sigh effect*, which affects staff immediately after the implementation of the software is completed. In this crucial phase, staff must return to their normal duties and have less time to tackle operational problems linked to the ERP systems. This results in a drop in motivation that has been experienced by most of the staff we interviewed.

Key Aspects of the Relationship with the Implementer

Based on the accounts of both software distributor staff and implementing organization staff, we concluded from our study that, as time goes by, organizations' perceptions and expectations about the software they acquired fluctuate. We were able to model that the mood of the staff in the client organization follows a curve as represented in Figure 1.

In the initial section of the curve, expectations rise steadily, and the perception of the software product being purchased comes into sharper focus as a state-of-the-art solution to old problems is in sight. Managers are excited about getting new tools to achieve their goals, and their belief in the ERP system rises. Thus, organizational actors become increasingly committed to the project.

Then, as the two organizations (client and implementer) begin to negotiate the fine detail of the implementation plan, staff members realize the extent of work and change to current practices involved in the project, and their fears grow steadily. They culminate when the workload allocation is completed, and they must face new responsibilities, while strangers invade the organization asking all sorts of detailed questions about the ways staff members handle their duties.

However, as the implementation gets under way, early benefits are delivered, and when obstacles are encountered, staff members in both organizations (who know each other much better by then) are active in trying to solve them. In this phase, staff members in the client organization reported that they got a real feeling of being at the leading edge of IT and collaboration developed between the two sides. Spirits are high, and the commitment of staff to the project reaches its highest. Unfortunately, this dynamic period does not last as, in the postimplementation phase, the ERP team is soon disbanded, and staff must return to their usual tasks of dealing with customer queries or processing sales orders.

The turning point in the relationship between the two firms is the management of this postimplementation phase, when the relation moves from an active hands-on role to a support role through the intermediary of a service desk or call center. At that stage, the implementer loses track of the general perception of the product they installed, because the communication that develops as part of the support relation is too rigidly structured around capturing and processing problems with the software, and this support relationship cannot capture the business dimensions of the project—i.e., whether the organization is achieving its targets or whether the site is ready to move to the next stage of development of its IT capability.

Clients noted how significantly the moods of users and project leaders dipped in the postimplementation period. As the burden of their everyday tasks took over, and customer inquiries again became a priority, their perceptions of the system tended to crystallize around the problems that emerged, and the attention of all actors involved became focused on the problems resulting from the software, which they acknowledged as being a negative orientation. The challenge for the implementer, as perceived by the implementing staff, is in maintaining the active relationship as long as possible in order to redress the postimplementation dip as quickly as possible. This is done by maintaining a type of communication that is based on a discussion of what the software achieved and how to take it further, rather than move to a restricted and

Figure 1. Evolution of Staff and Management Motivation for the ERP Project

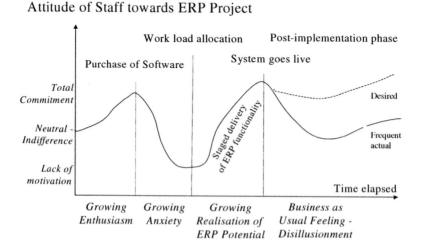

typically tension-laden software support situation (as is suggested with the dashed curve in Figure 1).

The project leader for the implementer firm, who played an active role in most of the projects we reviewed, was of the opinion that the fact that so many of the client organizations had no resident IT staff was another incentive to try to stay in touch with the evolution of the site. In organizations that have full-time IS staff, there is an obvious channel of communication, but in organizations where the ERP leader is essentially a user of the system as opposed to an administrator, the communication can quickly be restricted to matters of proper operation of the system that may be crucial in terms of the operations of the firm but are not conducive to an analysis of how the usage of the ERP functionalities can evolve or what kind of business development it could allow.

Thus, a rich, continued, and business-oriented communication between the implementer and the managers in charge was seen by both organizations as suitable for a better and more effective deployment of IT in the client organization. This may be the only way that the disillusionment mood of the postimplementation phase can be shortened and reversed quickly, so the company can take full advantage of its newly acquired ERP functionality and develop more effective business processes. It seems to make good business sense for the software vendor to prepare for the after-ERP projects, but the lack of time and the pressure of tight implementation schedules mean that these discussions are often overlooked.

Such communication is also necessary for a proper review of the projects to take place. The review phase of decision-making processes has long been highlighted as critical to proper evaluation of the effectiveness of organizational decision making and to learning about key managerial issues, most notably by Simon (1977) and Mintzberg et al. (1976). There is empirical evidence that not enough organizations undertake the review of their IS investments (Ward & Griffiths, 1996). The IS investments are largely regarded as badly analyzed and justified from the outset (Farbey, Land, & Targett, 1992). These findings were confirmed in our study, where some managers could not indicate to what extent the benefits sought were achieved. It seems that implementers can play crucial roles in this stage of the project, because they can help managers identify the benefits that may materialize and those that are unlikely. Later in the project, they can also help managers identify the next steps in deploying IT capabilities and exploiting the ERP systems acquired to the fullest.

CONCLUSION

This study of Irish experiences with ERP implementation shows that SMEs are just as likely to be interested in ERP as the larger organizations that were studied by previous researchers. The only reason why SMEs have not been the primary target of software vendors so far seems to be that vendors and consultants perceive that the arguments in favor of ERP would be stronger in companies such as Microsoft, Dell, or McKesson. However, in Ireland, where SMEs are a primary target on the software market (because organizations are much smaller on average), SMEs already went down the ERP route in significant numbers and successfully implemented ERP systems. Our study indicates that the duration and complexity of large ERP projects as portrayed in the literature may be due as much as to the complexity of the organizations where they are implemented as to the complexity inherent in ERP systems. This is good news for managers in SMEs who are interested in ERP, because it means that the route to ERP may well be shorter and cheaper for them. ERP implementations remain large IS projects (above the average of typical IS projects), but they can be quicker if the organization is pursuing clear managerial objectives and if it works in collaboration with an experienced implementer.

Thus, the ASP offerings recently introduced in the ERP market are not the only route for SMEs. The relatively short duration of ERP projects for SMEs is also good news for ERP solution providers, because it means that their market can be extended to a large group of organizations with less-developed IT infrastructures in place, and where the potential for selling total software solutions is high. This development of the ERP market may actually be timely for the suppliers of ERP solutions, if the predictions reported in the media that large multimillion IT projects will soon become a thing of the past turn out to be accurate (Robineau, 1998).

It is important to note that a large proportion of the companies in the sample have been pursuing a strong managerial rationale in implementing ERP rather than just following a trend, as found in previous studies (Caldas & Wood, 2000). If the four subsidiaries of international groups are excluded, all companies were pursuing definite managerial goals or had reframed their projects to include specific, new managerial targets. Even in the companies where ERP implementations were imposed by headquarters, there was a chance that managers would adopt the systems and try to exploit their potential.

The evolution of the managerial targets in the sites we investigated confirms the trends analyzed in the media toward CRM and toward e-business. ERP systems are seen as suitable total systems to support these new managerial strategies. This highlights the major conclusion of this study: Managers implementing ERP systems should pursue specific managerial targets through the acquisition of such systems, and deciding to acquire ERP software may not be sufficient in itself. At least, once the software is implemented, managers should undertake an accurate review of what was achieved, and think creatively about the ways that the robust platform implemented could be used to develop current business or pave the way toward new interests.

Finally, this study indicates the importance of having experienced implementation partners in ERP projects. The implementation of the software can be sped up, and, more importantly, the postimplementation disillusionment experienced by many companies can be shortened and diminished. An experienced implementation partner can also play a critical part in ensuring that organizations exploit their ERP platforms to the fullest and develop their IT capability beyond the mere utilization of ERP functionality.

REFERENCES

Bancroft, N. (1996). *Implementing SAP/R3: How to Introduce a Large System into a Large Organization.* Greenwich, CT: Manning.

Berger, P. (1998). PGI: Les services valent cher. *Le Monde Informatique*, (September 25), 779.

Besson, P. (1999). Les ERP à l'épreuve de l'organization. *Systèmes d'Information et Management*, 4(4), 21-52.

Bingi, P., Sharma, M., & Godla, J. (1999). Critical issues affecting an ERP implementation. *Information Systems Management*, (Summer), 7-14.

Caldas, M., & Wood, T. (2000). *How consultants can help organizations survive the ERP frenzy.* Retrieved from the World Wide Web: http://www.gv.br/prof_alunos/thomaz/ingles/paper6.htm.

Farbey, B., Land, F., & Targett, D. (1992). Evaluating investments in IT. *Journal of Information Technology*, 7(2), 109-122.

Fitzgerald, B. (1998). An empirical investigation into the adoption of systems development methodologies. *Information and Management*, 34, 317-328.

Gros, M. (1999). Les editeurs de PGI se ruent sur le client. *Le Monde Informatique*, (May 28), 812.

Harvard Business School. (1997). Vandelay Industries Inc. Harvard Business School case study reference 9-697-037, revised April 1997.

Jeanne, F. (1999). Progiciels: Pas d'ASP sans SAP. *Le Monde Informatique*, (September 24), 822.

Kalatoka, R., & Robinson, M. (1999). *E-business — Roadmap to Success*. Reading, MA: Addison-Wesley.

Lampel, J. (1995). Innovation as spectacle: Dramaturgical construction of technological change. *Conference on the Social Construction of Industries and Markets*. Chicago, IL.

Mintzberg, H., Raisinghani, D., & Theoret, A. (1976). The structure of "unstructured" decision processes. *Administrative Science Quarterly*, 21, 246-275.

Robineau, O. (1998). Les nouvelles facettes de l'infogerance. *Le Monde Informatique*, (October 16), 782.

Rowe, F. (1999). Cohérence, intégration informationnelle et changement: Esquisse d'un programme de recherche à partir des Progiciels Intégrés de Gestion. *Systèmes d'Information et Management*, 4(4), 3-20.

Simon, H. (1977). *The New Science of Management Decisions*. Englewood Cliffs, NJ: Prentice Hall.

Terrand, C. (1998). De la production aux services commerciaux: Synchroniser les rouages de la chaîne d'approvisionnement. *Le Monde Informatique*, (November 27), 788.

Terrand, C. (1999). La nouvelle guerre sainte des éditeurs de PGI. *Le Monde Informatique*, (July 2), 817.

Ward, J., & Griffiths, P. (1996). *Strategic Planning for Information Systems*. New York: John Wiley & Sons.

White, B., Clark, D., & Ascarely, S. (1997). Program of pain. *Wall Street Journal*, (March 14), 6.

Wood, T., & Caldas, M. (2000). Stripping the "Big Brother": Unveiling the backstage of the ERP fad. Retrieved from the World Wide Web: http://www.gv.br/prof_alunos/thomaz/ingles/paper5.htm.

ENDNOTES

[1]   Ninety-one percent (91%) of respondents to this study sought assistance from consultants in their ERP projects.

[2]   Sixth periodic report on the social and economic situation and development of SMEs. Retrieved June 2000 from the World Wide Web: http://www.inforegio.cec.eu.int/wbdoc/docoffic/official/radi/page31_en.htm.

[3]   The implementers could obviously not be relied upon exclusively in justifying the investment because of the conflict of interest inherent in the investment decision. It is, however, clear that project leaders in the implementer organizations must, as part of their task, differentiate between sites where implementing ERP is likely to succeed and sites where it should not be undertaken. It is ultimately in no one's interest to get involved in a project that will never succeed and will generate a lot of problems.

Chapter VIII

Implementing ERP — What Happens to Competitive Advantage?

David Sammon
University College Cork, Ireland

Frédéric Adam
University College Cork, Ireland

Kevin Higgins
Ulster Bank, Ireland

Mark Synnott
Intel, Ireland

ABSTRACT

Over the last 30 years, the enterprise-wide systems movement has been gathering momentum and has now reached a global dimension, with companies across the world and, more importantly, across very different industries jumping on the ERP/SCM/CRM bandwagon. The pace of implementations has been such that SAP alone have now implemented their software in 30,000 sites and have a user population well in excess of 10 million. However, studies carried out since the ERP epidemic broke out have revealed that the rationale pursued by managers in acquiring ERP packages has sometimes been weak and not well informed. Moreover, the track record of ERP implementations has not been good with many examples of implementation failures. It is our contention that the problems reported in ERP projects are due to a failure to link the business model underlying ERP packages and the unique assets of organisations. In this research study, we carried out two in-depth case studies of organisations having just implemented ERP packages and focused on the preparation stage of their projects. We also carried out a survey of organisations having implemented ERP to confirm quantitatively how well managers prepare themselves for ERP. Based on these, we uncover patterns of ERP project preparation which may explain the low success rate of ERP projects and put forward some proposals which should help managers and researchers to increase the likelihood that ERP projects are successful.

INTRODUCTION

ERP systems are enterprise-wide information systems that cater to many aspects of an organization's business processes (Holland, Light & Kawalek, 1999). The popularity of ERP software began to rise in the early 1990s and has grown to become one of the most widespread software applications used in managing enterprise-wide business processes (Light et al., 1999). One of the dominant features of the ERP market is that enthusiasm for ERP systems stretches across a broad industrial spectrum. Implementations are taking place in industries, such as chemicals, IT, electronics, textiles, and even in the public sector (Holland, Light & Kawalek, 1999; Chang & Gable, 2001). Perhaps the most resounding endorsement for ERP systems is that software giants IBM and Microsoft are using ERP packages produced by other software vendors (Martin, 1998).

However, there are concerns with the track record of ERP implementations and with the level of benefits that accrued to organizations having implemented ERP. We contend that many of the problems that arose in relation to ERP are due to the lack of preparation of many companies and to the weakness of the analysis carried out prior to implementing software packages. In order to discover how much preparation organizations make when implementing ERP, we carried out two in-depth case studies and a survey of companies focusing on the preparation stages of their projects.

IMPLEMENTING ERP

While ERP packages have the potential to bring tremendous benefits to organizations, these benefits do not come without considerable risks. A significant number of companies encounter problems, and managers are becoming increasingly wary of ERP packages (Davenport, 1998; Martin, 1998). Holland et al. (1999) estimate that over 90% of ERP implementations are late or more costly than first anticipated. In addition, there have been some high-profile failures: Fox Meyer drug company sued their ERP consultants after their attempted implementation led to bankruptcy, while both Dell, Hershey, Waste Management Inc., Allied Waste Industries, Unisouce Worldwide, and Mobil One were forced to abandon implementation after investing substantial resources (around $100 million each) in their respective ERP projects (Adam, 2000).

Thus, implementing ERP systems is now widely regarded as highly complex, very expensive, time-consuming, and risky (Martin, 1998; Davenport, 1998; Holland, Light & Kawalek, 1999; Koch et al., 2000). This complexity is largely due to the need for integration between the newly implemented software and existing applications and data sources (Holland, Light & Gibson, 1999), although in most cases, the ERP package replaces up to 80% of existing systems (Rowe, 1999). This means that any ERP implementation will have implications for the entire organization (Davenport, 1998) and, in particular, key business processes and most staff. Many authors concluded that the complexity of ERP implementations makes them organizationally disruptive and resource intensive and necessitate substantial investments of time, money, and people.

Ultimately, the greatest problem associated with ERP implementation is the failure of the management of an organization to understand the business problem raised by the ERP packages they buy. The technical risk associated with the ERP implementation is lower than that experienced in the development of bespoke systems (Holland, Light & Kawalek, 1999; Martin, 1998), but critical business-related difficulties remain (Davenport, 1998). The main implementation risks associated with ERP projects are related to change management and the business reengineering that results from integrating an organization's business model and the ERP standard software and switching to the ERP software's underlying business model (Holland, Light & Kawalek, 1999). Unsurprisingly, the main benefits of ERP implementation are derived from solving these business problems, with one AMR executive stating that, "80% of the benefit comes from what you change in your business. Software is just an enabler" (Martin, 1998).

IMPLEMENTATION STRATEGIES

A number of methodologies have been put forth to help organizations when they decide to implement an ERP package (Martin, 1998). One feature of these methodologies relates to the timing of incorporating functionality into the system. Over the last few years, managers sought one of the following:

- A compact implementation scenario: In this strategy, a skeleton or vanilla software package is implemented and extra functionality is added over time as user familiarity with the system grows (Holland, Light, & Gibson, 1999).
- A comprehensive implementation scenario: This strategy involves implementing the system incorporating all the required functionality in one go.

Both models have strengths and weaknesses. The comprehensive scenario has been the preferred strategy of many organizations (Westrup & Knight, 2000; Shankarnarayanan, 2000). However, its popularity declined, because often, the ERP model and functionality were poorly aligned, forcing customizations and longer implementation time, leading to higher costs and a decline in overall user confidence (Shankarnarayanan, 2000). A second reason why this strategy declined was because of the need to reduce the costs of consultancy relative to those of the software. Software vendors believed that the escalating consultancy costs [estimated by Westrup and Knight (2000) at between 20 to 50 times the cost of the software] were having a prohibitive effect on software sales and subsequently forced consultancy firms to alter their strategies. With the compact implementation approach now being deployed, most often the cost of implementation declined to lower than 3:1, on average (Westrup & Knight, 2000). However, this strategy also has its problems, because it requires the development of many patches to fill in the blanks left in the skeleton. For most companies, developing software is not their core activity, and having to develop many interfaces and additional modules reintroduces significant risks of failure. In addition, companies may have to carry out development using new platforms they are not familiar with or to integrate applications that are not designed to "talk" to one another. Getting support for such development may also be impossible in case of problems. For instance, many companies discovered that integrating specialized CRM software with SAP is tricky (though the rationale for doing so is clear given the weakness of SAP's CRM offering at this point in time).

Another implementation choice that management faces is whether to phase in the ERP system or whether to go with a so-called *big bang* approach

(Holland, Light, & Gibson, 1999). Due to the modular design of ERP systems (Davenport, 1998), organizations can choose to implement some of the modules initially and interface them with remaining legacy systems. This approach allows ERP software to be implemented in parallel with existing systems (Holland, Light, & Gibson, 1999). The phased approach is less risky than the big bang; however, it is more expensive in the long run (Hirt et al., 1999). This is as a result of temporary software that has to be written to interface with the legacy system. By contrast, the big bang is riskier, because it forces an organization to go live with the entire new software at once. Additionally, the big bang approach requires greater resources at one time, because the implementation process must occur in parallel instead of sequentially (Hirt et al., 1999). Managers are, therefore, facing a trade-off between the amount of up-front disruption and the amount of temporary work-arounds that may have to be developed.

Finally, companies, especially multinationals, face a choice between using their ERP as a standardization tool or preserving (rather tolerating) some degree of local independence in software terms (Davenport, 1998). A generic ERP strategy is rigid, and an organization may risk losing market share to competitors willing to provide greater flexibility (Davenport, 1998) when asking local managers to sacrifice their specific processes for the good of the ERP project. As a result, companies that compete on a global scale or in diverse markets where business units do not share common processes often adopt a federal (Davenport, 1998) or franchising (Koch et al., 2000) strategy. The franchising strategy implies that a company will implement different versions of the same ERP software among business units. This ensures that common processes, such as financial bookkeeping, are linked, while also ensuring that regional diversity is catered for (Koch et al., 2000). This strategy amounts to a compromise between the purity of the system and the need for better market responsiveness (Davenport, 1998).

PROJECT MANAGEMENT
FOR ERP PROJECTS

Project management for ERP projects is little different from project management for any IS project, and traditional frameworks for project management are applied to ERP projects. However, certain areas of traditional project management require greater emphasis, while others can be discarded. PMBOK (2000) describes project management as the "application of knowledge, skills, tools and techniques to a broad range of activities in order to meet the requirements of a particular project" (p. 6). Project management is accomplished through the employment of processes such as initiating, planning, executing, controlling, and closing. The following are ways the project team manages the work of a project:

- Balancing competing demands for scope, time, cost, risk, and quality.
- Satisfying the different needs and expectations of stakeholders.
- Meeting identified requirements.

Project management is an aid to project managers, because it helps them to standardize routine tasks and to reduce the number of tasks that could potentially be forgotten. It also ensures that available resources are used in the most effective and efficient ways. The application of project management principles allows senior managers to establish and use more appropriate measures of success, to quantify value commensurate with cost, and to optimize the use of organizational resources.

Project management is also an integrative endeavor, and action or lack of action in one area will usually affect other areas, e.g., sometimes it is obvious, i.e., where a change in the scope of the project will impact the cost and time and may also impact the morale of the project team. Understanding these interdependencies is critical for a project leader.

Thus, the purpose of project management is to provide a uniform way of planning, executing, controlling, and closing out a project. Planning and control are key: project planning means determining the work to be performed and organizing required resources. Project control means determining what was accomplished, what remains to done, and where necessary, taking corrective action.

However, Maylor (2001) warned that project management lacks a strong theoretical base; it is not based on a series of premises from which consistent theory can be delivered but rather on empirical evidence, which has built up over time to form a body of knowledge. Thus, project management is learned through experience, and this earned it the title of the "accidental profession."

The Nine Knowledge Areas of Project Management

Project management as a discipline is only a recent concept, yet, over the past 50 years, a considerable body of knowledge has built up around project management tools, skills, and techniques. The purpose of the PMBOK is to identify and describe best practices that are applicable to most projects most of the time (see Table 1). PMBOK (2000) identified nine knowledge areas upon which project management is based. These nine areas, although presented as distinct features, are usually integrated, as are their component processes.

In the next sections, we propose a description of the activities identified in ERP implementation literature categorized under the nine knowledge areas of project management.

ERP Project Integration Management

Slevin and Pinto (1987) argued that project managers must be capable in both strategic and tactical aspects of project management in order to manage projects successfully. Holland et al. (1999) developed a framework for managing an ERP implementation, which expanded Slevin and Pinto's (1987) model (see Table 2). The framework is based on the critical success factors (CSF) of ERP projects and their integration. The CSFs are grouped under strategic and tactical headings, and they are vital for the successful planning, execution, and control of the ERP project.

Naturally, strategies and tactics are not independent of each other; strategy should drive tactics in order to fully integrate the three main management processes (planning, execution and control).

ERP PROJECT SCOPE MANAGEMENT

Davenport (1998) stated that the single biggest reason that ERP projects fail is because companies are unable to reconcile the technological necessities of the system with their own business needs. An ERP system imposes its own logic on a company's strategy, organization, and culture. If a definite scope statement is not articulated early in the project, the ERP system will drive the company toward full integration, even though a certain degree of business unit segregation may be the optimal solution. This will result in generic processes, even if customized processes were an original source for competitive advantage. A lack of understanding of the scope of the system may result in a conflict between the logic of the system and the logic of the business (Davenport, 1998).

The primary consideration when implementing an ERP system is that the ERP system will impose itself on the business and not vice versa. The key to ERP scope management is balancing the way you want to work with the way

Table 1. Nine Knowledge Areas of Project Management

1 Project Integration	2 Project Scope	3 Project Time
1.1 Project Plan Development 1.2 Project Plan Execution 1.3 Integrated Change Control	2.1 Initiation 2.2 Scope Planning 2.3 Scope Definition 2.4 Scope Verification 2.5 Scope Change Control	3.1 Activity Definition 3.2 Activity Sequencing 3.3 Activity Duration Estimating 3.4 Schedule Development 3.5 Schedule Control

4 Project Cost Management	5 Project Quality Management	6 Project Human Management
4.1 Resource Planning 4.2 Cost Estimating 4.3 Cost Budgeting 4.4 Cost Control	5.1 Quality Planning 5.2 Quality Assurance 5.3 Quality Control	6.1 Organizational Planning 6.2 Staff Acquisition 6.3 Team Development

7 Project Communications Management	8 Project Risk Management	9 Project Procurement Management
7.1 Communications Planning 7.2 Information Distribution 7.3 Performance Reporting 7.4 Administrative	8.1 Risk Identification 8.2 Quantitative Risk Analysis 8.3 Risk Response Planning 8.4 Risk Monitoring and Control	9.1 Procurement Planning 9.2 Solicitation Planning 9.3 Solicitation 9.4 Source Selection 9.5 Contract Administration 9.6 Contract Closeout

the system will let them work. Davenport (1998) put forward a two-stage model for deciding on the scope of the ERP system. First, most ERP systems are modular in nature; this means the system can be implemented for some functions and not for others. Most clients will adopt some modules, e.g., accounting and finance, while many clients will ignore other modules, such as HR. The second step is using the configuration tables to tailor particular aspects of the system to the way the company does business, e.g., using a FIFO rather than a LIFO inventory system. Customization is limited, and companies with an unconventional method of doing business are likely to find it impossible to reflect their business processes.

Bingi et al. (1999) commented that the scope of an ERP project affects not only the number of modules being implemented but also the number of functional units affected, the number of sites in which the system is to be implemented, the extent of customization, and the number of interfaces with legacy applications.

Thus, in complex organizations, such as multinationals, this scope management stage is crucial and requires a preliminary determination of what configu-

Table 2. CSFs for Project Management and ERP Project Management

Critical Success Factors for Project Management[a]	
Strategic	Tactical
Project mission	Communication
Top management commitment	Recruitment/personnel
Project schedule	Technology
	User acceptance
Critical Success Factors for ERP Project Management[b]	
Strategic	Tactical
Legacy systems	Client consultation/acceptance
Business vision	Business process change
Project schedule	Monitoring and feedback
	Troubleshooting

[a]*Source: Slevin and Pinto (1987)*
[b]*Source: Holland et al. (2000)*

ration will be rolled out in the different sites. This vision of the software is sometimes referred to as a template.

Minahan (1998) argued another point with respect to scope. He stated that companies try to "automate existing redundant or non-value-added processes" (p. 3), rather than choose what existing methods are relevant to their ERP experience. Only when companies begin implementation do they realize that they are missing some of the value of the ERP system; thus, it is vital that the scope of the system be open for controlled change. Scott et al. (2000) expanded this point, stating that most implementers find that at least 20% of their needed functionality is absent from the package. This should typically have been identified in developing the template for the ERP implementation.

Sherman (2000) stated that companies that implement an ERP system and pursue a growth-by-acquisition strategy are likely to find that they have to continue to perform implementations into the future, e.g., Lyondell Chemical Company acquired two new companies in the last two years, which necessitated two more SAP implementations.

Wood and Caldas (2000) found that of the 91% of their respondents who said they would implement again if faced with the situation again, 25% would significantly change the scope or the implementation methods of the project.

Shanks et al. (2000) stated that 90% of ERP implementations end up over time and over budget due to, among other factors, changes in the project scope. We argue that these bad results go back to a lack of preparation before projects are implemented.

ERP Project Time Management

Depending on the size of the organization and the scope of the project, implementing an ERP system may take years because of the need to be rolled out across multiple sites, lines of businesses, and countries. McKie (1999) stated, "nobody is capable of implementing financial, distribution and manufacturing software across a range of statutory, operational, linguistic and cultural parameters in a short time frame" (p. 2). Krumbholz et al. (2001) cited a Standish Group Report on ERP implementation project that revealed that organizations were "on average, 178% over budget, took two and a half times as long as intended and delivered only 30% of promised benefit" (p. 2).

A typical implementation of an ERP system takes, on average, 14 months. Corning Inc. estimated that rolling out its ERP system to 10 of its manufacturing divisions would take between five and eight years (Bingi et al., 1999; Stedman, 1998). The length of implementation is greatly affected by the scope of the project, i.e., more activity regarding modules, sites, and functions means a longer process. A large proportion of the implementation time is consumed by customizing the package, so the length of time could be substantially reduced by keeping the system "plain vanilla" and reducing the number of packages that require customization in order to be bolted onto it (Bingi et al., 1999).

Minahan (1998) claimed that a typical ERP implementation takes between two and three years, while larger ones can stretch to five years. On top of this, because most ERP systems are not very user friendly, considerable more time must be spent establishing rules for use of the system and training employees to follow them. Stefanou (2000) stated that unrealistic time frames add unnecessary pressure and lead to project failures.

In Chapter 7, we reported on a survey of 14 Irish organizations that covered a broad range of sizes and industries. We concluded that ERP implementations averaged eight and a half months in duration. This indicates that ERP projects do not have to be as long and as complex as previously described, though this may be realized to the smaller size of the organizations in our sample.

Osterland (2000) suggested that the best time to go live with an ERP system is at the end of the first month of a quarter, because the company finished its reporting procedure from the previous quarter, and there is still time for troubleshooting the new system before the reporting process begins again.

SAP recognized that the implementation time is a big disadvantage and introduced a number of new products for smaller companies, e.g., Ready-to-Run, which is a scaled-down version of its R/3 suite, and Accelerated SAP

(ASAP). Other vendors are following suit by offering industry-specific applications to cut down on the implementation time.

ERP Project Cost Management

The total costs of implementing an ERP system include the cost of licensing, training, implementation, maintenance, customization and hardware requirements (MacVittie, 2001), extra costs for the retention of newly skilled employees via bonus schemes, company perks, salary increases, and continual training (Bingi et al., 1999). Berger (1998) added that for every pound spent on ERP software licences, companies must spend a further £5-7 on related services, most of which are consultancy costs. Scott et al. (2000) stated that the complexity of ERP projects generated a lucrative consulting support industry, and this caused considerable controversy over the risks of escalating implementation costs.

Like most software, ERPs are priced based on the functionality of the system and the number of users who will access it. ERP systems also require companies to invest in migrating data, modifying existing systems, overhauling network infrastructures, and hiring a multitude of consultants whose fees can run as high as five or 10 times the price of the software. The costs quickly add up, and Chevron spent nearly $160 million implementing their ERP system over a five-year period. Jones of the Gartner Group stated that it is not unusual for big complex implementation projects to cost between $50,000 and $75,000 per user (Minahan, 1998).

Stedman (1998) stated that 10% to 20% of the total project cost is spent on training the end users, e.g., Baan charge $5,000 per head to train users. The problem with using external trainers is that they are perfectly familiar with the ERP system, but they are unable to answer questions regarding the business processes that underpin the system. Thus, buyers are designing and conducting their own training programs. Visio used a strategy of training "superusers" who were then used to train the rest of the workforce in the company (Breen, 1997). This type of strategy has since become commonplace (Adam & Twomey, 2001).

ERP Project Quality Management

An ERP system is not just an office automation software package that can be bought off the shelf and implemented with the aid of a step-by-step user manual. It is a serious transformation process that requires fundamental changes in the way business processes are designed and conducted. Various methodologies were put forward to ensure the package is implemented in a manner that ensures the quality of the final system, i.e., that the system is implemented in an efficient way and the objectives (both implied and stated) are met.

One such methodology is a 10-step program put forward by the TheSpot4.com:

1. Match the program objectives with the business objectives.
2. Match the program culture with the business culture.
3. Match the program organization with the business organization.
4. Define key objectives, benefits, and expectations before you start.
5. Ensure that you have top-level management buy-in.
6. Create a change management team.
7. Create an integration team.
8. Pick your best and brightest for the implementation team.
9. Build a milestone-based program-wide plan, publish it widely, and stick to it.
10. Use rapid prototyping methods.

Minahan (1998) promoted a seven-step program to a better ERP project:

1. Look at yourself first, the goal should be to improve your business — to identify, examine, and improve your existing business processes.
2. Plan ahead, establish business goals, and map out a strategy for achieving them.
3. Prove the need for ERP: spell out how the system will support overall business strategy and how it will work with the new business processes.
4. Choose partners wisely: select the ERP vendor right for you and engage consultants with the requisite knowledge of your business processes and the ERP technology.
5. Pick the best people for the job: a good rule for selection is to examine which people are key to each of the operations, and they are the people that should be on the team.
6. Start off slow: install ERP on a rolling basis and start with the small but highly visible business units first.
7. Change everything, remain flexible, and be prepared to roll with the punches as new information becomes available.

Stefanou (2000) advanced a three-phase model for ERP selection. The first phase considers the business vision as a beginning point for ERP initiation. The nest phase consists of performing a detailed examination and defining business needs and constraints. It is the commitment of the organization to change that bridges the gaps between the constraints and business goals. The final phase considers the selection of modules for the core system that supports critical business practices.

ERP Project Human Resource Management

An ERP implementation is a major undertaking that requires management to assemble the best possible team to plan, execute, and control the project. Top management must be visible in their commitment to the project, clarifying the exact goals of the project. Responsibility for the implementation should be given to those individuals who have a high degree of knowledge of the business and the way that its component parts interact. This implies reassigning the few people who are most likely to be missed from their duties to the ERP project team on a full-time basis (Maher, 1999).

Frequently, companies do not fully comprehend the impact of choosing internal employees with the correct skill sets. The right employees for the team should not only be experts in the company's processes but also be knowledge-able of the best business practices in the industry. The large consulting agencies provide guidelines for selecting employees for ERP projects, but companies often do not carefully follow these exercises. Ignorance of the project needs and an inability to provide leadership and guidance to the project by the company's team is a major reason for failure of ERP projects. It is easy to find functional areas reluctant to sacrifice their best resources to the project; this is a difficulty that must be overcome (Bingi et al., 1999).

Wood and Caldas (2000) stated that ERP implementation teams are "multidisciplinary, dedicated teams, comprised normally of Information Technology specialists, key users and operations personnel, as well as consultants with process redesign and change management skills" (p. 4). They stated that their findings suggested that the support given by consultants is less than adequate, this despite the fact that they are extensively used. Consultants are seen to be of little relevance and insufficiently prepared for the task. In 1995, the ERP consultancy market was insignificant, but by 1998, it grew to a $10 billion industry. Thus, Wood and Caldas suggested that ERP consultants are simply jumping in the ERP bandwagon and, for the most part, they do not possess the requisite skills for the job, e.g., their survey revealed that only 47%

of respondents believed that their consultants were operative and influential during the implementation process. Only 23% stated that the consultants had the necessary skills and experience for the project.

Bingi et al. (1999) added a final point, stating that team morale is a vital component for the success of the project. Team members are required to put in long hours (as much as 20 hours per day), and this stress coupled with their regular duties could quickly diminish team morale. Thus, support from upper management and the project leader is crucial to maintaining a focused team.

ERP Project Communications Management

Scott et al. (2000) performed an in-depth analysis of an ERP implementation, and they discovered that companies find it difficult to communicate internally, because each department views its information as its own, and they are reluctant to share it. Implementation team members have often discovered that it was easier to learn and share experiences with people from outside their organization than within intraorganizational teams. This is where the chief benefit of using consultants to aid implementation is apparent. They add value to the project by "facilitating meetings as open discussions of requirements, preparing agendas, prioritising issues… providing objectivity and avoiding bias, conflicts of interests and possible confusion" (p. 112). Thus, consultancy agencies are important in ERP projects, despite the possible lack of technical experience or knowledge (as discussed earlier in the HR section), because they facilitate open and productive communication.

Palaniswamy et al. (2000) stated that the higher the levels of communication and interaction in the implementation team, the higher the performance of the team. The members of the team must be able to communicate between themselves, with the clients, the suppliers, and all other stakeholders.

A global ERP implementation can also cause communication problems. Stedman (1998) gave an example of Meritor Heavy Vehicles Systems LLC, which had to transfer a team of U.S. employees to Europe for nine months in order to eliminate communications breakdowns caused by time-zone difficulties. This is a very common difficulty for mutinational firms.

ERP Project Risk Management

Even the high-profile companies experienced difficulties in implementing ERP systems. According to Weston (1998), ERPs "are tremendously advantageous in the hands of someone who knows what to do with them, but can be dangerous in the hands of someone who doesn't" (p. 1). According to

Davenport (1998), an ERP system "by its very nature imposes its own logic on a company's strategy, organization and culture" (p. 122). Wood and Caldas (2000) expanded on this point by stating that ERP implementations involve "broad organizational transformation processes with significant implications on the organization's management model, organization structure, management style and culture and particularly on people" (p. 6). Thus, as MacVittie (2001) put it, ERPs require a radical change in the business processes of organizations. Radical change means risks, and risks mean more time and money.

Sammer (2000) cited the example of Bournes Inc., a manufacturing company in California, which encountered resistance to their new ERP system. Prior to the implementation, the local managers were used to tailoring financial information and reporting to meet their needs, but postimplementation, there was consistent reporting across regions, and thus, local managers were deprived of their autonomy and reacted negatively toward the new system.

ERP systems are complex, and they require reliance on many different types of expertise, which may also need to be sourced outside the organization. Good, experienced consultants are difficult to find, thus employing a consultancy firm is no guarantee that the project will be a success. As a result, companies that trained their employees in the art of ERP implementation stand a great risk of losing their investment, because personnel with such experience are in great demand by consulting agencies.

Another difficulty with ERP implementations is that, typically, companies can only hold onto 20% of their previous applications, which can be viewed as a benefit on one hand because it allows for "house cleaning" and a fresh start, but it also means that it is impossible to return to a preimplementation situation (Rowe, 1999).

In Europe, ERP projects are more complex than in North America, because of diverse national cultures that influence organizational culture and make successful implementations of multinational ERP solutions difficult. Thus, failure to adapt packages to fit the national culture leads to projects that are expensive and late (Krumbholz, 2001). Stefanou (2000) posited that organizational factors seem to be more important than technological factors for the success of an implementation.

Holland et al. (1999) contended that ERP implementations are complex because of the high levels of integration required and the need for enterprise-wide consensus in the reengineering of the organization's core business processes in line with the processes implicit in the system. Managers argue that the ERP's business model is not representative of their model, and reengineering the business to suit the model is fraught with risks.

Also, Wood and Caldas (2000) discovered low levels of satisfaction among firms that successfully implemented ERP systems; 45% of firms perceived no improvements; and 43% stated that no cycle reduction was obtained. In brief, the risks associated with ERP implementation projects are very high and the rewards are possibly very low. Yet, as Wood and Caldas put it: "ERP systems seem to have simply conquered hearts and minds throughout the business realm" (p. 5).

ERP Project Procurement Management

Because ERP software is largely considered to be packaged software, it needs to appeal to the discretionary customer, it is generic, parameterized, and flexible (Scott et al., 2000). Thus, the choice of vendor is extremely important and subject to much discussion in academic literature.

Maher (1999) stated that the different packages on the market have different strengths in different areas. It is important for the customer to recognize this and select the package with the strengths that are appropriate. Only when top management reaches consensus on what the business requires can package vetting and selection begin. When selecting the package, the customer must recognize that there will never be a perfect match between the company's needs and the package's abilities. The key is implementing the packaged software in a customized manner so as to address the specific business needs of the company. KPMG notes that of the two factors, effective implementation is far more significant than the choice of the package. A last point made by Maher is that the chosen system must be flexible enough to accommodate the changing needs of the business.

Shanks et al. (2000) conducted a comprehensive survey of successful ERP implementations, and they discovered that ERP product selection is based on the following factors in order of importance:
1. Business fit
2. Ease of implementation
3. Vendor services and support
4. Special industry or applications capabilities
5. Product affordability
6. Compatibility with existing systems

Minahan (1998) suggested using cross-functional and cross-business unit teams to ensure that the correct package is procured, i.e., a suite, which will support the long-term goals of the organization. Later chapters in this book expand this point that the successful selection of an ERP system begins with an understanding of the external and internal business environments and also of the technological environment. Failure to integrate the business and technological needs will result in an ill-scoped system or selection process, which is not business driven.

Stefanou (2000) stated that when considering from which vendor to purchase, it is vital to consider the availability of experts in the system, the partnering company that will aid in the implementation, and the training courses available from either the vendors or third parties.

ERP projects executed using this framework as a tool for planning the implementation are likely to find that they omitted some important factors that are possibly unique to ERP implementation projects. Nonetheless, it is a comprehensive framework that is particularly useful for focusing attention on some of the core issues that arise during the implementation of an enterprise-wide system — issues such as the construct of the implementation team, the hidden costs of ERP implementation, the scope of the implementation, the use of consultants in the implementation process, etc.

PROBLEM AREAS SPECIFIC TO ERP PROJECTS

The nine knowledge areas of project management may not fully cover the characteristics of ERP systems, which need to be considered to ensure successful management of an ERP project. Three more areas are outlined below.

ERP Project Rationale Management

Wood and Caldas (2000) found some dubious reasons for implementing an ERP system. These included the following: "the need to follow a trend," "the need to meet the pressures of the IT function," and "the pressures of the head office." They found that 36% of respondents declared: "The firm didn't know exactly what it was buying" or "what could be expected from the system." They observed a scarcity of rationality in the decision process but a high degree of emotion accompanied by a high degree of euphoria during implementation, which they believed is consistent with "managerial fads and fashions" (p. 7).

Another prominent reason for implementing an ERP system was as a reaction to the Y2K problem (Minahan, 1998; Brown et al., 2000; Bingi et al., 1999). This presents skewed reasoning for engaging in an "organizational revolution." ERPs involve broad organizational transformation processes that have a huge impact on the organization's management and organizational model. The Y2K issue should have had a comprehensive yet simple technological solution.

Davenport (1998) suggested a number of questions that management need to ask to ensure that they are engaging in an ERP project for the right reasons and not from some knee-jerk reaction to their competitors' actions or something that they heard about in the media:

1.   How might an ERP system strengthen our competitive advantage?
2.   How might it erode our competitive advantage?
3.   What will be the system's effect on organizational culture?
4.   Do we need to extend the system across all functions?
5.   Should we only implement certain modules?
6.   Would it be better to roll out the system globally or restrict it to certain regional units?
7.   Are there other alternatives for information management that might suit us better than an ERP system?

Top management need to answer these questions to ensure that they understand what an ERP system implies. Wood and Caldas (2000) discovered that many organizations failed to implement their ERP systems, because they viewed them as just another IT project or some type of IT-meets-reengineering project. Once top management are committed to the project, it is vital that they be able to document the reasons for choosing to implement that system and that they publish the reasons widely across the organization (Minahan, 1998). Clear and unambiguous statements by top management regarding why the ERP system is being pursued are vital in ensuring the success of the project.

ERP Project Review Management

There are various strategies for implementing an ERP system into a multinational company (as outlined by Holland et al., 1999), and with each method, there is a series of repeated steps involved, e.g., implementing a finance module in one location is similar to implementing the same module in another site, even allowing for regional variations. There is a high degree of correlation between the implementation process in one site as in another, but the PMI defines a project as a "temporary endeavour to create a unique product or service" (p. 4) and so does not recognize the need to learn from experience.

Maylor (2001) disputed the claim that a project is "a one-off activity," because it implies a degree of novelty, which is often misplaced, and because it discourages the consideration of projects as a business process, focusing instead on the technical or physical aspects of the work involved. The Deming Cycle (plan – do – check – act) or Simon's 1977 Decision Making Model (Intelligence – Decision – Implementation – Review) as applied to project management is disputed by some project managers, because if projects are unique, there should be no need for a review, because nothing can be learned from it that can be applied to new projects in the future. But, Maylor (2001) discovered that as a result of the lack of a review process, the same mistakes were made repeatedly in different projects by the same people. Maylor (2001) suggested using projects as a business process, where the first step in each new project is to review and evaluate similar projects completed in the past or similar steps completed previously in the same project.

Global ERP Project Management

Production and manufacturing operations have become more complex, automated, and geographically dispersed, according to Palaniswamy et al. (2000). ERP systems are designed to cope with the complexity inherent in geographical dispersion, but a global ERP implementation confronts many issues, which are particular to worldwide implementation projects, e.g., decision making involving different time horizons and geographical dispersion (Palaniswamy et al., 2000).

Edburg et al. (2001) outlined some practical issues (shown in Table 3) that must be confronted when implementing an IT system on a global basis.

Davenport (1998) asked, for a multinational, how much uniformity should exist in the way it does business in different regions or countries. For most companies, differences in regional markets remain so profound that strict process uniformity would be counterproductive. Companies must remain flexible and allow regional units to tailor their operations to local customer requirements and regulatory structures. Davenport recommended a type of federalist system, where different versions of the same system are rolled out to each regional unit, e.g., Monsanto, Hewlett-Packard, and Nescafe found this approach successful. This raises its own problems for the company, i.e., deciding on what aspects of the system need to be uniform and what aspects can be allowed to vary (Horwitt, 1998).

Bingi et al. (1999) stated that multinational companies need to make sure that the ERP vendor has the same package available in all the regional locations.

Vendor claims regarding this issue should be investigated, because they may be exaggerating the readiness of the package for global implementation.

CASE STUDIES OF ERP IMPLEMENTATIONS

We carried out two in-depth case studies of organizations that just implemented ERP packages from two leading ERP vendors. In one of the organizations we studied (a multinational with production facilities in many countries), the IS manager described how a small production unit based on a remote island in the Caribbean was forced to implement SAP in order to comply with the IT strategy drawn up by the head office. This facility manufactures the company's products for the local market and has around 50 staff members. The business case for the implementation of such a large ERP package in such a small production unit was reduced to a single consideration: the need to be able to report to HQ using the same format as everyone else and the need to share information. No alternative way to achieve the level of system integration required for basic information sharing was examined, and it seemed uncertain whether it made good economic sense to invest such amounts of money (especially given the lack of local expertise with the platform, which meant that specialists had to travel considerable distances to set up the system). In the Caribbean site, as in the site we visited in Ireland, the implementation of

Table 3. Global Management Issues

Type of Problem	Issues
Language	Appropriate language is difficult to identify Transition is complex and time consuming Differing formats for different languages
Systems development and support	Differing national standards Training and compensation of employees Different terminology Hours and availability of support
Legal regulations and enforcement	Different forms of protectionism Employee hiring, firing, etc. Intellectual property laws Accounting, tax, customs, and contract law
Level of technology	Levels of technology and knowledge Availability of facilities and support Differing uses of technology
Culture and geography	Prejudices Behavioral differences Different symbolic formats Security and disaster planning

SAP was not a matter of choice. Sites were included in the five-year roll-out worldwide plan and had to abide by the schedule they were given. Naturally, from an HQ point of view, the economic rationale may be sound given the small incremental costs involved in equipping one more site. However, the disruption to local business and the costs (proportional to local turnovers) must also be considered.

In the Irish site, the IS manager and the Financial Controller (who was the ERP project leader) were satisfied with the ease with which SAP was implemented, but the IS manager was less impressed with the amount of soul-searching the integration with their Siebel package involved. He was also concerned that the corporate IT plan involved standardization around SAP modules, including the CRM module. This would mean that the Siebel application would have to be replaced by the SAP CRM module. He felt this would be a real pity given the way that the Siebel package currently performed and given the perception of users that using Siebel was a real treat in comparison with using SAP. The maintenance of the two applications also seemed to reflect these views, with Siebel offering a level of simplicity in its operation that was far superior to the complexity inherent in any operation in the SAP software.

Another site we investigated, a specialized manufacturer of components of telecom products working mostly on contracts on behalf of large suppliers of telecom solutions, was purchased by a much larger player in the industry. The IS manager explained how they were forced to switch to Baan to comply with the IT strategy of the U.S. firm that bought them. In the interview, he admitted that, given the choice, he would not have moved to Baan, as the current system gave perfect satisfaction.

The implementation, which lasted two years, was just finished when we talked to him. The first 18 months were spent implementing in the U.S. sites and briefing local representatives of all other sites on the methodology pursued. After this initial phase, the software was rolled out in the other sites, including the one we studied. By comparison to other reported instances of ERP implementations, the project has run smoothly, but the IS manager, now in charge of further roll-outs in some of the other European facilities, described how the Austrian site had to implement three different ERP packages in a five-year period. When they were still independent, they acquired a specialized package developed by a local software house. Soon afterward, they were purchased by the Irish company and implemented Manman so as to be able to integrate their production systems and coordinate the manufacturing of subcontracted components. New work methods had to be put in place so the collaboration between the two sites could take place. This required some fine tuning before it delivered satisfactory results. Now that they were both bought by a larger player, the Austrian site must upgrade all its systems to Baan and again change its work methods to be able to maintain the integration of the production scheduling systems. This means that, in total, staff at the Austrian plant have practically been implementing ERP software nonstop for the last five years. One can legitimately wonder how counterproductive such an amount of constant change is for the productivity of the plant and the morale of the staff. Even in the case of smooth implementations, the level of disruption brought into everyday activities by three successive ERP implementations was considerable, and the costs of these disruptions must be taken into account when judging the success or otherwise of the whole project.

In another European site of the same company, the story became even more complicated, when local IS staff were asked to abandon their Baan 4 implementation because it was felt that Baan 5 should be considered as a totally new product and not merely an upgrade of Baan 4. Thus, even when a site is using the software required for integration, staff members may be asked to undertake implementation from scratch if a new version must be introduced. This makes the whole ERP scene unstable, as local companies may be asked to change their methods not only to adopt a corporate platform but also even to move to new versions of the same software, because differences between versions are too great to enable proper integration.

The IS manager we talked to concluded that the only benefits he could see in implementing Baan were that some of the customization made in their Manman software would be better catered for by the standard Baan system, and that Baan was excellent for commodity management, an important area for the company. When we talked to him, he could see no benefits other than these in the whole Baan implementation project.

Another fact that we found striking about these two cases, and others involving multinational corporations, was that once the initial analysis was carried out, no more consideration was given to how likely the ERP projects were to yield economies of scale or returns on investment at a local level. To illustrate this fact, it is useful to recall that at this site, no investment appraisal was made when Baan was implemented, even though the new Baan-based system would cost 16 times as much as the Manman system it replaced in terms of maintenance. Given the similarities between the Baan solution and the system it replaced, we would have expected the IS manager to be able to identify significant productivity gains or reductions in operating costs before we regarded the investment as properly justified. However, in this case, as in many others, it seemed that implementing a particular piece of software to comply with the corporate policy was the most important and overriding target.

In line with these reports, Saint-Leger and Savall (2001) described how operators on the assembly line at a large manufacturer of components and equipment for the car industry were unable to properly describe the use of the data entry scanner they were told to use. Interviews with a dozen different staff members revealed as many different interpretations of what data should be captured, and none proved to be totally correct. As a result of this permanent wrong data entry, production was recorded completely haphazardly, and the production scheduling module of the system ran every night based on incorrect data. More interviews identified that one (temporary) staff member was responsible for the device, and she turned out to be spending all her time correcting the errors made by the operators of the device. Even at that, she admitted she was able to correct about 5% of the errors made everyday, with the consequence that the data were always incorrect by a considerable margin. She did not seem to have time to do anything else but correct whatever small proportion of the overall error she was able to tackle and had no idea how the situation would be sorted out in the long term.

These types of stories are consistently reported about ERP implementations. Broadly speaking, they can be broken down into stories that indicate the weakness of the business case made before the system was implemented and stories that indicate the extreme weakness of the implementation methodologies followed. In some cases, one wonders how organizations can possibly operate lasting businesses given the nature of the problems reported. Arguably, it would be more efficient to have an imperfect scheduling system that required some ad hoc decision making, rather than a perfect system consistently running MRP and resource requirements schedules on the basis of incorrect data, as was the case in Saint-Leger and Savall]s (2001) study.

As regards the weakness of the business case, the case studies reported here indicate that companies rush to the implementation phase, and that they seem to put the implementation of their ERP before any other serious business considerations. Thus, the implementation of the system, rather than the achievement of the goals they seek when buying an ERP becomes the horizon of most managers. This is evidenced by the findings that multinationals do not hesitate to ask local sites where managers would never dream of introducing any kind of ERP system to do full-scale implementations of such complex pieces of software as SAP. Asking the staff members of a site to change an ERP platform three times in five years, when there is ample evidence that each of the packages implemented actually worked perfectly is not rational from a managerial point of view.

This lack of focus when it comes to analyzing why an ERP package should be implemented can also be observed in the lack of a clear methodology at implementation time. Although it seems that roll-out implementation mirroring the way things were done in one key site works well for multinationals, a more detailed analysis often reveals that problems arise on the ground when it comes to training operators to use their new systems. We were able to collect anecdotal evidence that describes a level of frustration among users of many implemented ERPs, which seems to surpass anything we ever observed with other computerized systems. This is a matter of concern, given the importance of having full employee cooperation for the proper operation of an ERP package. As noted by Saint Leger and Savall (2001), the inputting of correct data at the correct times into each of the modules is the real Achilles heel of the mightiest ERP package.

A SURVEY OF ERP PROJECTS

In order to broaden the range of our findings, we also carried out a survey of ERP projects and received 50 replies (out of 400 contacts we initiated — a response rate of 12.5%) to our questionnaire. Respondents were from all over the world, and most were on the customer listings made available by ERP package vendors (which we obtained on their web sites). The key finding was that companies do not seem to be overly worried that they run the risk of sacrificing unique competitive advantage by implementing ERP packages. They seem to be certain that acquiring and implementing a complete business solution and applying it to their company is the main source of advantage in an ERP project. This is corroborated by the fact that 80% of our respondents did not consider any alternative to an ERP package.

Even more interesting was the finding that companies used cost and functionality as their priorities when selecting software, and only 15% considered the issue of *fit* between the package and their operations. This is a staggering statistic that seems to indicate that companies adopt ERP as a basis for a radical change rather than as a tool to protect and optimize their current competitive advantage. This approach seems to be misguided, given Lee and Adams' (1990) warning about generic recipes:

> *...if all firms could use a cookbook approach to identifying strategic use of IT, then none of these firms would hold an edge*

*over other firms (...) It is a matter of concern that many existing
applications presented as strategic by the literature have quickly
turned to a necessity or competitive liability rather than a
competitive advantage. (p. 179)*

To our way of thinking, the situation with ERP packages can be illustrated
with the diagram in Figure 1, where an asset is shown to have to be valuable,
not too widely available, and to require specific know-how for its proper use
before it can confer sustainable competitive advantage (Mata et al., 1995).

In the case of ERP, given that ERP packages are widely available and can
now be obtained in ASP mode, it is difficult to see how an organization can
derive any kind of sustainable advantage without a serious analysis of how the
package bought will complement its unique assets or processes. Competitive
parity is likely to occur in many industries, where the rate of ERP uptake is quite
high, as far as enterprise-wide software is concerned. This is in slight opposition
to the message currently relayed by most ERP vendors. As noted by Watson
and Schneider (1999), ERP systems are sold to top managers as strategic
solutions rather than as operational computer software.

In spite of these observations, 66% of the managers in our survey felt that
their organizations were better placed vis-à-vis their competitors after implementing their ERP software. Some (31%) felt that the ERP had not changed
anything, and 3% felt their companies' positions worsened as a result of
implementing the ERP software. One manager who felt that his organization's
position was not affected by the ERP implementation stated that ERP was not
about gaining market share but about creating internal process improvements.
This may indicate that ERP systems are, to some extent, all things to all people
at this point in time.

DISCUSSION AND CONCLUSION

These observations confirm that organizations place the implementation of
an ERP at the forefront of their concerns, and that they lack focus in
understanding the reasons why they implement these packages in the first place.
This is in contrast to the findings reported in Chapter 7. However, the fact that
the organizations in Adam and O'Doherty's survey were mostly SMEs may
explain the differences in the results. We can hypothesize that SMEs are far
more careful when investing large amounts in a software project, and that,
unlike multinationals where decisions are often rolled out in subsidiaries without
much consultation, these smaller organizations analyze their needs far more

accurately. They also consider the issue of investment appraisal and cost justification far more carefully than do multinationals. In these large companies, the focus seems to be on ERP as a tool for integration and standardization rather than on ERP as a competitive weapon. This is in sharp contrast with the findings of studies that looked at smaller companies, where a much more focused analysis of the needs of the organization was carried out to determine how best to exploit the functionalities of ERP packages.

In the face of a market where managers find in ERP packages whatever they want to find, integration, standardization, reengineered business processes, or aggressive search for competitive advantage, ERP vendors must be wondering how to best market their products. Sammon, Adam and Elichirigoity (2001) observed that the messages on the web sites of leading software vendors reflect these uncertainties. To our way of thinking, though, benefits from enterprise-wide software will only come to those who perform a rigorous analysis of their needs and attempt to build upon the specificities of their companies with ERP functionalities, rather than merely apply a cookbook approach to ERP implementations.

Figure 1. Competitive Advantage Versus Competitive Liability

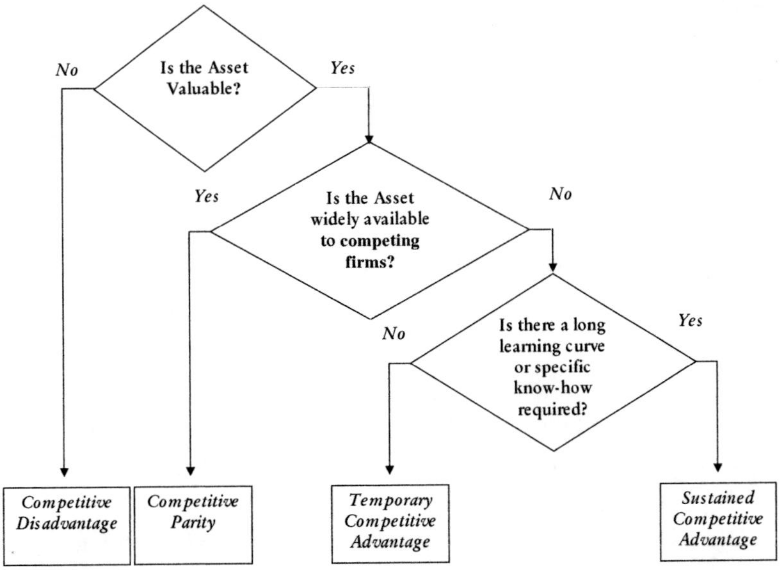

Source: After Mata et al. (1995)

REFERENCES

Adam, F. (2000). Réflexions sur le mouvement ERP—Risques et opportunités. *Congrès de la Net-Economie*, (March), Paris, France.

Adam, F., & O'Doherty, P. (2000). Investigating the reality of ERP implementations. *Journal of Information Technology*, *15*(4), 305-316.

Adam, F., & Twomey, D. (2001). Purchasing critical information systems — The Bord Gais case study. *Systèmes d'Information et Management*, *6*(3), 75-96.

Berger, P. (1998). PGI: Les services valent cher. *Le Monde Informatique*, (September 25), 779.

Bingi, P., Sharma, M., & Godla, J. (1999). Critical issues affecting an ERP implementation. *Information Systems Management*, (Summer), 7-14.

Breen, C. (1997). Improving your business vision. *Irish Computers*, (September).

Brown, C., Vessey, I., & Powell, A. (2000). The ERP purchase decision: Influential business and IT factors. In *Proceedings of AMCIS*.

Chang, S.-I., & Gable, G. (2001). A Delphi examination of public sector ERP lifecycle implementation, management and support issues. *Journal of Decision Systems*, Special Issue on ERP and their implications for Decision Making.

Davenport, T. (1998). Putting the enterprise into the enterprise system. *Harvard Business Review*, (July/August), 131-131.

Edburg, D., Grupe, F., & Kuechler. (2001). Practical issues in global IT management. *Information Systems Management*, *18*(1).

Hirt, S., & Swanson, E. (1999). Adopting SAP at Siemens Power Corporation. *Journal of Information Technology*, 14, 243-251.

Holland, C., Light, B., & Kawalek, P. (1999). Beyond ERP systems: Innovative strategies for competitive advantage. In *Proceedings of the Seventh European Conference on Information Systems*. Copenhagen, Denmark: Copenhagen Business School.

Holland, C.P., Light, B., & Gibson, N. (1999). A critical success factors model for enterprise resource planning implementation. In *Proceedings of the Seventh European Conference on Information Systems* (pp. 273-287). Copenhagen, Denmark: Copenhagen Business School.

Horwitt, E. (1998). Enduring a global rollout — and living to tell about it. *Computerworld*, (March).

Koch, C., Slater, D., & Boatz, E. (2002). The ABC's of ERP. Retrieved from the World Wide Web: http://www.cio.com/research/erp/edit/erpbasics.html.

Krumbholz, M., Galliers, J., Coulianos, N., & Maiden, N. A. M. (2000). Implementing enterprise resource planning packages in different corporate and national cultures. *Journal of Information Technology*, 15, 267-279.

Lee, M., & Adams, D. (1990). A manager's guide to the strategic potential of information systems. *Information and Management*, 19, 169-182.

Light, B., Holland, C., Kelly, S., & Willis, K. (1999). Best of breed IT strategy: An alternative to ERP systems. In *Proceedings of the Seventh European Conference on Information Systems*. Copenhagen, Denmark: Copenhagen Business School.

McKie, S. (1999). The great leap forward. *Business and Finance*, (January).

McVittie, L. (2001). Buckle up: Implementing ERP takes time and patience. Retrieved March 2001 from the World Wide Web: www.network computing.com/.

Maher, J. (1999). ERP in industry: Automate and integrate. *The Engineers' Journal*, (November).

Martin, M. (1998). Smart managing. *Fortune*, (February 2).

Mata, F. J., Fuerst, W. L., & Barney, J. B. (1995). IT and sustained competitive advantage: A resource-based analysis. *MIS Quarterly*, (December), 487-501.

Maylor, H. (2001). Beyond the Gantt chart: Project management moving on. *European Management Journal*, *19*(1).

Minahan, T. (1998). Enterprise resource planning. *Purchasing*, (July 16).

Osterland, A. (2000). Blaming ERP. *CFO*, (January).

Palaniswamy, R., & Frank, T. (2000). Enhancing manufacturing performance with ERP systems. *Information Systems Management*, *17*(3), 43-55.

PMBOK. (2000). *Project management institute body of knowledge*. Retrieved from the World Wide Web: www.pmi.org.

Rowe, F. (1999). Cohérence, intégration informationnelle et changement: Esquisse d'un programme de recherche à partir des Progiciels Intégrés de Gestion. *Systèmes d'Information et Management*, 4(4), 3-20.

Sammer, J. (2000). The ERP continuum. *Business and Finance*, (December), 343.

Sammon, D., Adam, F., & Elichirigoity, F. (2001). ERP dreams and sound business rationale. In *AMCIS Conference*, (August). Boston, MA.

Scott, J., & Kaindl, L. (2000). Enhancing functionality in an enterprise software package. *Information and Management*, 37.

Shankarnarayanan, S. (2000). *ERP systems: Using IT to gain a competitive advantage.* Retrieved from the World Wide Web: www.expressindia.com/newads/bsl/advant.htm.

Shanks, G., Parr, A., Hu, B., Corbitt, B., Thanasankit, T., & Seddon, P. (2000). Differences in critical success factors in ERP systems implementation in Australia and China: A cultural analysis. In *Proceedings of the Eighth European Conference on Information Systems* (July 3-5, pp. 537-544). Vienna, Austria.

Sherman, E. (2000). ERP attitude adjustments. *Computerworld*, (February).

Simon H. (1977). *The New Science of Management Decisions.* Englewood Cliffs, NJ: Prentice Hall.

Slevin, D. P., & Pinto, J. K. (1987). Balancing strategy and tactics in project implementation. *Sloan Management Review*, 29(1), 33-41.

Stedman, C. (1998). Global ERP rollouts present cross-border problems. *Computerworld*, (November).

Stefanou, C. (2000). The selection process of enterprise resource planning, ERP, systems. In *Proceedings of the Sixth Americas Conference on Information Systems* (August 10-13, pp. 988-991). Long Beach, California.

Weston, R. (1998). ERP users find competitive advantages. *Computerworld*, (January 19).

Westrup, C., & Knight, F. (2000). Consultants and ERP systems. In *Proceedings of the Eighth European Conference on Information Systems.* Vienna, Austria.

Wood, T., & Caldas, M. (2000). *Stripping the "Big Brother": Unveiling the backstage of the ERP fad.* Retrieved from the World Wide Web: http://www.gv.br/prof_alunos/thomaz/ingles/paper5.htm.

Chapter IX

Examining the Influence of ERP Systems on Firm-Specific Knowledge Assets and Capabilities

Tom Butler
University College Cork, Ireland

Aidan Pyke
Cork Institute of Technology, Ireland

ABSTRACT

There is a paucity of in-depth research on the effects that enterprise resource planning (ERP) systems have on firm-specific intangible assets, such as knowledge, and associated capabilities. Accordingly, this chapter explores the implementation of SAP in two operational units of the Boxit Group—a global player in the manufacture of chapter and packaging. Leonard-Barton's (1995) theory of knowledge creating activities, knowledge sets, and core and non-core capabilities is employed as a conceptual framework to examine the implementation and use of SAP modules in the firm studied. The findings of this in-depth exploratory case study illustrate that the introduction of SAP-specific business routines can threaten established core, enabling and supplemental capabilities and related knowledge sets. The integration of SAP's embedded business routines and reporting functionality contributed to the creation of (a) highly rigid reporting structures; (b) inflexible managerial decision-making routines; and (c) reduced autonomy on the factory floor in the firm studied. SAP thus endangered the firm-specific knowledge creating activities that underpinned operational core capabilities in this organization. Finally, Leonard-Barton's conceptual framework is extended to incorporate insights into the manner in which ERP systems such as SAP affect the various aspects of organizational knowledge sets.

INTRODUCTION

There is a paucity of in-depth research on the effects that enterprise resource planning (ERP) systems have on firm-specific intangible assets, such as knowledge, and associated capabilities. Accordingly, explored in this chapter is the implementation of SAP in two operational units of the Boxit Group — a global player in the manufacture of paper-based packaging. Leonard-Barton's (1995) theory of knowledge-creating activities, knowledge sets, and core and noncore capabilities is employed as a conceptual framework with which to examine the implementation and use of SAP modules in the firm studied. The findings of this in-depth exploratory case study illustrate that the introduction of SAP-specific business routines can threaten established core, enabling, and supplemental capabilities and related knowledge sets. The integration of SAP's embedded business routines and reporting functionality contributed to the creation of highly rigid reporting structures; inflexible managerial decision-making routines; and reduced autonomy on the factory floor in the firm studied. SAP thus endangered the firm-specific knowledge-creating activities that underpinned operational core capabilities in this organization. Finally, Leonard-Barton's conceptual framework is extended to incorporate insights into the manner in which ERP systems such as SAP affect the various aspects of organizational knowledge sets.

Previous research on ERP systems centered on business modeling, product development issues, the life cycle of ERP systems, and the knowledge required to manage the implementation of ERP systems (Esteves & Pastor, 2001). Studies of ERP system implementation and use, which focus on knowledge and its management, address such issues as change management around ERP system implementation (Al-Mashhari, 2000); senior managers' perspectives on knowledge management in ERP environments (Klaus &

Gable, 2000); knowledge requirements for ERP systems implementation and management (Jones & Price, 2001); the relationship between ERP, knowledge, and organizational effectiveness (Hedman, 2000); and ERP systems and the integration of knowledge in an organization (Esteves & Pastor, 2001). There is, nevertheless, a paucity of research on how ERP systems influence extant *knowledge-creating activities* and associated *core capabilities* in organizations.

This lacuna is addressed in the present chapter, which deepens the IS field's understanding of the relationship between the introduction of ERP systems and the core capabilities of manufacturing organizations. Leonard-Barton's (1995) research illustrates that knowledge-creating activities, such as problem solving, experimentation, importation of external expertise, and the introduction of new methodologies and tools, underpin the development of firm-specific *knowledge sets*. She argued that such knowledge sets give rise to core capabilities. The following analysis of the ERP literature helps illustrate the relevance of Leonard-Barton's theoretical perspective as this study's conceptual framework.

ERP SYSTEMS: PROMISE AND PRACTICE

An ERP system is composed of several software packages or modules that help automate, informate, and integrate cross-functional business processes such as human resources, sales and marketing, finance, and production (Parr & Shank, 2000). Firms implementing ERP systems hope to enhance the firm's competitive position by improving levels of efficiency and effectiveness within and across core business processes (Davenport, 1998; Wagle, 1998). Consequently, the rate of ERP system implementation across a range of industries has been extremely rapid (Bancroft et al., 1998). So much so, that Pozzebon (2001) argued that the implementation of an ERP system has become a technological imperative for many organizations. However, Chung and Snyder (2000) reported that the implementation of an ERP system currently represents the firm's largest IT investment. The impact of such systems on the knowledge-creation process is unclear, as the subsequent analysis of the ERP literature elucidates.

The Promise and Reality of ERP Systems

More firms are turning to ERP to leverage knowledge assets at all levels in the organization, to the extent that ERP systems replaced legacy systems in informating and automating core business processes (Holland et al., 1999). Davenport (1998) emphasized the significance of this trend when he stated that: "the business world's embrace of enterprise systems may in fact be the most important development in the corporate use of Information Technology in the 1990s" (p. 122). By 1999, a total of 53,000 firms worldwide had implemented ERP systems (Cerullo & Cerullo, 2000). SAP is the current leader in the ERP systems market, with approximately 33% of the market share, while the other leading vendors are Peoplesoft, Oracle Applications, and JD Edwards (Holsapple & Sena, 2001). Unlike legacy systems, ERP systems tend to take the form of customizable software packages (Holland et al., 1999). Cooke and Peterson (1998) contended that the principal reasons why firms implement an ERP system are to standardize business processes and to support globalization. Each module of an ERP system, for example, SAP R/3, accesses more than 1,000 in-built business processes based on industry best practices (Bancroft, 1998).

Despite its popularity, SAP does not have a reputation for being user-friendly (Stedman, 1999). For example, Caldwell and Stein (1998) found that managers in one major organization refused to operate the system, because they found it to be user-unfriendly. Another drawback concerns customization — Holsapple and Sena (1999) observed that while software modifications of SAP modules are possible, they are not recommended. The rationale for this is that organizations implementing ERP systems wish to improve their business processes by importing optimized business routines embedded in systems like SAP (Curran & Ladd, 1998). For this reason, firms rarely attempt customization: for example, only 5% of the Fortune 1000 companies customized an ERP system to support their idiosyncratic business processes (Davis, 1998). This prompted some to argue that the implementation of an ERP system should be considered a business project rather than an IS project (Shanks et al., 2000), as improved company performance is the key criterion for assessing the success of ERP system implementations (Ross, 1998; Markus & Tanis, 1999).

ERP systems are indispensable due to the complexity of modern organizations and to the diversity of their operational environments (Holland et al., 1999; Brehmer, 1991). Human imperfections, in terms of limited cognitive abilities, act as inhibitors, limiting actors in their attempts to formulate and implement appropriate business strategies and solutions (Simon, 1961). The existence of bounded rationality provides a powerful argument for the use of ERP systems in support of management activity. However, the power of ICT to *informate* is dependent upon a recipient's ability to interpret the information provided (Zuboff, 1988). In addition, there are dangers inherent in the passive and unreflective use of the organization's information resource (Orlikowski, 1991). Significantly, interpretation is made especially difficult in ERP systems, as the information provided is frequently decontextualized, abstract, and explicit (Nonaka & Nishiguchi, 2001). The consequence of a shift from embodied knowledge to encoded knowledge associated with ERP implementations was anticipated by Spender (1989), who questioned the following:

> *...modern trend away from tacit and towards explicit [Knowledge], from craft to system while [firms] remain dependent upon their employees' skilled practices, hunches and intuition or on judgments captured in the industry's recipe. (p. 51)*

It is also apparent that information systems, such as ERP, are often externally imposed disruptive mechanisms capable of changing a firm's structure and routines, thereby influencing the actions and interpretations of the organization's actors (Orlikowski, 1991). Such external mechanisms may be *culturally alien* (Orlikowski, 1991; Poster, 1990), as organizations adapt or reengineer their business processes to accommodate those embedded in the ERP systems (Davis, 1998). Hence, as an ERP system's capabilities impose specific and rigid performance of organizational routines, it commits a firm to completing tasks in a preordained way. Spender (1996) warned that such change can be problematic, as "far from being a tool, technology becomes our master when it shapes the systemic aspects of our systems" (p. 58).

Thus, ERP systems generate an imperative to establish integrated business processes across diverse functional boundaries in organizations (Davenport, 1998). The implementation of any technology in organizational environments characterized by functional differentiation specialization requires collective learning, coordination, and significant organization (Pavitt, 1991). A process of collective socialization and knowledge creation occurs when an ERP system is implemented, as it links formerly disparate knowledge and creates a new knowledge-creating dynamics within an organization. This has major consequences for the role-related activities of organizational actors (Hanseth & Braa, 1998). Furthermore, it has enormous implications for the firm-specific knowledge sets, as researchers in the resource-based view hold that a firm's knowledge is embedded in its organizational and managerial processes and business routines and practices (Teece et al., 1990; Leonard-Barton, 1995). These themes are further explored in the following subsection.

KNOWLEDGE, LEARNING,
AND CAPABILITY DEVELOPMENT
IN ORGANIZATIONS

Leonard-Barton (1995) argued that a firm's core capabilities arise out of its knowledge-creating activities. In articulating her theory, Leonard-Barton integrates several theoretical perspectives with her own empirical research. Indicated in Figure 1 are the related disciplines, theories, and research streams

Figure 1. Foundations of Leonard Barton's Theory of Knowledge-Creating Activities, Knowledge Sets, Core Rigidities, and Capabilities

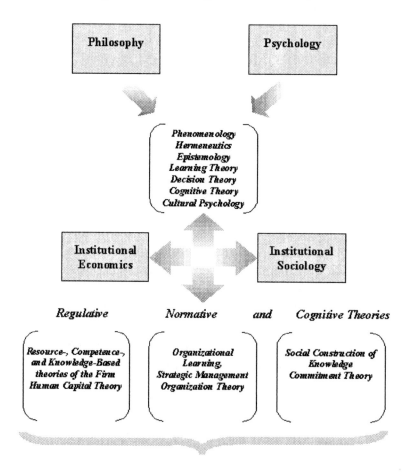

that she draws upon to build her conceptual framework. The following subsection provides an overview of seminal thought from Leonard-Barton's immediate theoretical influences. The second subsection then delineates Leonard-Barton's (1992, 1995) theoretical framework of *core*, *enabling* and *supplemental capabilities*, and the knowledge-creating activities and knowledge sets that underpin them.

Perspectives on Learning, Knowledge, and Organizational Routines

The resource- and the knowledge-based views of the firm attempt to unpack the macro perspective of the organization into its constituent elements (Spender, 1996). The theoretical foundation of the resource-based view of the firm emanates from the seminal work of Penrose (1959). Penrose considered that the firm is an amalgam of resources configured in a way that creates firm-specific advantage. In essence, the firm-specific advantage flows not from the organization's resources, per se, but from the knowledge that enables it to deploy such resources to leverage maximum benefit within its operational environment. Selznick's (1957) concept of *distinctive competence* adds to the resource-based view, as it acknowledges the uniqueness of each firm. Nelson and Winter's (1982) work on the evolutionary aspect of firm-specific development enriched the resource-based view. According to Nelson and Winter (1982), an organization's practiced routines determine what it is capable of doing. Firms can, therefore, be understood in terms of a hierarchy of organizational routines. As Nelson and Winter (1982) put it, "we propose that the routinization of activity in an organization constitutes the most important form of storage of the organizations specific operational knowledge" (p. 99). At higher levels in the hierarchy, routines provide mechanisms for managerial decision making. At lower levels, practiced routines define organizational skills and how they are coordinated. Higher-order routines are looked to when choosing which combinations of lower-order routines are to be applied to accomplish a particular task. An organization's capabilities, therefore, depend on the possession of established and well-practiced higher- and lower-order routines. Following March and Simon (1958), Nelson and Winter (1982) argued that the search activities for new routines are rule-based activities. Hence, they maintain that it is the purposeful search for and selection of new routines that illustrates the diversity of options available to a firm and that enhances its stock of firm-specific knowledge. This evolutionary perspective is the hallmark of Nelson and Winter's *"simple and stylized"* theory of the firm.

Wernerfelt's (1984) theory developed the notion that a firm must possess firm-specific resources viz. competencies and capabilities. Such theories formed the theoretical foundations for the concept of *dynamic capabilities* (Teece et al., 1990). In order to attain and to sustain a competitive advantage, the firm's competencies and capabilities must be difficult to imitate and be durable and valuable (Barney, 1991). In their search for rents, organizations should seek to nurture firm-specific capabilities (Rumelt, 1982). Montgomery and Wernerfelt (1988) submitted that the resource-based view of the firm provides a conceptual basis for understanding and predicting significant organizational events.

Spender (1996) considered that the resource-based view does not sufficiently acknowledge the key role that knowledge plays in the organization and argued for a knowledge-centric approach to the management of organization's resources. To support this argument, Spender (1996) cited the Penrosian argument that the development of experience and knowledge is core to the firm's ability to respond to change. Drucker (1995) contended that knowledge rightfully attained a dominant position in the hierarchy of organizational resources, which finds expression in the knowledge-based view of the firm. Knowledge was elevated to this primary status, because it is regarded as pivotal in determining how the other resources of the firm are combined in order to create a competitive advantage (Spender, 1996). Davenport and Prusak (1998) viewed knowledge as a framework, providing a platform for the assessment and assimilation of new information and experiences. They developed this thesis arguing that the framework is constructed from a dynamic combination of contextualized information, experience, and values and norms. The requirement to separate knowledge from other resources stems from its intrinsic qualities; it emanates from individual cognitions, which shape and are, in turn, shaped by the social dynamic within the organization, resulting in a fusion of cognitive and societal processes (Berger & Luckmann, 1967). The recognition of the key role, which knowledge plays in the life of the individual and community, led to the knowledge-based view of the firm (Spender, 1996; Nonaka & Takeuchi, 1995; Grant, 1996). Grant and Baden-Fuller's (1995) synopsis of the knowledge-based view of the firm is a useful construct that illustrates the streams of research that contributed to the knowledge-based view of the firm.

Knowledge and Capability Development in Organizations

Nonaka (1994) considered knowledge to be justified true belief. Davenport and Prusak (1998) broadened this definition significantly and argued that knowledge is as follows:

...a fluid mix of framed experience, values, contextual information, and expert insight that provides a framework for evaluating and incorporating new experiences and information...in organizations it often becomes embedded not only in documents and repositories but also in organizational routines, processes, practices and norms. (p. 5)

Polanyi (1962, 1967) contended that explicit knowledge is knowledge in the abstract, while tacit knowledge incorporates experience and intuitive knowledge, which results from subconscious learning. However, an organization's cultural perspective may influence the value it places upon its tacit and explicit knowledge assets (Alavi & Leidner, 2001). Nonaka (1994) observed that firms tend to place a value premium on explicit knowledge at the expense of tacit knowledge. Accordingly, Kim and Manborgne (1997) noted that such an approach leads to "a preoccupation with allocating resources, ...monitoring and measuring performance, and manipulating organizational structures to set lines of authority."

Spender (1996) defined learning as "the process of experiencing and analyzing, or the process of communicating the knowledge previously generated by others" (p. 47). Learning is influenced by the individual's perception of his or her environment (Lave, 1988; Lave & Wegner, 1991). Daft and Weick (1984) argued that interpretation molds the environment more than the environment molds perception. Lave (1988) argued that the purpose, needs, and goals of an actor shape the individual's perception, so that what is perceived does not necessarily equate with accuracy and truth. The interpretation of information is a subjective process, which is capable of producing distinct and different realities for the individual (Daft & Weick, 1984). This is due to the influential role of the individual's schema or frame, which drives the perceptual process. Webster (1983) defined schemas as "a mental codification of experience that includes a particular organized way of perceiving cognitively and responding to stimuli." Berger and Luckmann (1967) contended that humans are only capable of perceiving phenomena rather than *numena*, that is, the things in themselves. Phenomena are reconciled by cognitive structures, so that the confusing material flux becomes interpretable. As the cognitive structures interpret the material, they are influenced by "mindsets" that forge multiple perspectives concerning the way a problem is formulated, the motives of the actors involved, and the implications of proposed solutions (Janis, 1989).

Ciborra and Lanzarra (1996) contended that individual perceptions or mindsets are but constituents in the formative context, which they defined as:

"the set of preexisting institutional arrangements, cognitive frames and imageries that actors bring and routinely enact in a situation of action." The creation and nurturing of a sympathetic formative context is key to capability development, as organizations become both frames for action and the products of action (Holm, 1995). The work of Lave (1988) and Lave and Wegner (1991) includes an ontological dimension to the theory of learning, arguing that individuals learn within a social context, and that both the stage of the individual's development and position in the firm impact the learning process. An organization's ability to learn and cultivate its knowledge asset is dependent upon its capability, through its evolving social character, to influence its employees' sense-of-self (Nelson & Winter, 1982; Spender, 1996). Nonaka and Takeuchi (1995) considered that individual intuition is a source of organizational knowledge. Hence, organizational actors should be viewed as active participants in vibrant communities, where social, cultural, and past forces contribute to a collective learning process aimed at satisfying individual and communal needs (Barnes, 1985). Humans are gregarious animals and, as such, a herd instinct or an empathetic behavior pattern can develop within any firm. Boland et al. (1994) refer to this group instinct as distributed cognition, which they define as follows:

> ...the process whereby individuals who act autonomously within a decision domain make interpretations of their situation and exchange them with others with whom they have interdependencies so that each may act with an understanding of their own situation and others. (p. 475)

They further contend that when distributed cognition works well, it enables the production of beneficial coordinated outcomes. The corollary of this contention is that where distributed cognition does not exist or is distorted, then conflict may ensue, and goal congruence is problematic. Hedberg (1981) argued that organizations are engaged in a cycle of learning as the organization's actors perceive and respond to environmental stimuli.

Argyris and Schon (1978) identified two approaches to learning. They described single-loop learning as learning that achieves incremental change in the actions of the individuals and organization. The second approach is double-loop learning, the outcome of which is to create paradigm shifts in the way actors perceive and relate to their environments. Argyris (1982) contended that learning loops unfold spontaneously and are strongly dependent on the individual and group perceptions of the environment, the business mission, and even their own learning abilities. Argyris argued that the actions of management must provide direction to the learning process. Notably, Attewell (1992) argued that organizations learn by incorporating individual values, skills, practices, and insights into organizational routines, which exist independently of the originating individual. Such organizational routines are essentially knowledge repositories, which are indispensable to the operation of the firm due to bounded rationality (Nelson & Winter, 1982). Consequently, Levitt and March (1988) spoke of "encoding references from history into routines that guide behaviour" (p. 319). Such organizational routines are defined by Nelson and Winter (1982) as a "relatively complex pattern of behavior…triggered by a relatively small number of initiating signals or choices and functioning as a recognizable unit in a relatively automatic fashion" (p. 165). Levitt and March (1988) contended that routines "include the forms, rules, procedures, conventions, strategies, and technologies around which organizations are constructed and around which they operate" (p. 320). Nelson and Winter (1982) outlined how, over time, firms develop distinctive organizational routines and that such routines may be viewed as the product of each firm's history, experience, and administrative heritage.

Brown and Duguid (1991) warned organizations of the dangers in concentrating on abstract knowledge, which is knowledge that is divorced from actual practice. They stated the following:

> *[A]bstractions detached from practice distort or obscure intricacies of that practice. Without a clear understanding of those intricacies and the role they play, the practice itself cannot be fully understood, engendered (through training), or enhanced (through innovation). The central issue is learning to be a practitioner not learning about the practice. (p. 40)*

Accordingly, Brown and Duguid (1991) observed that a purely Tayloristic approach divorces the methodology of doing from the philosophy that underpins the act. This inhibits the practitioner's ability to cope with the *"tricky interpolations"* inherent in the doing.

In light of the foregoing observations, it is clear that learning does not always produce the desired behavior (Leavitt & March, 1988). They argue that learning may instead produce *rigidities*, as firms seek to replicate the knowledge sets to which they attributed their past successes, and *superstitious learning*, the result of a subjective ill-defined process that does not conform with the organizational objectives.

Leonard-Barton's (1995) theory of firm-specific competencies posits three types of organizational capability, viz., core, enabling, and supplemental (see Figure 2). She argued that core capabilities provide a firm with a sustainable competitive advantage; hence, they are distinguished from supplemental and enabling capabilities. Leonard-Barton (1992,) considered that "a core capability is a knowledge set that distinguishes and provides a competitive advantage" (p. 113). This view originates in Selznick's (1957) seminal work in the area and argues that a *distinctive competence* (i.e., a core capability) is firm-specific and strategic in nature. Stalk et al. (1992) argued that firm-specific capabilities "are collective and cross-functional—a small part of many people's jobs, not a large part of a few...because a capability is everywhere and nowhere, no one executive controls it entirely" (p. 63). Accordingly, Prahalad and Hamel (1990) stated the following:

> ...*core competencies are the collective learning in the organization...especially how to co-ordinate diverse production skills and integrate multiple streams of technologies... Core competence does not diminish with use...competencies are enhanced as they are applied and shared. (p. 82)*

Figure 2. A Taxonomy of Capabilities: Core, Enabling and Supplemental

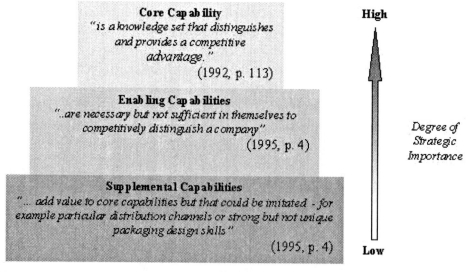

Source: Adapted from research by Leonard-Barton (1995)

Likewise, Teece et al. (1990) considered a core capability to be a set of special skills, complementary assets, and routines that enable the firm to attain and sustain a competitive advantage. Both Barney (1991) and Hamel (1994) consider that core capabilities cannot be imitated and, therefore, constitute a competitive advantage for a firm. Hamel (1994) argued that a core competence is "an activity, a messy accumulation of learning…(and) will comprise of both tacit and explicit knowledge" (p. 12). Winterschied (1994) stated that they are comprised of tangible and intangible resources, arranged in integrated clusters, which span individuals and communities to enable distinctive activities to be performed in unique ways. It may be deduced from this that core capabilities are fragile in nature and that the social webs that enable learning are delicate and require careful handling.

Toward a Framework for Examining Organizational Knowledge-Creating Activities, Knowledge Sets and Firm-Specific Capabilities

Drawing on such observations, and in line with seminal perspectives on learning in organizations, Leonard-Barton (1995) conceptualized a core capability as a firm-specific knowledge set. This, she argued, is reflected in a firm's *values and norms, physical technical systems, employee knowledge and skills,* and *managerial systems.* Figure 3 captures these four dimensions to firm-specific knowledge sets. Leonard-Barton contended that embodied knowledge and personal skills underpin capability development. Teece et al. (1990) observed that employee knowledge and skill includes firm-specific and industry-specific knowledge, while Itami (1989) argued that it is impossible to separate the individual from the knowledge he or she possesses, as they are inextricably linked. Nevertheless, Leonard-Barton argued that an organization's *physical technical systems* result from the application of employee knowledge and skills and therefore encapsulate them and permit their widespread dissemination and application. Hence, she argued that the information content of such systems exceeds the information value of their contributing constituents. A question therefore arises as to the value of information systems that are not founded on tried and tested, unique, and firm-specific employee knowledge and skills. Managerial systems are also the product of employee knowledge and skills, in that they represent established routines for obtaining or building resources and then allocating and deploying them. They also include the formal and informal approaches to knowledge creation through sabbaticals, apprenticeships, and, of stimulating learning and encouraging knowledge application

Figure 3. Values and Norms, Physical Technical Systems, Employee Knowledge and Skills, and Managerial Systems as Firm-Specific Knowledge

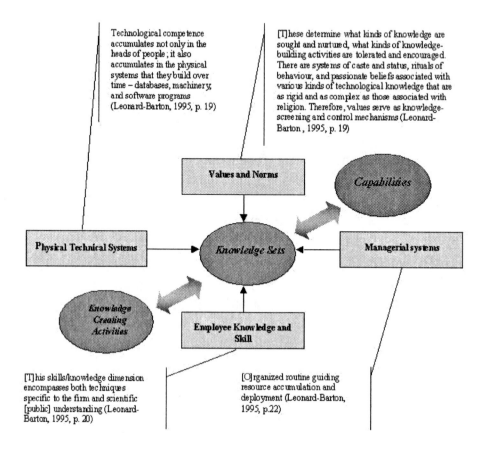

through incentives systems and reporting structures (Leonard-Barton, 1995). However, the creation and application of knowledge and skills is underpinned by the values and norms of an organization. These determine what kinds of knowledge and skills are created and developed and how such knowledge and skills are applied. Leonard-Barton (1995) categorized organizational values as *V* values and *v* values. *V* values originate from the company founder who inculcates his or her personal values and management style, and as a firm expands, recruits specialists who identify and support the values of the founder. *V* values coexist with *v* values that relate to products or services and are dynamic and temporal in character. The importance of social and organizational norms is well acknowledged in the literature. Scott (1995), for example, stated the following:

> *Social norms and values are essential ingredients of any social situation; behaviour is guided not only by natural endowments and interest but by moral beliefs and normative obligations.* (p. 139)

Consequently, O'Reilly (1989) warned that failure to develop new norms supportive of the organization's strategy means that a firm will have to engage in close monitoring of activities or direct rewards in order to consolidate new practices. Badaracco (1991) therefore argued that knowledge cannot migrate and become useful to an organization unless the system possesses the *social software* — values and norms — to create and exploit it. With some notable exceptions (e.g., Barney, 1986), the influence of values and norms is not usually associated with the creation of core capabilities. Leonard-Barton (1995) illustrated that values and norms can be dynamic and positive, or they can act to preserve outmoded routines and capabilities, contributing to the creation of core rigidities.

Leonard-Barton (1992) argued that core rigidities are essentially outmoded and inefficient organizational practices and routines. These are shaped by dysfunctional values and norms that fail to evolve and to meet the challenges in a dynamic and changing environment. Hence, dysfunctional values and norms are argued to constrain the development of new knowledge sets and associated productive capabilities.

Developing the concept of the *dominant coalition*, proffered by Cyert and March (1963) and used extensively by Thompson (1967), Leonard-Barton (1992, 1995) argued that within organizations, some knowledge sets are more valued than others and gain dominant positions, thereby creating a knowledge hierarchy. The knowledge set most valued attracts practitioners of that discipline, thereby reinforcing the dominance of the prevailing knowledge set. This has implications for the creation and development of capabilities and the self-propagating nature of knowledge sets within certain organizational environments. Unmanaged, this process can lead to the development of an imbalanced portfolio of capabilities, increasing the risk of reinforcing core rigidities. Leonard-Barton (1992) defined and described core rigidities as follows:

...inappropriate sets of knowledge. Core rigidities are the flip side of core capabilities. They are not neutral; these deeply embedded knowledge sets create problems. While core rigidities are more problematic for projects that are deliberately designed to create new, nontraditional capabilities, rigidities can affect all projects — even those that are reasonably congruent with current core capabilities. (p. 118)

Child (1972) and Miller and Minzberg (1972) argued that organizations operating in benevolent environments do not have strong incentive to change and are, therefore, susceptible to strategic stagnation. A successful firm may have difficulty in executing such attitudinal transformations, as many firms have difficulty in comprehending that "a firm's strengths are also—simultaneously—its weakness" (Leonard-Barton, 1995, p. 30; see Selznick, 1957). Crisis fuels and drives the process of change (Nystrom & Starbuck, 1984; Bartunek, 1988). Nonaka et al. (2001) promoted the concept of creative chaos as a method of countering the threat of rigidities, because chaos can do the following:

...focus people's attention and encourage them to transcend existing boundaries, to define a problem, and resolve it. Facing chaos, organization members experience a breakdown of routines, habits and cognitive frameworks. (p. 26)

They described creative chaos as an intentional creation of the organization's leaders. Management nurture creative chaos to promote a sense of crisis, which is intended to create new challenges and sunder the sense of inertia that may exist within the organization. Hedberg (1981) contended that such activity supports the process of unlearning:

...the discarding activity — unlearning — is as important a part of understanding as is adding new knowledge. In fact, it seems as if slow unlearning is a crucial weakness of many organizations. (p. 1)

Such unlearning and subsequent reframing can be facilitated by crises, upheavals, conflicts, and innovation (White, 1969; Nystrom et al., 1976; Bartunek, 1988). Even minor innovations can render deeply embedded knowledge valueless (Hederson & Clark, 1990; Leonard-Barton, 1995).

Nevertheless, Leonard-Barton (1995) argued that dynamic knowledge-creating activities counter the problem of core rigidities by ensuring that new knowledge circulates and revitalizes a firm and the communities-of-practice that constitute it.

Presented in Figure 4 is a model of the knowledge-creating activities that underpin the development of firm-specific knowledge in each of the dimensions of an organization's knowledge set. In respect of shared, creative problem solving, Leonard-Barton (1995), contends, "in a learning environment, progress must be everyone's business — not just the province of a few specialists" (p. 8). She contended that problem solving of this type is internally focused and distributes ownership of the problem, which facilitates invention and innovation as opposed to localizing expertise. For Leonard-Barton (1995), the knowledge-creating activities of formal and informal experimentation involve incremental innovation. She stated (1995): "creating knowledge require constant pushing beyond the familiar" (p. 12). Implementing and integrating new methodologies and tools involves the creation, integration, and application knowledge and skills at the lowest possible level within an organization: accordingly, she (1995) said that the "implementation of new technical processes can move beyond merely increasing efficiency when managed for learning" (p. 90). When pulling in expertise from the outside, it is recognized that an important source of knowledge comes from external sources and in

Figure 4. Knowledge-Creating Activities

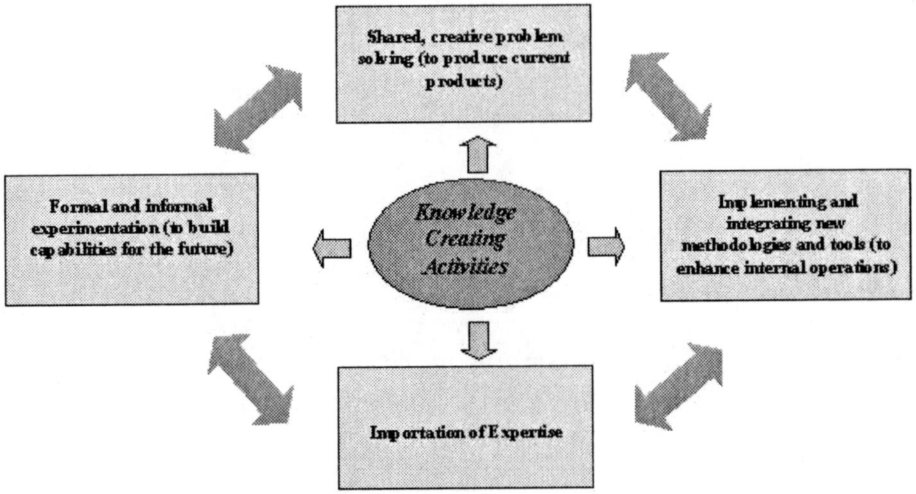

Source: Adapted from Leonard-Barton (1995)

other organizations. Hence, in line with extant perspectives on the resource-based view of the firm, Leonard-Barton highlighted the role that problem solving, experimentation, importing expertise from outside the firm, and implementing and integrating new methodologies plays in shaping a firm's knowledge set by acting on all four of the dimensions previously delineated.

RESEARCH OBJECTIVE

This study's objective is to explore the organizational consequences and outcomes of importing "best practice" embedded in ERP systems, such as SAP, as non-firm-specific organizational routines. Of special interest is the organizational ability to maintain successful knowledge-creating activities and knowledge sets relevant to its core capabilities, while at the same time, overcoming potential core rigidities. Formally stated, this study's research objective is as follows:

> *To deepen the IS field's understanding of SAP's influence on firm-specific knowledge-creating activities, knowledge sets, and associated core, enabling, and supplemental capabilities through the importation and implementation of non-firm-specific routines, embodying industry-wide best practice.*

Leonard-Barton's (1992, 1995) theory of knowledge-creating activities and the resultant knowledge sets that underpin core, enabling, and supplemental capabilities is used as a conceptual framework to structure the case report and its findings. This operates to direct attention on the operational core capabilities, knowledge-creating activities, and knowledge sets in order to evaluate the affect that SAP has on each.

A CASE-BASED RESEARCH STRATEGY

A naturalistic research approach was adopted for the present study. Accordingly, a qualitative, interpretive, case-based research strategy was implemented with reference to constructivist thought in the social sciences (see Lincoln & Guba, 1985; Stake, 1995) and interpretivist approaches in the IS field (Walsham, 1995). Stake (1995) contended that case studies can be *intrinsic, instrumental,* or *collective* in focus. An instrumental case study is one where the case forms a backdrop or context and is of secondary importance. Such a study is undertaken to validate a theory or to explore a particular phenomenon as it is manifested in the case. Yin (1994) argued that a case may "involve more than one unit of analysis…such as meetings, roles, or locations" (p. 42), this he terms an "embedded case study design." The present study incorporates an instrumental case study incorporating two embedded units of analysis.

The case selected for study is the Boxit Group, an Irish-owned and - managed transnational corporation specializing in the manufacture of packing cases and associated materials. Boxit Group and its affiliates employ over 43,000 people in 23 countries worldwide. Two production facilities constitute the embedded units of analysis — Boxit Corrugated Cases (BCC) and Boxit Corrugated Services (BCS). The embedded units were purposively selected, because they possess different operational core capabilities, knowledge sets, and knowledge-creating activities and were in different stages of development — BCC was established in 1973 and BCS in 1998. Both participated in the roll-out of the corporate ERP system, which involved the implementation of SAP's Financial and Purchasing modules — the latter of which included support for the engineering maintenance of production equipment at both plants.

Purposeful sampling was employed throughout. Research was conducted in 2001 at two sites. Social actors (20 of them) participated in the study, through formal and informal interviews over a period of several months. Each of the formal interviews was tape-recorded, while extensive case notes were taken on informal conversations and observations while on-site at the research locations. A wealth of documentary evidence was also gathered. Naturalist techniques were employed to analyze and report on the research data (see Lincoln & Guba, 1985; Stake, 1995).

THE BOXIT GROUP

In 2002, the Boxit Group of companies was the leading producer of paper-based packaging in the world. Boxit is a transnational corporation, with major markets and production facilities located in Europe and the Americas. The Group and its affiliates currently employ some 43,000 people in 23 countries. Boxit's European operations are located in Ireland, the United Kingdom, France, Spain, Italy, The Netherlands, Germany, Belgium, Portugal, and Sweden. Boxit's European operations are comprised of 23 paper and paperboard mills together with 125 conversion facilities, of which approximately 90 produce corrugated cases. In 1997, Boxit produced over 1.5 million tons of corrugated cases, together with approximately 250,000 tons of other packaging products, including paper sacks and folding cartons. Based on volume, Boxit was the largest producer of corrugated cases in Europe, with an estimated market share of 15%. Boxit was the market leader in France and Ireland, and one of the leading three producers in Italy, the United Kingdom, Spain, and The Netherlands. The paper-based packaging markets in Europe are defined primarily by geographical distance from the relevant operations, without reference to national boundaries. Many large organizations negotiate their packaging requirements on a Pan-European basis, the Irish firms within the group benefit from such deals.

Management Decision Making and Learning — The Boxit Way

During the 1990s, Boxit's management philosophy provided regional and local management teams of its operating subsidiaries significant autonomy to run their production and marketing activities in response to local conditions. Boxit found that this strategy helped develop strong local management teams whose members understood and were responsive to the demands and cycles of their local markets and customers. The regional businesses were monitored and controlled by Boxit's senior management through a system of regular financial reporting and review, together with tight capital and cash controls. This regional decentralization and close central monitoring in combination with performance-related incentives provided strong motivation for local management to improve performance. The purpose of this strategy was to encourage the improvement of the production processes and the reduction of costs, as well as to allow dissemination of successful ideas throughout the Boxit Group. Information flow is considered important to the Boxit Group's success, as it impacts upon its ability to react effectively to changes in the multiplicity of markets in which it operates. This philosophy is encapsulated in the *The Boxit Way*, which states:

> *Our objective is to sell to our customers products that conform to their requirements, on time, at a competitive price. We will do this by providing the encouragement and the means for continuous improvement in our processes, technology, products and services.*

For that reason, Boxit had a strong and inclusive commitment to the education and training of its employees.

Thus, organizational actors were to contribute to the firm's growth through the application of formal learning to evolve operational processes in innovative ways. Training was viewed as a sine qua non for the achievement of success through improving quality and controlling costs. Accordingly, the company supported a wide variety of initiatives that provided relevant education, training, and development opportunities to its staff. Formal training was advanced through a combination of in-house and external programs. The focus of this was on the development of team skills and production techniques, and in supporting employees in attaining qualifications in their chosen profession from the professional or academic institutions. For example, the company operated a graduate training program for developing top executives. The aim of this program was to identify and develop managerial talent and bring it to a world-class standard. Admission to the program was by interview, and its duration was two years. During this time, the trainees were assigned four positions in different units of the Boxit organization, each for a six-month period. They were then posted permanently as heads of operations to a unit within the group or to positions at corporate headquarters. This mix of formal training coupled with the latitude to innovate at an operational level, down to the level of manufacturing teams, resulted in Boxit developing the characteristics of a true learning organization (Stata, 1989; Senge, 1990).

CORE OPERATIONAL CAPABILITIES
AT BCC AND BCS

The Boxit Corrugated Cases (BCC) manufacturing plant supplies the dairy and food sectors with packaging materials. The packaging requirements of such customers are easily projected and facilitate large production runs by BCC with minimum changes in its standard operational routines. The emergence of a dynamic and highly successful electronics industry in Ireland during the early 1990s presented new market opportunities for the Boxit Group. Firms in this emergent sector had radically different, more sophisticated, and varied packaging requirements than those of BCC's traditional customer base. While exciting new opportunities were presented, so too were possible negative consequences associated with the dynamic, market-led production schedules and idiosyncratic needs of the electronics industry. This arose because firms operating in the electronics sector could not provide suppliers with exact delivery schedules. Suppliers had to respond quickly and on short notice. However, the production capabilities of BCC were not aligned with the needs of firms operating in the electronics industry, as BCC's Customer Services Manager pointed out:

> *...customers' requirements [in the electronics sector] range from pallets to foam inserts to cartons — this is not BCC's core business and is not cost effective for us to engage in this work.*

BCC's core capabilities were de facto core rigidities when it came to servicing the requirements of the electronic industry, while altering values and norms in the company. After several unsuccessful attempts to reconfigure its production routines, BCC's management considered that smaller production runs and products with nonstandard specifications were too disruptive to the efficient operation of the plant. Thus, due to the need to maintain its lucrative revenue flows from existing markets, management at BCC were unable and unwilling to adapt its production activities to service the electronics market. The choice was clear to BCC, cede the new niche market to other companies or establish a production facility with core production capabilities to deliver the product and service in a way that met customer's requirements. Hence, Boxit Corrugated Services (BCS) was established to service the packaging needs of the dynamic electronics industry.

While the BCC was unable to reconfigure its asset and capability portfolios to meet the dynamic demands of the electronics sector, it possessed a tradition of introducing technical innovation in its production processes through the knowledge-creation activities of its employees coupled with the introduction of new technology. For example, BCC pioneered the process of four-color printing on corrugated packaging. Consequently, it was five to 10 years ahead of the competition in terms of its technical capabilities. Evidence of this firm-specific knowledge set comes from BCC's Production Manager:

> *[Competitors] cannot get the same print quality from the four-colour machines, despite having very good machinery. The difference is down to skills. They have four-colour machines in Lurgan and Dublin and they cannot produce the same quality as we can in [BCC]. They would have broadly the same machines, so it's down to skills.*

BCC's management was aware that capability-based advantages erode over time; hence, it upgraded production equipment on a regular basis. Significantly, the installation, operation, and customization of new technology provided a platform for knowledge creation and capability development, as the production manager commented:

> In the past, operators quickly mastered the knowledge and skills required to run new technologies. When a technological investment has matured, in terms of quality and efficiency of output, we assess our competitors' positions and when we determine that they are closing the gap, in terms of quality and output, we invest again.

Thus, BCC coupled *learning-by-doing* with the experiential knowledge of long-serving staff to produce and retain skills and related knowledge in a tacit form — in the production area, this method of learning was known as *Standing-by-Nanny*. Group learning was critical here, as production operators worked in teams of four. In this scheme of things, a lead operator assumed responsibility for training other members of the team. This helped build and reinforce a team's norms and values and enabled knowledge and skill transfers. This approach to mentoring was widely used in all Boxit's production facilities. A training manager usually facilitated the process, as management was mindful that success in such endeavors could not be left to the communication skills of the lead operator. This approach to organizational learning created a highly idiosyncratic production-oriented knowledge and skills resource within the Boxit group of companies. Thus, knowledge and skills developed over time through learning-by-doing and was transmitted through socialization within and between communities-of-practice.

When the BCS facility was established in 1998 to meet the idiosyncratic needs of the electronics sector, BCS's plant manager opted not to replicate BCC's operational routines by transferring workers and work practices from BCC. Thus, BCS did not directly import the knowledge and skills and associated values and norms of BCC's workforce. His aim was to introduce more flexible operational routines that would help BCS meet the particular needs of the electronics sector. To achieve this, he felt that a radically different set of values and norms needed to be established in the new plant — values and norms that were congruent with the use of emergent technologies, like SAP. By so doing, he wished to avoid introducing rigidities associated with outdated conditions of employment, including, for example, pay differentials and demarcation. He clearly recognized that this might prevent the attainment of flexibility in the manufacturing process deemed to be critical to the success of BCS. Nevertheless, the knowledge and skills of workers at BCC were recognized as being valuable to the new operation at BCS. The problem was how to import much-needed knowledge and skills while filtering out the rigidities and inappropriate knowledge sets associated with the managerial systems, values, and norms at BCC. Accordingly, BCS's new plant manager decided to use technology to import the required experiential knowledge and skills, while, at the same time, instituting a different set of values and norms through the process of socialization. However, his first task was to install the production plant. This was sourced from BCC, which was in the process of upgrading its production facilities. In order to operate the machines, workers had to adopt appropriate operational routines: this constituted the importation of explicit knowledge and skills from BCC. The importation of tacit knowledge proved to be difficult to address; however, explicit knowledge of efficiency levels, quality parameters, and maintenance routines proved easier to import. This was a task made all the easier when SAP was introduced, as these were eventually programmed into SAP's purchasing module.

While the foregoing describes operational routines at both plants, an understanding of the forces underpinning managerial decision making is also important. Before the introduction of SAP, Boxit Group's general management philosophy ensured that operational managers had significant autonomy to run their logistics, production, and marketing activities, with respect to local conditions. Boxit found that this strategy helped develop strong local management teams whose members understood, and were responsive to, the fluctuations in demand for the products produced in their plants. Regional manufacturing and sales operations were monitored and controlled by Boxit's corporate management team through a system of regular financial reporting and review, coupled with tight capital and operating expense controls. This regional decentralization and close central monitoring coupled with performance-related incentives for local managers provided motivation for improvements in performance. The implementation of SAP changed both the reporting structure and the way in which the organization measured and improved performance at the plant level.

IT SYSTEMS AS ENABLING AND SUPPLEMENTAL CAPABILITIES AT BOXIT

Boxit's Information Technology Support Center, based in Paris, was responsible for new systems, maintenance, service, and upgrades for the company's European operations. This service was delivered and supported on a regional basis. For example, the needs of Irish operational units were serviced by the IT center based in Dublin. The IT center's primary activity was to provide help desk facilities to corporate HQ and manufacturing facilities. The Boxit Group outsourced the maintenance of its ICT systems to an U.K.-based company called Vanco. Vanco constantly monitors the traffic on the network. Boxit Ireland's IT manager stated: "Vanco manages the network in real-time, we are only aware that problems have occurred post solution, without such support Boxit could not manage."

The IT manager noted that the outsourcing of the maintenance of the ICT systems freed the IT department to "concentrate on the tactical and strategic end of the business." The ICT department is heavily involved in the selection and deployment of systems at the corporate level and at the plant level.

In the late 1990s, Boxit's operational units employed a computerized shop floor data collection system called PC-TOPS. This system replaced the traditional job cards, which were filled in manually by the lead operator on each of the manufacturing machines. With the PC-TOPS, each processing machine had a PC for data input. This enabled data concerning current production runs to be accessed in real time. The PC-TOPS system also calculated the costs incurred in producing each job. This could then be compared with the price charged to the customer to ensure that profit targets were being met. However, at an operational level, this system provided real-time production details concerning the following:

- The job currently being processed on each machine
- The speed at which each machine is operating
- Machinery failure and the cause of the failure
- The start and estimated finish times of jobs being currently processed

While PC-TOPS was an effective tool, it was not integrated with the AS400 MRP-based logistic applications in use at operational plants, which supported customer services, production planning, and transport activities. Operational managers were enthusiastic users of the PC-TOPS system, as they could monitor events on the production floor in real time, enabling staff to respond quickly to customer queries concerning the status of goods on order. However, because of the lack of integration between the AS400 logistics system and PC-TOPS, staff members sometimes neglected to update the AS400 system. The result was that managers and staff members could not rely on the information relating to job completion, which originated from the AS400 system. It was hoped that the introduction of SAP would eliminate this problem, as SAP provided a more comprehensive and integrated reporting capability than PC-TOPS.

The customer service manager with responsibility for production planning considered that the information provided by the PC-TOPS system was so effective that:

> *[W]e no longer need a program chaser in planning. The program chaser used to go down on the factory floor to see what was happening, to check that the production was operating to plan. The role has changed to production assistant, whose duties include inputting relevant information and monitoring the execution of the plan, in real time, on the system.*

This manager felt that the principle benefits that flowed from the system were immediate access to quality information and more productive use of staff time. The tenuous human contact, which existed prior to the introduction of PC-TOPS, between those on the shop floor and those in the manager's office, was severed. This was regarded as inevitable and almost natural. The ability of the office staff to journey onto the factory floor and gather and interpret information was eliminated. This opportunity to gain physical cues and have face-to-face contact was not valued by the customer service manager. However, this was not a universally held belief, as some managers acknowledged the power and usefulness of IT tools but also valued personal contact. The following narrative illustrates.

While PC-TOPS supported operational capabilities on the factory floor, another innovative IS supported product design and sales and marketing activities. Innobook was the first global database of packaging designs and was available on the organization's extranet. Innobook was essentially a knowledge management repository of packaging designs, the chief contributors and users of which were Boxit's European plants. BCC and BCS were enthusiastic users of Innobook, as it permitted them to give up-to-the-minute advice to customers during the packaging design phase. Consequently, it enabled customers to select from a range of expertly designed packaging solutions and tailor them for their own requirements. It also enabled BCC and BCS to accept orders for product designs used by firms across Europe for local and national production. This system also facilitated the procurement of specialized raw materials. It also removed uncertainty from the production process. Boxit's competitors did not have the resources to develop such capabilities, as the size of its European operation and its distributed knowledge resource were significant. The BCS plant manager viewed this as a value tool. He stated:

> *[W]e would have the edge in terms of design and innovation, which provides access to all the design departments across Europe in all our plants. None of our competitors have this capability. Such a facility gets us in the door, which is important at this stage.*

Innobook was especially suited to developing new business. It was, therefore, more highly prized by managers at BCS than by managers in the more mature BCC.

Boxfit's strategy of growth through acquisition required the assimilation and integration of vast amounts of knowledge, information, and data. The databases of recently acquired former competitors provided an information-rich source for organizational learning and a source of additional designs for inclusion in the Innobook database. However, managers at BCC and BSC were concerned that the implementation of SAP and its embedded decision-making routines would put constraints on their innovative use of the Innobook IS.

The Dublin-based IT function acted as a hub for communications between the group's nominally independent firms. All internal e-mails were routed through a server located in Dublin. This enabled the IT center to provide virus checking, to generate reports to inform individual firms of their top 10 users, and to monitor content. While this approach was an efficient and effective method of communication in Europe, companies in the United States are less integrated than in Europe. This was attributable to the group's strategy of forming strategic alliances with firms in the packaging industry. The Group's strategy of joint ownership of companies in the United States is also a determining factor. This evolving business structure means that maintaining an up-to-date e-mail database is a constant challenge. Therefore, the telephone rather than e-mail is the preferred means of communication between the European and non-European firms. Some managers found that e-mail was useful to connect with other managers who have similar responsibilities within the group. Nevertheless, they organized face-to-face meetings four times a year. As the production manager stated:

> *All the production managers in the UK and Ireland meet four times a year to share information and experiences. Experience*

*relating to new machinery, work practices, or shift patterns
exists within the group.*

Such meetings were considered vital. Managers considered that they
provided an opportunity to learn from the experience of others. A valuable pool
of knowledge existed and was exchanged in a friendly environment among
colleagues who understood the industry's processes. In fact, the process was
so successful that managers at BCC felt that they rarely needed to import
knowledge or expertise. They could avail of the knowledge existing within the
group. BCC was a successful operational unit, and the confidence that this
engendered was evident from the comments of one of the senior managers: "We
seldom go outside for expertise, we have what we need in-house, we know our
industry."

BSC and BCS also leveraged IT to expedite processes that support its
production activities. For example, production dies used to cut the corrugated
sheet into the required shapes were designed and fabricated using a CAD/
CAM system. The process most commonly used to print corrugated board is
flexographic printing. It is an effective printing method for color retail packaging
and other print products. The use of ISDN lines to transfer artwork designs also
reduced the turnaround time for design acceptance from four days to just one.

THE IMPLEMENTATION OF SAP AND ITS EFFECT ON CORE CAPABILITIES, KNOWLEDGE SETS, AND KNOWLEDGE-CREATING ACTIVITIES

As with most organizations that introduce SAP, Boxit's corporate management employed a firm of consultants to help implement the system—this
constituted an importation of expertise. However, Boxit management considered that it was necessary for consultants to be familiar with Boxit's industry
and culture, if they were to leverage fully their knowledge and skills. Hence,
Boxit attempted to train the consultants in its business routines and inculcate
them in its values and norms. This proved unproductive and expensive, and
consequently, Boxit's IT function opted to train selected end users to the level
of SAP superusers. The rationale behind this was to have superusers provide
one-on-one training to other staff, thereby increasing the skill level and
commitment of end users. Managers noted that superusers developed a

Copyright © 2004, Idea Group Inc. Copying or distributing in print or electronic forms without written permission of Idea Group Inc. is prohibited.

valuable and unique knowledge set. They understood Boxit's business processes, industry dynamics, and the capabilities of SAP. The role of the superuser evolved to one of redesigning the way in which staff implemented business routines and of integrating SAP's routines with the "Boxit way."

An Examination of SAP's Influence on Operational Capabilities at Boxit

One of Boxit's primary goals was to use SAP to standardize the performance of each of its manufacturing plants. As the Human Resource Manager noted:

> *[W]e have identified approximately 25 key performance criteria for our plants. If we could transpose the average of the top 10 across all firms, then our bottom line would be transformed.*

While recognizing that each manufacturing plant has its own values and norms, the HR manager expected that SAP would help to define the appropriate mix of resources to ensure that plants improved their performance, as measured by these key performance indicators. Hence, through SAP, production outputs from the same make and model of machine operating in production plants in different locations were compared and analyzed for efficiencies. Performance that varied from the accepted norm was the subject of remedial action. Once the best practice was identified, it was adapted and applied to all of the firm's operations. SAP, therefore, facilitated the identification of "slacks" through benchmarking activities, although the managers of individual plants argued that such "slacks" were beneficial for competence development.

The implementation of SAP provided Boxit's management with an opportunity to attempt operational change in structure and process in several areas, as the IT manager pointed out:

> *[W]e have seen a major change in the structure of the organization since SAP has been introduced. For the first time in the corporation's history a Senior Vice President with responsibility for purchasing was appointed.*

The information SAP provided enabled the Senior Vice President to negotiate the purchase of raw materials, such as starch, in bulk, for Boxit's entire European operation. The savings were significant at the corporate level, but centralized purchasing prevented plant managers from sourcing raw materials locally, thereby introducing time efficiencies and cost savings at the plant level. Thus, they felt that SAP prevented them from lowering the overall cost of production at their plants. Worse still, according to the plant managers, SAP's dynamic reporting capability enabled corporate management to make ad hoc inquires and to drill down and examine performance in greater detail than ever before. As a manager of BCS explained:

> *Now the theory is that we will all run on SAP...from a sheet plant point of view SAP is a nightmare, I mean it is an enormous amount of work for no benefits at all. In fact it adds cost to the operation here. For a corrugated plant it has obvious benefits, for an accountant sitting in Paris it is brilliant because he can see everything and he can drill-down into any level of detail he wants, down to what machines are producing what. Obviously, this leaves comparison wide open.*

Local managers were concerned that variances attributable to fluctuations in local demand were not understood at corporate headquarters. Analyzing performance using limited criteria, they argue, risked producing misleading results; especially if SAP's nonfirm-specific operational routines were misaligned with local conditions. BCS managers, therefore, contended that in order to assess the performance of plants in disparate locations, local factors must be taken into account. For example, inventory was sometimes maintained at high levels due to local agreements with customers, while underutilized production capacity was often due to seasonal fluctuations in the firm's customer base. Hence, some plants might not compare favorably with others serving different customer groupings, or when compared with the requirements of firms in the same industry operating in different regions. Managers at BCC and BCS feel that such a process might be used as a lever to increase operating efficiencies, irrespective of local contingencies. They also argued that SAP-enabled benchmarking of units acted as a barrier to innovation.

In order to compare favorably with other units, managers at BCS and BCC were under pressure to commit their resources to maximize current performance; however, as resources were finite, they were unable to dedicate sufficient "slacks" to help maintain plant-specific innovation through knowledge-creating activities. The temptation for local managers was to leave their successors allocate the required resources to develop the capabilities necessary to address future problems and opportunities. Hence, managers underlined that SAP-enabled benchmarking had to involve more than comparing the costs of a series of activities or services required to produce the products. Using this criterion, there was no accounting for intangible resources such as knowledge and skills. Under SAP, this was considered a cost rather than a learning opportunity. It is long recognized that knowledge redundancy is essential for the well-being of a learning organization and its knowledge-creating activities. Managers and operational staff at BCS and BCC were of the opinion that SAP endangered the organizational learning process, as it led managers to concentrate on attaining short-term quantifiable gains, thereby depleting the firm's wellsprings of knowledge.

Transferring Explicit Knowledge and Operational Skills Through SAP

Attitudes toward SAP varied, however, BCC's production manager identified that it had the potential to solve problems that were emerging in the workforce by educating technicians as they performed their duties. When experienced maintenance technicians found solutions to problems with manufacturing equipment, they recorded them using the facility supplied by SAP. Thus, SAP permitted the explicit experiential knowledge of technicians to be captured and transferred to less-experienced coworkers. This was seen as supporting Boxit's learning-by-doing philosophy — except in this case, *Standing-by-Nanny* was effectively augmented by a *"Standing-by-SAP"* approach. SAP's capabilities in effecting knowledge transfers were reported by the BCC's production manager viz.:

> *We [were] starting to lose maintenance personnel [to other companies] and the information which the [SAP] system provide[d] help[ed] new maintenance personnel, who ha[d] no experience of working with packaging equipment. The information on the system provide[d] points of reference to help technicians to diagnose and rectify problems. Consequently, each technician [was] aware of work previously undertaken on each machine.*

Ironically, the manager at BCS, who later was highly critical of SAP, exploited this facility early on to help transfer explicit knowledge of the operation and maintenance of former BCC plant to BCS, thus avoiding the importation of what were operational core rigidities at BCC. Nevertheless, the maintenance community perceived the introduction of SAP as an additional method of supervision and quality control. They objected to the implementation of SAP on the basis that it required them to do additional clerical work and it distorted the existing chain of command within their department.

As previously stated, communities-of-practice in the Boxit organization possessed a long-held belief in the supremacy of experiential knowledge and the knowledge-creating routine of learning-by-doing. The implementation of SAP caused a change in the values and norms of the organization in regard to the long-established primacy of tacit over explicit knowledge. Indeed, Boxit's CEO was famous (or infamous) for his application of tacit knowledge in sizing up a competitor for potential takeover. However, the consensus on the importance of tacit knowledge that existed prior to the implementation of SAP was no longer evident in 2001. Local managers were concerned that this shift to SAP's prepackaged solutions would ultimately dehumanize the manufacturing process and eliminate opportunities (or the motivation) for problem solving at plant level. Without such opportunities, much-prized problem-solving activities and core capabilities could be lost.

CONCLUSION

This study showed that SAP can have a significant effect on an organization's knowledge-creating capabilities. Based on this study's findings, presented in Figure 5 is an integrative model of ERP system implementation that captures the salient issues surrounding, and consequences of, such endeavors. Briefly, the findings illustrate that the introduction of routines of "best practice" via SAP had unanticipated consequences for knowledge-creating activities at management and operational levels that challenged the knowledge sets on which unit-specific core capabilities were based. When imaginatively applied, SAP helped negate potential core rigidities, particularly where explicit knowledge was transferred between manufacturing units. Nevertheless, managers and operational staff felt that SAP endangered tried and tested learning routines; attenuated valuable knowledge-creating activities; depleted the firm's intangible knowledge assets; and threatened established core, enabling, and supplemental capabilities. The dynamic reporting capability of SAP to make ad hoc inquires, to drill down, and to examine managerial and operational performance in greater detail than ever before contributed to the creation of a rigid, centralized management structure and further reduced the autonomy of plant managers and operational staff. This signaled a shift in emphasis from tacit to

Figure 5. An Integrative Model of ERP System Implementation

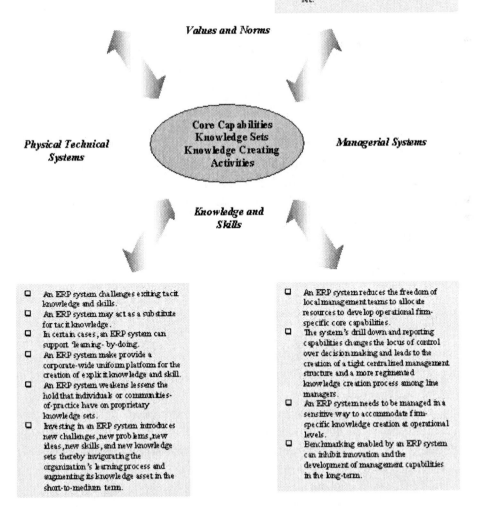

❑ An ERP system is a powerful management tool.
❑ When combined with human intuitiveness and experiential knowledge the capabilities of an ERP system can enable management to sunder core rigidities.
❑ An ERP system supports the importation and dissemination of explicit knowledge in a sanitized, structured format.
❑ If the routines of best practice embedded in an ERP system do not fit core capabilities, or the knowledge creation activities of operational units, they are misaligned.

❑ An ERP system produces a change in a firm's values and norms.
❑ An ERP system places an emphasis on explicit knowledge over tacit knowledge by changing the perceptions and cognitive processes of organizational actors.
❑ The dehumanisation of knowledge creation processes may occur with ERP systems.
❑ A perceived shift from implicit to explicit knowledge may result in a perceived devaluation of knowledge sets that were previously prized.
❑ Local management teams may experience a lack of ownership over the ERP system.
❑ The perception of ERP systems as being user-unfriendly militates against full acceptance and efficient use of the system.
❑ An ERP system may become a *core rigidity* and the new dominant knowledge set.

Values and Norms

Physical Technical Systems

Core Capabilities Knowledge Sets Knowledge Creating Activities

Managerial Systems

Knowledge and Skills

❑ An ERP system challenges exiting tacit knowledge and skills.
❑ An ERP system may act as a substitute for tacit knowledge.
❑ In certain cases, an ERP system can support 'learning-by-doing.
❑ An ERP system make provide a corporate-wide uniform platform for the creation of explicit knowledge and skill.
❑ An ERP system weakens lessens the hold that individuals or communities-of-practice have on proprietary knowledge sets.
❑ Investing in an ERP system introduces new challenges, new problems, new ideas, new skills, and new knowledge sets thereby invigorating the organization's learning process and augmenting its knowledge asset in the short-to-medium term.

❑ An ERP system reduces the freedom of local management teams to allocate resources to develop operational firm-specific core capabilities.
❑ The system's drill down and reporting capabilities changes the locus of control over decision making and leads to the creation of a tight centralized management structure and a more regimented knowledge creation process among line managers.
❑ An ERP system needs to be managed in a sensitive way to accommodate firm-specific knowledge creation at operational levels.
❑ Benchmarking enabled by an ERP system can inhibit innovation and the development of management capabilities in the long-term.

explicit knowledge and changed the system of values and norms within the organization.

In conclusion, it is argued in this chapter that organizations should take extant knowledge-creating activates, such as tried-and-tested firm-specific routines for problem solving, organizational learning, and decision making into account when implementing SAP modules. Hence, senior management must regard SAP as a means to an end, rather than an end in itself. Accordingly, business and IT managers should apply SAP in a sensitive and judicious manner, rather than be driven by its capabilities. Finally, it is clear that SAP has the potential to become the dominant knowledge set within an organization and, therefore, has the potential to become a core rigidity.

REFERENCES

Al-Mashari, M. (2000). Constructs of process change management in ERP context: A focus on SAP/R3. In *Proceedings of the Americas Conference on Information Systems* (AMCIS) (August 10-13). Long Beach, CA.

Alavi, M., & Leidner, D. (2001). Knowledge management and knowledge management systems: Conceptual foundations and research issues. *MIS Quarterly*, March, 25(1), 107-136.

Argyris, C. (1982). The executive mind and double-loop learning. *Organizational Dynamics,* (Autumn), 5-22.

Argyris, C., & Schon, D. (1978). *Organizational Learning*. Reading, MA: Addison-Wesley.

Attewell, P. (1992). Technology diffusion and organizational learning in industrial settings. *Organization Science*, *3*, 1-19.

Badaracco, J. (1991). *The Knowledge Link: How Firms Compete Through Strategic Alliances*. Boston, MA: Harvard Business School Press.

Bancroft, N., Seip, H., & Sprengel, L. (1998). *Implementing SAP/R3*. Greenwich, CT: Manning.

Barney, J. B. (1986). Organizational culture: Can it be a source of sustained competitive advantage? *Academy of Management Review*, *11*(3), 656-665.

Barney, J. B. (1991). Firm resources and sustainable competitive advantage. *Journal of Management*, *19*, 99-120.

Bartunek, J. K. (1988). The dynamics of personal and organizational reframing. In R. E. Quinn, & K. S. Cameron (Eds.), *Paradox and Transformation:*

Towards a Theory of Change in Organization and Management (pp. 137-162). Cambridge, MA: Ballinger.

Berger, P. L., & Luckmann, T. (1967). *The Social Construction of Reality*. New York: Doubleday.

Boland, R. J. Jr., Ramkrishnan, V. T., & Dov. T. (1994). Designing information technology to support distributed cognition. *Organization Science, 5*(3), 456-475.

Brehmer, B. (1991). Distributed decision making: Some notes on the literature. In Rasmussen et al. (Eds.), *Distributed Decision Making: Cognitive Models in Cooperative Work*. New York: John Wiley & Sons.

Brown, J. S., & Duguid, P. (1991). Organizational learning and communities of practice: Towards a unified view of working, learning and innovation. *Organization Science, 2*(1), 40-57.

Caldwell, B., & Stein, T. (1998). Beyond ERP: New IT agenda. *Information Week*, (November).

Cerullo, M., & Cerullo, V. (2000). The internal auditor's role in developing and implementing enterprise resource planning systems. *Internal Auditing*, 15, 25-35.

Child, J. L. (1972). Organizational structure, environment, and performance: The role of strategic choice. *Sociology, 6*, 1-22.

Chung, S. H., & Snyder, C. A. (2000). ERP adoption: A technological evolution approach. *International Journal of Agile Management Systems, 21*(2), 24-32.

Ciborra, C., & Lanzara, G. F. (1996). *Designing Dynamics Artifacts: Computer System as Formative Contexts*. Berlin: De Gruiter.

Cooke, D. P., & Peterson, W. J. (1998). *SAP Implementation: Strategies and Results*. New York: The Conference Board.

Curran, T. A., & Ladd, A. (1998). *SAP R/3. Business Blueprint*. Englewood Cliffs, NJ: Prentice Hall.

Cyert, R. M., & March, J. G. (1963). *A Behavioural Theory of the Firm*. Englewood Cliffs, NJ: Prentice-Hall.

Daft, R. L., & Weick, K. E. (1984). Towards a model of organizations as interpretation systems. *Academy of Management Review, 9*(2), 284-295.

Davenport, T. (1998). Putting the enterprise into the enterprise system. *Harvard Business Review*, (July/August), 121-131.

Davis, J. (1998). Scooping up vanilla ERP: Off-the-shelf versus customized software. *InfoWorld, 20*(47), 4.

Drucker, P. (1995). *The Post-capitalist Executive, Managing in a Time of Great Change*. New York: Penguin.

Esteves, J., & Pastor, J. (2001). Enterprise resource planning systems research: An annotated bibliography. *Communications of the Association for Information Systems, 7*(8), 1-51.

Grant, R. M. (1996). Towards a knowledge-based theory of the firm. *Strategic Management Journal, 17*, 109-122.

Grant, R. M., & Baden-Fuller, C. (1995). A knowledge-based theory of interfirm collaboration. *Academy of Management Best Paper Proceedings*, 17-21.

Hamel, G. (1994). The concept of core competence. In G. Hamel, & A. Heene (Ed.), *Competence Based Competition* (pp. 11-34). New York: John Wiley & Sons.

Hanseth, O., & Braa, K. (1998). Technology as a traitor: Emergent SAP infrastructure in a global organization. In T. J. Larsen, L. Levine, & J. I. DeGross (Eds.), *Information Systems: Current Issues and Future Changes. Proceedings of the IFIP WG 8.2 and 8.6 Joint Working Conference* (pp. 155-174), Helsinki, Finland. IFIP, Laxenburg, Austria.

Hedberg, B. (1981). How organizations learn and unlearn. In P. C. Nystrom, & W. H. Starbuck (Eds.), *Handbook of Organizational Design*. London: Oxford University Press.

Hederson, R., & Clark, K. B. (1990). Architectural innovation: The reconfiguration of existing product technologies and the failure of established firms. *Administrative Science Quarterly, 35*, 9-30.

Hedman, J. (2000). The CES framework for discussing ES. In *Proceedings of the Americas Conference on Information Systems* (AMCIS), (August 10-13). Long Beach, CA.

Holland, C. P., Light, B., & Kalwalek, P. (1999). Beyond enterprise resource planning projects: Innovative strategies for competitive advantage. In J. Pries-Heje, C. Cibarra, K. Kautz, J. Valor, E. Christiaanse, D. Avison, & C. Heje (Eds.), *Proceedings of the 7th European Conference on Information Systems* (June 23-25, Vol. I-II, pp. 273–287). Copenhagen, Denmark.

Holm, P. (1995). The dynamics of institutionalization: Transformation processes in Norwegian fisheries. *Administrative Science Quarterly, 40*, 398-422.

Holsapple, C., & Sena, M. (1999). Enterprise systems for organizational decision support: A research agenda. In *Proceedings of the Americas*

Conference on Information Systems (AMCIS) (August 10-13). Long Beach, CA.

Itami, H. (1989). Mobilising invisible assets: The key for successful corporate strategy. In E. Punset, & G. Sweeney (Eds.), *Information Resources and Corporate Growth*. Floral Street, London: Punset and Sweeney, Printer Publishers Ltd.

Janis, I. L. (1989). *Crucial Decisions: Leadership in Policymaking and Crisis Management*. New York: The Free Press.

Jones, M. C., & Price, R. L. (2001). Organizational knowledge sharing in ERP implementation: A multiple case study analysis. In *Twenty-Second International Conference on Information Systems*.

Kim, W. C., & Manborgne, R. (1997). Fair process: Managing in the knowledge economy. *Harvard Business Review*, (July/August), 71-84.

Klaus, H., & Gable, G. (2000). Senior manager's understandings of knowledge management in the context of enterprise systems. In *Proceedings of the Americas Conference on Information Systems* (AMCIS) (August 10-13). Long Beach, CA.

Lave, J. (1988). *Cognition in Practice: Mind, Mathematics, and Culture in Everyday Life*. Cambridge, MA: Cambridge University Press.

Lave, J., & Wenger, E. (1991). Situated learning: Legitimate peripheral participation. *IRL Report 90-0013*, Palo Alto, CA, Institute for Research on Learning. Cambridge, MA: Cambridge University Press.

Leonard-Barton, D. (1992). Core capabilities and core rigidities: A paradox in managing new product development. *Strategic Management Journal*, 9, 41-58.

Leonard-Barton, D. (1995). *Wellsprings of Knowledge: Building and Sustaining the Sources of Innovation*. Boston, MA: Harvard Business School Press.

Levitt, B., & March, J. (1988). Organizational learning. *Annual Review of Sociology*, 14, 319-340.

Lincoln, J. L., & Guba, E. G. (1985). *Naturalistic Inquiry*. Thousand Oaks, CA: Sage.

March, J. G., & Simon, H. A. (1958). *Organizations*. New York: John Wiley & Sons.

Markus, M. L., & Tanis, C. (1999). *The Enterprise Systems Experience — From Adoption to Success*. Claremont, CA: Claremont Graduate University.

Miller, D., & Minzberg, H. L. (1972). *Strategy formulation in context*. Working Paper. Montreal, Quebec, Canada: McGill University.

Montgomery, C. A., & Wernerfelt, B. (1988). Diversification, Ricardian rents, and Tobin's Q. *Rand Journal of Economics, 19,* 623-632.

Nelson, R. S., & Winter, S. G. (1982). *An Evolutionary Theory of Economic Change.* Cambridge, MA: Harvard University Press.

Nonaka, I. (1994). A dynamic theory of organizational knowledge creation. *Organizational Science, 5*(1), 14-37.

Nonaka, I., & Nishiguchi, T. (2001). *Knowledge Emergence: Social, Technical, and Evolutionary Dimensions of Knowledge Creation.* Oxford, UK: Oxford University Press.

Nonaka, I., & Takeuchi, H. (1995). *The Knowledge Creating Company: How Japanese Companies Create the Dynamics of Innovation.* Oxford, UK: Oxford University Press.

Nystrom, P. C., & Starbuck, W. H. (1984). To avoid organizational crises, unlearn. *Organizational Dynamics, 12*(4), 53-65.

Nystrom, P. C., Hedberg, B. L., & Starbuck, W. H. (1976). Interacting processes as organization design. In R. H. Kilman, L. R. Pondy, & D. P. Sleviin (Eds.), *Management of Organization Design* (Vol. 1, pp. 209-230). New York: Elsevier North-Holland.

O'Reilly, C. A. (1989). Corporate culture considerations based on an empirical study of high growth firms in Silicon Valley. *Economia Aziendale, 3*(3).

Orlikowski, W. J. (1991). Integrated information environment or matrix of control? The contrary implications of information technology. *Accounting, Management, and Information Technologies, 1,* 9-42.

Parr, A., & Shanks, G. (2000). A taxonomy of ERP implementation approaches. In *Proceedings of the 33ʳᵈ Hawaii International Conference on Science Systems, HICSS.* Maui, Hawaii.

Pavitt, K. (1991). *Key characteristics of the large innovating firm. Science Policy Research Unit*, University of Sussex. New York: John Wiley & Sons.

Penrose, E. (1959). *The Theory of the Growth of the Firm.* London: Blackwell.

Polanyi, M. (1962). *Personal Knowledge: Towards a Post-Critical Philosophy.* Chicago, IL: University of Chicago.

Polanyi, M. (1967). *The Tactic Dimension.* New York: Anchor Books.

Poster, M. (1990). *The Mode of Information Structuralism and Social Organization.* Cambridge, UK: Polity Press.

Pozzebon, M. (2001). Demystifying the rhetorical closure of ERP packages. In the *Twenty-Second International Conference on Information Systems*, 329-338.

Prahalad, C., & Hamel, G. (1990, May/June). The core competence of the corporation. *Harvard Business Review, 68*(3), 79-91.

Ross, J. W. (1998). *The ERP Revolution: Surviving versus Thriving*. Cambridge, MA: Centre for Information System Research, MIT Sloan School of Management.

Rumelt, R. P. (1982). Diversification strategy and profitability. *Strategic Management Journal*, 359-369.

Scott, W. R. (1995). *Institutions and Organizations*. Thousand Oaks, CA: Sage.

Selznick, P. (1957). *Leadership in Administration: A Sociological Perspective*. New York: Harper and Row.

Shanks, G., Parr, A., Hu, B., Corbitt, B., Thanasankit, T., & Sheddon, P. (2000). Differences in critical success factors in ERP systems implementation in Australia and China: A cultural analysis. In *Proceedings of the Eighth European Conference on Information Systems* (ECIS 2000). Vienna, Austria.

Simon, H. A. (1961). *Administrative Behavior* (2nd ed.). New York: MacMillian.

Spender, J. C. (1989). *Industry Recipes: The Nature and Sources of Managerial Judgement*. Oxford: Blackwell.

Spender, J. C. (1996). Making knowledge the basis of a dynamic theory of the firm. *Strategic Management Review, 17*, 45-62.

Stake, R. E. (1995). *The Art of Case Study Research*. Thousand Oaks, CA: Sage.

Stalk, G., Evans, P., & Shulman, L. (1990). Competing on capabilities: The new rules of corporate strategy. *Harvard Business Review, 70*, 57-69.

Stedman, T. (1999). SAP, ERP rivals will add simpler interfaces: Upgrades target biggest sore spot for users. *Computerworld*, (March 22), 4.

Teece, D. J., Pisano, G., & Sheun, A. (1990). Firm capabilities, resources and the concept of strategy. *Consortium on Competitiveness and Cooperation, Working Paper*. Berkley, CA: University of California, Berkley, Center of Research in Management.

Thompson, J. D. (1967). *Organizations in Action*. New York: McGraw-Hill.

Walsham, G. (1995). Interpretative case studies in IS research: Nature and method. *European Journal of Information Systems, 4*(2), 74-81.

Webster. (1983). *Webster's Dictionary of English Usage.* Springfield, MA: Merriam-Webster.

Wernerfelt, B. (1984, April/June). A resource-based view of the firm. *Strategic Management Journal, 5*(2), 171-180.

White, O. F., Jr. (1969). The dialectical organization — An alternative to bureaucracy. *Public Administration Review, 29*, 32-42.

Winterscheid, B. C. (1994). Building capability from within the insiders' view of core competences. In G. Hamel, & A. Heene (Eds.), *Competence-Based Competition.* New York: John Wiley & Sons.

Yin, R. K. (1989). *Case Study Research: Design and Methods.* Thousand Oaks, CA: Sage.

Zuboff, S. (1988). *The Sources of Innovation.* New York: Oxford University Press.

Chapter X

Toward a Model of Organizational Prerequisites for ERP: Reintroducing the Concept of Data Warehousing

David Sammon
University College Cork, Ireland

Frédéric Adam
University College Cork, Ireland

ABSTRACT

Data Warehousing was the 'hot topic' of the early-to-mid 1990's but it became unfashionable through the mid-to-late 1990s with the widespread implementation of ERP systems. However, in recent times, the re-emergence of Data Warehousing, to address the limitations of ERP systems, provides researchers with a new challenge and the ability to test the validity of old notions in solving new problems. This chapter lays the foundation for a model of organizational prerequisites for ERP project implementation. The model is aimed at the 'Intelligence' phase of managerial decision making for ERP projects. It draws on the increasing volume of organizational ERP literature now being published and past research into Data Warehousing project implementations is introduced in an attempt to highlight the re-emerging need for the concept of organizational prerequisites. The chapter documents the early stages of a larger research study, which is currently in progress. The main objective of the chapter is to present a literature-based model, the need for which emerges from a number of 'issues of concern' around the implementation of ERP, which integrally covers the phases which organizations go through when purchasing ERP packages.

INTRODUCTION

To date, researchers looked at the ERP market as the place where organizational needs, in terms of integrated enterprise-wide systems, were met by the packages proposed by ERP vendors. However, current research in ERP (e.g., Hossain & Shakir, 2000; Wood & Caldas, 2001; Sammon & Adam, 2002) found that the ERP market is characterized by a strong vendor and consultant push, whereby organizations appear to have little choice but to *jump on the bandwagon* (as described for activity-based costing by Jones & Dugdale, 2002; and IT outsourcing by Michell & Fitzgerald, 1997; and to some extent for e-commerce development by Howcroft, 2001). Reflecting on the current sales bias in the ERP market, Esteves and Pastor (2001) indicated that "Research on ERP systems has been treated as a 'secondary' and its importance has been neglected by the IS community" (p. 3).

Furthermore, they called for future research and investigation on the role of each party (vendor, customer, and consultant) and their influence in ERP selection. A number of researchers backed up this call, such as Hossain and Shakir (2000), Wood and Caldas (2001), and Sammon and Adam (2002).

"Ignore history — condemned to repeat it" (Judge, 1997; Webster, 2000) seems to be an adequate statement when it comes to describing the mixed fortunes of organizations deploying IS and researchers' approaches to studying these IS evolutions. This may be due to the fragmentation of research in IS as described by Blanville and Landry (1989) and Adam and Fitzgerald (2000). Lucas (1991) suggested that, as a field, we need to think about interesting problems and look for underlying issues rather than focus on today's hot topic to keep up with the latest IS fashion. Therefore, addressing the suggestions of Kraemer and Dutton (1991) and Land (1995), the objective of this chapter is to build upon existing research carried out in the areas of data

warehousing (DW) and ERP, therefore, emphasizing a "continuity of ideas" and constructing a "cumulative" body of research.

INTEGRATING ERP INVESTIGATIONS WITH PREVIOUS RESEARCH

Although DW and ERP represent two alternate approaches to IS in organizations, a number of common defining factors exist between these two types of IS project implementations, as illustrated in Table 1.

Due to the constant regeneration and redefinition of the Data Warehousing concept, there is yet to evolve an 'inclusive' definition of Data Warehousing. However, proposed definitions identify the goal of Data Warehousing as enabling the provision of better corporate information to support an organization. As a result, the main objective of a Data Warehousing solution is to turn data into information. Therefore, by design, Data Warehousing is informational, analysis and decision support oriented, rather than oriented towards transaction processing (Babcock, 1995). However, there is also no agreed upon definition for ERP systems, although their characteristics position these systems as integrated, all-encompassing (Markus and Tanis, 2000), complex mega-packages (Gable et al., 1997) designed to support the key functional areas of an organization. Therefore, by design, an ERP is an operational-level system (see Chapter 1).

Reflecting on the early-to-mid 1990s Data Warehousing can be described as an informational solution to an operational problem in terms of data integration, as illustrated in Figure 1. The emergence of the Data Warehousing

Table 1. Defining Characteristics of DW and ERP

Characteristics of IS Approach	ERP	DW
Focus/origin	Operational	Informational
Benefit	Efficiency	Effectiveness
Design	Implement best practice	Create best practice
Development system	Software package	Evolving concept
Industry	Dominated by a few big players	Fragmented, hundreds of vendors
Characteristics of IS Project Implementation	ERP	DW
Project complexity	High	High
Project failure rate	High	High
Clarity and understanding of project initiative by organization	Low	Low

concept can be viewed as an evolution of Management Information Systems (Wu and Buchmann, 1997). The limitations of the traditional Management Information Systems (MIS), perceived as being unable to maintain a consistent view of an organization's reconciled data, was identified as the potential benefit of a Data Warehousing system. To overcome the problems with traditional approaches of accessing large amounts of data in heterogeneous, autonomous distributed systems, the emergence of Data Warehousing introduced the concept of a 'logically centralised data repository'. Therefore, the concept of Data Warehousing emerged due to the evolution of IS objectives within organizations (emerging from concerns with operational efficiency to considerations of market competitiveness), and further due to the growing demand within organizations to analyse (internal and external) business information.

However, by the mid-to-late 1990s ERP provided an alternate operational solution to the operational integration problem, and furthermore, ERP systems also promised to deliver on the informational requirements of an organization, such is its scope, therefore, the perceived need and along with it, the rate of Data Warehousing project implementations, was reduced. As further illustrated in Figure 1, and referencing the insights of Wood and Caldas (2001), ERP can be described as:

> *... a comprehensive information technology package built on the promise that all critical information should be totally integrated in one single information database [p.387]*

Unfortunately, as organizations moved toward the post-implementation phase of ERP project implementations, post Y2K for the vast majority of organizations, the real issue of benefit realisation emerged and with it came the re-emergence of the need for Data Warehousing, as illustrated in Figure 1. Due to the monolithic style integration of the mid-to-late 1990s, many organizations are now discovering that the solution to leveraging investment decisions in, and retrieving useful data from, an ERP system is to undertake a Data Warehousing initiative in conjunction with the implemented ERP system (Sims, 2001; Raden, 1999; Inmon, 2000; Radding, 2000; Hewlett-Packard, 2002). The harsh reality of ERP systems implementation, to the expense of those organizations that invested resources in the initiative, is that ERP only gets data into the system, it does not prepare data for use and analysis (Inmon, 2000).

To our way of thinking, this creates a *double learning curve* for implementing organizations, undertaking in quick succession both an ERP project and a DW project, in an attempt to finally achieve the benefits expected but

Figure 1. IS Integration Approaches

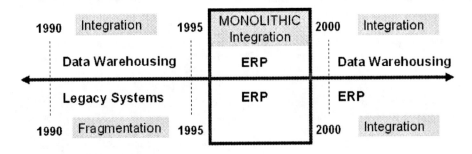

never realized. This was referred to as a "dilemma" by Inmon (1999). As a result, the significance and benefit of generating a set of organizational prerequisites for ERP project implementations, facilitated by an examination of existing research in DW may be greater than previously considered in our approach to research in this area.

UNDERSTANDING ORGANIZATIONAL PREREQUISITES

Organizational Prerequisites are generated through an examination of critical factors throughout the lifecycle of an IS project (planning, implementation, post-implementation). However, in use, organizational prerequisites are concerned with the 'pre-planning' or 'intelligence' phase of a project implementation life-cycle.

Finnegan and Sammon (1999, 2000, 2002) proposed the concept of organizational prerequisites in their study of DW project implementations. They defined *organizational prerequisites* as follows:

> *[N]ecessary elements existing within the organization, which are examinable [internally] by the implementing organization, prior to the organization undertaking the initiation of a data warehousing project.*

Table 2. The Need for Organizational Prerequisites in DW Project Implementations

Factor	Description
[1] Every organization that initiates a DW project encounters its own unique "set of issues" around a common set of factors.	Given that, there are numerous similarities in all DW projects. And, given that, 50% of all DW projects undertaken experienced some degree of failure and for remarkably similar reasons. If this common set of factors can be identified and its occurrence sign-posted in a structured format, then organizations could determine their suitability for DW project initiation.
[2] There are a high number of DW project failures.	Even though all of the causation factors associated with DW project implementation failure are not concerned with the initial stages of the project directly, they can lead to failure at some stage of the implementation, and should be taken into account at the start of the project.
[3] The level of clarity and understanding of the DW project initiative that exists within the organization needs to be determined.	If the causes of likely future problems can be identified in advance, then they can be addressed, or at least sign-posted and worked around, thus improving the DW project's chances of success, prior to implementation initiation.
[4] The use of a corporate readiness model in a DW project implementation is incorporated into the *preparatory stage* of an implementation methodology.	The organization cannot assess its readiness prior to the initiation of the project, due to the fact that the project is initiated once the readiness tests are introduced. Furthermore, these models are complex and not suited for internal use within the organization.
[5] The format of the model does not lend itself to internal use within the implementing organization.	The existing readiness models are specifically related to external consultancy use in DW implementations and require the external consultants to interpret the meaning of each readiness check and identify the areas of focus for the organization. The structural meaning and interpretation of the models is complex and involves a lot of computation in use. The lack of academic research in the area of enterprise readiness for the successful implementation of a DW project is evident in the lack of methodological "*scholarly rigour*" being applied to the existing models.

Finnegan and Sammon (1999, 2000, 2002) highlighted a number of factors that legitimize the need for a model of organizational prerequisites in relation to DW project implementations, as illustrated in Table 2.

Therefore, an organization should be empowered to assess its readiness and preparedness for the successful implementation of a DW system prior to project initiation, in a vendor/consultant-independent, methodology-independent, and preimplementation thought process. As a result, Finnegan and Sammon (2000) stated that "there is a need to identify a method of assessment that is structured in an easily understood and interpretable format, and is directed at use internally by the implementing organization."

USING THE PREREQUISITE MODEL

The critical areas of Finnegan and Sammon's (1999, 2000, 2002) research model are structured into a five-factor table (as illustrated in Table 3) under the following headings (Systems Factors, Data Factors, Skills Factors, Organizational Factors, and Project Management Factors). The factors are not mutually exclusive in relation to their influence on a DW project implementation. The "multiplicative effects" of these factors combine to drastically affect the implementation of the DW system, beyond the intentioned plan at the initial phase. Each of these factors contains the following: certain issues that were documented and refined from existing readiness models; other advocates' proposed research models; previous causes of documented failures; along with factors critical to the successful implementation of DW projects.

Each of these factors is examined within the organization through the examination of the logical process of going through three conceptual stages (*Existing, Planned, Implemented*), as illustrated in Table 3. The *Existing* stage relates to what the organization had in place prior to the initiation of the DW project. The *Planned* stage identifies what the organization felt they

Table 3. Research Model Structure

EXISTING	PLANNED	IMPLEMENTED	
SYSTEMS FACTORS The purpose of the systems factors is to identify the extent of the organisation's examination of the technical platform (hardware) and software, the knowledge of the legacy systems possessed and the extent of the provision of an integrated solution, to support the data warehousing project initiative, within the organisation			DEGREE TO WHICH FACTOR IS CRITICAL
DATA FACTORS The purpose of the data factors emerges with regard to the complexity of the data becoming apparent only once the project is under way. The data factors attempt to identify the level of understanding of the base data and the establishment of a sound enterprise-wide data model in designing the data warehousing system			
SKILLS FACTORS The purpose of the skills factors is to identify the skills and competencies that exist within the organisation, due to the fact that the scale of a data warehousing project is greater than experiences have prepared the organisation for. It identifies the organisations level of extraction in relation to the knowledge and experience gained from previous data warehousing projects			
ORGANISATIONAL FACTORS The organisational factors propose to identify the organisation's method of ensuring total commitment to the project along with the achievement of effective sponsorship of the project. This factor further identifies the effects of people and politics within the project's scope			
PROJECT MANAGEMENT FACTORS The purpose of the project management factors is to identify the initial scope of the project. It attempts to identify the organisation's need to ensure that there is an agreement of what is meant by data warehousing and its objectives within the organisation. This factor also identifies the organisation's management of user expectations in relation to the projects implementation			

needed (and planned for) to achieve with the successful implementation of the DW system. Finally, the *Implemented* stage identifies what the organization ended up with, in the successfully implemented warehousing system. This progression highlights the organization's diversity of experiences in DW project implementation, and the "lessons learned" through the initial and subsequent warehousing initiatives within the organization. As a result, Finnegan and Sammon (1999, 2000, 2002) identified how and why certain factors are critical to a DW project implementation, and in effect, sign-posted their occurrence within organizations. As a result, a set of organizational prerequisites was generated, through an analysis of the degree of criticality of each of the factors to an organization's DW project implementation.

The research objective of the Finnegan and Sammon (1999, 2000, 2002) study was forward looking and addressed issues in relation to DW project implementation that are of significant practical value to organizations, who for the first time attempt to internally evaluate the plausibility of implementing a DW project. This observation was further highlighted by the most recent developments in DW, the advent of the convergence of DW and ERP (Inmon, 2000). These organizations are at the initial decision-making stage of the what, why, and how of DW. According to Finnegan and Sammon (1999, 2000, 2002), their knowledge and understanding of DW and the organization's suitability for project implementation at this point is at an unacceptable level. Therefore, the organizational prerequisites model can be viewed as a method of identifying the extent of the existence of necessary elements within the organization for a DW project implementation. This leaves us pondering whether the same approach can be taken for ERP project implementation.

REALITY OF ERP IMPLEMENTATION: AN EXTENSION OF CURRENT THINKING

Lucas (1981) defined implementation as the whole process of introducing a system into an organization, from conception of an idea, to analysis, design, installation, and operation. The inclusion of "conception of an idea" is something that seems to be overlooked throughout current research in ERP implementation, highlighting the issue that the decision-making process prior to ERP software selection is not considered within the scope of the implementation process models (Shanks et al., 2000). The analysis step of most ERP projects seems to skip the early stages and to focus a package evaluation exercise (Kelly et al., 1999). The phase of problem finding (Pounds, 1969), where organiza-

Figure 2. Understanding Research in ERP

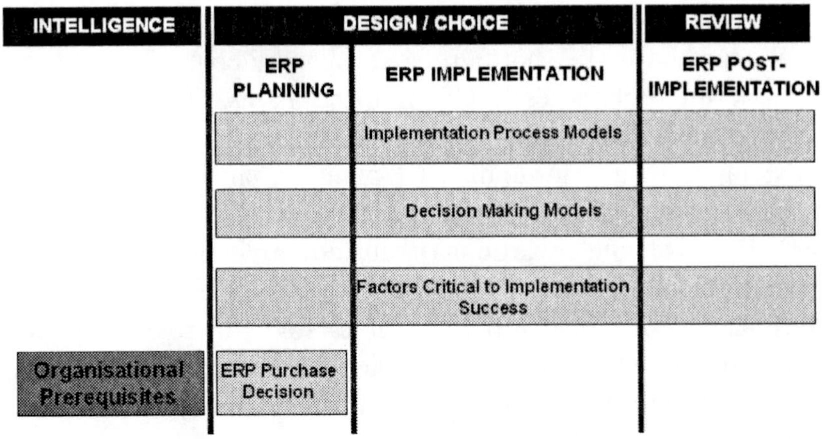

INTELLIGENCE	DESIGN / CHOICE		REVIEW
	ERP PLANNING	ERP IMPLEMENTATION	ERP POST-IMPLEMENTATION
		Implementation Process Models	
		Decision Making Models	
		Factors Critical to Implementation Success	
Organisational Prerequisites	ERP Purchase Decision		

tional actors identify stimuli in the environment that they come to perceive as problems requiring their attention, has not been a feature of any reported ERP projects. Sammon and Adam (2000) concluded that few research projects examined the first phase (intelligence phase), however, this stage of the decision-making process is crucial in ERP projects, as noted by Pomerol (1994), because ideas and alternatives not considered at this stage are unlikely to be considered in the later stages. Thus, decision-making processes in relation to ERP selection are inherently weak in many organizations. This is highlighted in Figure 1, using Simon's (1977) four-stage decision-making process (normative) model as a guide to locate the focus of existing research in ERP.

Several researchers developed process models for ERP implementation (Bancroft et al., 1998; Ross, 1999; Markus & Tanis, 2000; Shanks et al., 2000, Parr & Shanks, 2000; Shakir, 2000). From a synthesis of these models, planning is identified as the first phase, as illustrated in Figure 2, and the key activities undertaken can be identified as follows: assembly of a steering committee; development of a business case for ERP; ERP package selection; selection of a project team manager; and creation of a project plan. However, adopting these implementation processes returned a high rate of failure, both in terms of project implementation and the delivery of expected benefits. In addition, according to Somers and Nelson (2001), "broad-based empirical research in the CSFs that impact implementation is still very limited" (p. 1).

Furthermore, Nah et al. (2001) reported that the difficulties of ERP implementations were widely cited in the literature, but research on critical factors for initial and ongoing ERP implementation success is rare and fragmented. We contend that the shortfall of the available literature is highlighted by the fact that it simply classifies the CSFs into the phases of the ERP implementation process models and, in effect, does not extend to the inclusion of factors of critical importance, prior to the ERP planning phase, referred to as the *Intelligence* phase in Figure 2. To further illustrate this point, we identified a number of issues of concern around the current implementation of ERP, as illustrated in Table 4.

The issues of concern identified in Table 4 for ERP project implementation, mirror those identified for DW project implementation in Table 2, to legitimize the need for a model of organizational prerequisites. Therefore, this demonstrates our continuity of ideas in this research study.

Also, due to the fact that organizational prerequisites are concerned with the 'pre-planning' or 'intelligence' phase of a project implementation life-cycle, their need has been further legitimised by a number of researchers. Parr and Shanks (2000) call for an examination of the criticality of CSFs associated with a successful ERP project implementation and organizational prerequisites, by design, focus on an analysis of the '*degree of criticality*' of a factor to a project implementation. Markus et al. (2000) propose that while organizations experience problems at all phases of the ERP system life-cycle, many of these problems experienced in later phases originated earlier but remain unnoticed or uncorrected, therefore, researchers and organizations:

> *will do well to adopt broad definitions and multiple measures of success and pay particular attention to the early identification and correction of problems [p.245]*

TOWARD AN ORGANIZATIONAL PREREQUISITES MODEL FOR ERP PROJECT IMPLEMENTATION

In an attempt to fill this research gap, a theoretical framework was developed in order to further explore and clarify the research problem, as illustrated in Figure 2. The framework, represented in Figure 3, organizes the areas we identified in current ERP literature, which are further described in

Table 4. Issues of Concern in ERP Implementation

Issues of Concern	Description	Reference
[1] The planning phase of an ERP implementation project	The scale of ERP projects has rarely been tackled by most organizations, highlighted by an inadequate organizational analysis at the beginning of the project	Kelly et al., 1999
[2] The complexities of the ERP market	This issue is illustrated through the concept of the ERP "community" and the role of each actor (ERP vendor, ERP consultant, and implementing organization) in the ERP project implementation	Sammon & Adam, 2002; Esteves & Pastor, 2001; Wood & Caldas, 2001; Hossain & Shakir, 2000
[3] Complex implementation	Many ERP systems implementations fail, to a degree or completely, to meet project constraints due to their complexity; An ERP package is so complex and vast that it takes several years (lengthy) and millions of dollars (expensive) to roll out	Sammon & Adam, 2000; Davenport, 1998; Martin, 1998; Bingi et al., 1999; Holland et al., 1999; Shanks et al., 2000; Koch et al., 2000; Saint-Leger & Savall, 2001
[4] High rates of failure in ERP project implementation	The combined effect of [1], [2] and [3]; the high failure rate of ERP implementation calls for a better understanding of its CSFs	Somers et al., 2000
[5] Failure to deliver expected benefits	As a result of [4]; on average, ERP projects deliver only 30% of the promised benefits; only around 10% - 15% of ERP implementations deliver anticipated benefits	Bingi et al., 1999; Stefanou, 2000; Saint-Leger & Savall, 2001; Krumbholz et al., 2000; Rutherford, 2001
[6] Level of dependence	Once an ERP system is implemented, going back is extremely difficult; it is too expensive to undo the changes ERP brings into an organization; due to the *all-encompassing* nature of all ERP offerings, a level of dependence is created that far surpasses the dependence associated with prior technological regimes	Bingi et al., 1999; Markus & Tanis, 2000

Table 5. The research listing in Table 5 is not exhaustive and is continually updated throughout the research study.

As represented in Figure 3, there is a need for research into the *Intelligence* phase of the decision-making process for ERP software selection, highlighting the critical factors for selection and implementation of an ERP

Figure 3. The Research Problem Framework

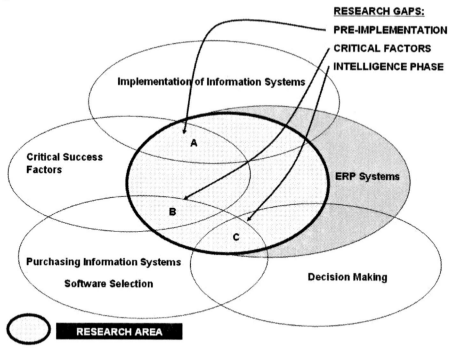

package in a preplanning phase environment, therefore, facilitating a vendor/ consultant-independent, methodology-independent, and preimplementation thought process. In support of this argument, Stafyla and Stefanou (2000) stated the following:

> ...given the cost and the permanent nature of ERP investments, an understanding of the way decisions are taken concerning the adoption, evaluation and selection of ERP software can be very useful for both academic research and practice. (p. 293)

However, Esteves and Pastor (2001) went one step further by highlighting the important issue concerning the definition of "those decisions" that organizations face prior to implementing an ERP system. Caldas and Wood (1998) and Wood and Caldas (2001) called for the following:

> ...the utilization of a broader [alternative] perspective to its [ERP implementation] comprehension, one that would challenge

Table 5. ERP Research Areas

Research Area	Description	Reference
A	Group CSFs into a strategic–tactical factors framework for assessing ERP project implementation; present several critical issues that must be addressed before implementing any ERP package; examine the CSFs in enterprise-wide systems projects; identify the risk factors in ERP project implementations that are unique to those projects; assess the CSFs that are critical throughout the stages of the ERP implementation process (The theoretical development of CSFs in ERP implementations remains embryonic.); classify CSFs of ERP implementation in the respective phases of a process-oriented ERP life cycle model	Holland et al., 1999; Bingi et al., 1999; Sumner, 1999, 2000; Somers & Nelson, 2001; Nah et al., 2001
B	Cite six common mistakes (factors) organizations make when choosing an ERP package; highlight the critical issues involved in the selection process of ERP systems; identify a set of factors that describe ERP package capabilities associated with the purchase of ERP systems	Kuiper, 1998; Stefanou, 2000; Brown et al., 2000
C	Focus on the decision-making processes concerned with ERP software selection; map decision-making models to the different phases of the ERP project life cycle (Evaluation, Selection and Implementation); demonstrate the influence of bias over requirements in the decision-making process; introduce the concept of nondecision-making and establish its existence in the ERP software selection process	Sammon & Adam, 2000; Shakir, 2000; Sammon & Lawlor, 2001; Sammon & Adam, 2002

the reductionism and Information Technology biases that have characterised the prevailing approach to the subject. (p. 5)

Therefore, addressing the recommendations made by Caldas and Wood (1998) and Wood and Caldas (2001), we propose that a key milestone in, and radical approach to, ERP research will involve the identification and development of an organizational prerequisites model for ERP project implementation.

CONCLUSION

We contend that the strong vendor push that characterizes the ERP movement inherently favors the *sales* discourse (that proposed by ERP vendors and ERP consultants) and replaces the *needs* discourse (that of the implementing organization). According to Westrup and Knight (2000):

> *...the deployment of ERP systems takes place in a marketplace*
> *of ERP vendors generally mediated by ERP consultants. Their*
> *aims, though never publicly formulated, are to sell ERP systems*
> *and consultancy services respectively. (p. 641)*

This contention can prove increasingly problematic for the implementing organization, leading to what we term a *double learning curve* for implementing organizations undertaking both ERP and DW initiatives. Furthermore, ERP vendors and ERP consultants are extending their range of products and services to provide these DW functionalities. As a result, this further strengthens the *sales* discourse and, in effect, reduces the implementing organization's chances of successfully implementing either ERP or DW. Therefore, an implementing organization needs to be empowered and made aware of the complexities of the ERP market, facilitating a vendor/consultant-independent, methodology-independent, and preimplementation thought process to ERP project implementation. This reiterates the point made by Finnegan and Sammon (1999):

> *...there is a need to identify a method of assessment that is*
> *structured in an easily understood and interpretable format,*
> *and is directed at use internally by the implementing organization.*

There is no doubt in the authors minds that initially, when organizations commenced the implementation of ERP systems they did not expect to have to invest in future Data Warehousing solutions to leverage their ERP investments. As a result of this, the early lessons learned by organizations, in relation to Data Warehousing, should not be dismissed. This new era of enterprise-wide systems integration projects introduces an increased level of complexity to an already complicated organizational initiative. In the past, in relation to ERP systems, organizations have been too accepting of the promises of the *sales* discourse.

To conclude, although organizational prerequisites were previously generated for DW (Finnegan & Sammon, 1999, 2000, 2002) and the "traditional" approach to project implementation, the current focus of the implementing organization is now on undertaking DW to complement ERP. So, as a first step, organizational prerequisites should be generated for ERP and further reexamined in the context of the "modern" approach to DW-type project implementations.

REFERENCES

Adam, F., & Fitzgerald, B. (2000). The status of the IS field: Historical perspective and practical orientation. *Information Research*, 4(July).

Babcock, C. (1995). Slice, dice & deliver. *Computerworld, 29*(46), 129-132.

Bancroft, N., Seip, H., & Sprengel, A. (1998). *Implementing SAP R/3* (2nd ed.). Greenwich, CT: Manning.

Bingi, P., Sharma, M., & Godla, J. (1999, Summer). Critical issues affecting an ERP implementation. *Information Systems Management, 16*(3), 7-8.

Blanville, C., & Landry, M. (1989). Can the field of MIS be disciplined? *Communication of the ACM, 32*(1), 48-60.

Brown, C. V., Vessey, I., & Powell, A. (2000). The ERP purchase decision: Influential business and IT factors. In *Proceedings of the Sixth Americas Conference on Information Systems* (August 10-13, pp. 1029-1032). Long Beach, California.

Caldas, M., & Wood, T. (1998). *How consultants can help organizations survive the ERP frenzy.* Retrieved March 28, 2000 from the World Wide Web: http://www.gv.br/prof_alunos/thomaz/ingles/paper6.htm.

Davenport, T. (1998). Putting the enterprise into the enterprise system. *Harvard Business Review*, (July/August), 121-131.

Esteves, J., & Pastor, J. (2001). Enterprise resource planning research: An annotated bibliography. *Communications of the Association for Information Systems, 7*(8), (August).

Finnegan, P., & Sammon, D. (1999). Foundations of an organizational prerequisites model for data warehousing. In *Proceedings of the Seventh European Conference on Information Systems (ECIS)*, (June). Copenhagen, Denmark.

Finnegan, P., & Sammon, D. (2000, Fall). The ten commandments of data warehousing. *DATABASE, 31*(4).

Finnegan, P., & Sammon, D. (2002). Presenting the organizational prerequisites for data warehousing implementation. In S. Barnes (Ed.), *Knowledge Management Systems: Theory and Practice*. UK: International Thomson Business Press.

Gable, G., van den Heever, R., Scott, J., & Erlank, S. (1997). Large packaged software: The need for research. *Proceedings of the Third Pacific Asia Conference on Information Systems (PACIS)*.

Hewlett-Packard. (2002). Strategic systems of the future: Integrating ERP applications and data warehouses. *DM Review*, (March).

Holland, C. P., Light, B., & Gibson, N. (1999). A critical success factors model for enterprise resource planning implementation. In *Proceedings of the Seventh European Conference on Information Systems* (pp. 273-287). Copenhagen, Denmark: Copenhagen Business School.

Hossain, L., & Shakir, M. (2001). Stakeholder involvement framework for understanding the decision making process of ERP selection in New Zealand. *Journal of Decision Systems, 10*(1), 11-27.

Howcroft, D. (2001). After the goldrush: Deconstructing the myths of the dot.com market. *Journal of Information Technology, 16,* 195-204.

Inmon, W. H. (1999). *Data warehousing and ERP.* Retrieved November 24, 2001 from the World Wide Web: http://www.billinmon.com/library.

Inmon, W. H. (2000). *ERP and data warehouse: Reading the tea leaves.* Retrieved October 18, 2001 from the World Wide Web: www.billinmon.com/library/articles/arterpfu.asp.

Jones, T. C., & Dugdale, D. (2002). The ABC bandwagon and the juggernaut of modernity. *Accounting, Organizations and Society, 27,* 121-163.

Judge, A. (1997). *The art of non-decision making and the manipulation of categories.* Retrieved October 24, 2001 from the World Wide Web: www.uia.org/uiadocs/nondec.htm.

Kelly, S., Holland, P., & Light, B. (1999). A departure from traditional systems development methodologies: Enterprise resource planning, ERP, systems and the use of process modelling tools. In *Proceedings of the Ninth Annual Business Information Technology Conference,* (November 3-4). Manchester, UK.

Koch, C., Slater, D., & Boatz, E. (1999). *The ABC's of ERP.* Retrieved from the World Wide Web: www.c10.com/fornms/erp/edit/122299_erp_content.html.

Kraemer, K., & Dutton, W. (1991). Survey research in the study of management information systems. In K. Kraemer, J. Cash Jr., & J. F. Nunamaker Jr. (Eds.), *The Information Systems Research Challenge: Survey Research Methods* (Vol. 3. pp. 3-58). Cambridge, MA: Harvard Business Press.

Krombholz, M., Galliers, J., Coulianos, N., & Maiden, N. A. M. (2000). Implementing enterprise resource planning packages in different corporate and national cultures. *Journal of Information Technology, 15,* 267-279.

Kuiper, D. (1998). The key to a custom fit. *Evolving Enterprise,* (Spring).

Land, F. (1995). The new alchemist: Or how to transmute base organizations into corporations of gleaming gold. In *Proceedings of the Third Euro-*

pean Conference of Information Systems (July, pp. 21-30). Athens, Greece.

Lucas Jr., H. (1981). *Implementation: The Key to Successful Information Systems*. New York: Guilford.

Lucas Jr., H. (1991). Commentary. In K. Kraemer, J. Cash Jr., & J. F. Nunamaker Jr. (Eds.), *The Information Systems Research Challenge: Survey Research Methods*, (Vol. 3, pp. 67-79). Cambridge, MA: Harvard Business Press.

Markus, M.L., & Tanis, C. (2000). *The Enterprise Systems Experience — From Adoption to Success*. Claremont, CA: Claremont Graduate University.

Markus, M.L., Axline, S., Petrie, D. & Tanis, C. (2000). Learning from adopters' experiences with ERP: Problems encountered and success achieved. *Journal of Information Technology, 15,* 245-265.

Martin, M. (1998). Smart managing. *Fortune*, (February 2).

Michell, V., & Fitzgerald, G. (1997). The IT outsourcing market-place: Vendors and their selection. *Journal of Information Technology, 12,* 223-237.

Nah, F. F. H., Lau, J. L. S., & Kuang, J. (2001). Critical factors for successful implementation of enterprise systems. *Business Process Management Journal, 7*(3), 285-296.

Parr, A., & Shanks, G. (2000). A model of ERP project implementation. *Journal of Information Technology, 15,* 289-303.

Pomerol, J. C. (1994). *Le monde de l'aide à la décision. LAFORIA —* Working Papers Series, #94/20, pp. 1–26.

Pounds, W. (1969). The process of problem finding. *Industrial Management Review, 10*(1), 1-19.

Radding, A. (2000). Knowledge management appears on ERP radar. *Datamation*. Retrieved October 18, 2001 from the World Wide Web: http://itmanagement.earthweb.com.

Raden, N. (1999). ERP and data warehousing. *Archer Decision Sciences*. Retrieved October 18, 2001 from the World Wide Web: www.archer-decision.com/artic11.htm.

Ross, J. W. (1999). *The ERP Revolution: Surviving versus Thriving*. Cambridge, MA: Centre for IS Research, Sloan School of Management, MIT.

Rutherford, E. (2001). ERP's ends justify its means. *CIO Online Quick Poll Report*. Retrieved July 18, 2001 from the World Wide Web: http://www.cio.com/poll/042401_erp.html.

Saint-Leger, G., & Savall, H. (2001). L'apres projet ERP: Retour d'experience sur un changement qui n'a pas eu lieu (Post-ERP phase: Feedback from experience regarding a change which did not occur). In *Conference de l'Association Information et Management*. Nantes, Italy.

Sammon, D., & Adam, F. (2000). Towards a model of ERP software selection — Widening the debate. In *Proceedings of the 10th Annual BIT Conference*, (November 1-2). Manchester, UK.

Sammon, D., & Adam, F. (2002). Decision making in the ERP community. In *Proceedings of the 10th European Conference on Information Systems*, (June). Gdansk, Poland.

Sammon, D., & Lawlor, D. (2001). An examination of an ERP software selection process: An Irish case study. In *Proceedings of the 11th Annual BIT Conference*, (October 30-31). Manchester, UK.

Shakir, M. (2000). Decision making in the evaluation, selection and implementation of ERP systems. In *Proceedings of the Sixth Americas Conference on Information Systems* (August 10-13, pp. 1033-1038). Long Beach, CA.

Shanks, G., Parre, E., Hu, B., Corbitt, B., Thanasankit, T., & Seddon, P. (2000). Differences in critical success factors in ERP systems implementations in Australia and China: A cultural analysis. In *Eighth European Conference on Information Systems*. Vienna, Austria.

Simon, H. (1977). *The New Science of Management Decisions*. Englewood Cliffs, NJ: Prentice Hall.

Sims, D. (2001). ERP integration strategies. *EA Community*. Retrieved October 15, 2001 from the World Wide Web: www.eacommunities.com/articles/art23.asp.

Somers, T., & Nelson, K. (2001). The impact of critical success factors across the stages of enterprise resource planning implementations. In *Proceedings of the 34th Hawaii International Conference on Systems Sciences* (January 3-6, pp. 1-10). Maui, Hawaii.

Stafyla, A., & Stefanou, C. (2000). ERP software selection: A study using cognitive maps. In *Seventh European Conference on Information Technology Evaluation ECITE (2000)*, (September). Dublin, Ireland.

Stefanou, C. (2000). The selection process of enterprise resource planning, ERP, systems. *Proceedings of the Sixth Americas Conference on Information Systems* (August 10-13, pp. 988-991). Long Beach, CA.

Sumner, M. (1999). Critical success factors in enterprise wide information management systems projects. In *Proceedings of the Fifth Americas*

Conference in Information Systems (AMCIS) (August 13-15, pp. 232-234). Milwaukee, WI.

Sumner, M. (2000). Risk factors in enterprise-wide/ERP projects. *Journal of Information Technology, 15,* 317-327.

Webster, F. (2000). Information, capitalism and uncertainty. *Information, Communication and Society, 3*(1), 69-90.

Westrup, C., & Knight, F. (2000). Consultants and enterprise resource planning (ERP) systems. In *Proceedings of the European Conference on Information Systems* (pp. 637-644). Vienna, Austria.

Wood, T., & Caldas, M. (2001). Reductionism and complex thinking during ERP implementations. *Business Process Management Journal, 7*(5), 387-393.

Wu, M.C., & Buchmann, A.P. (1997). Research issues in data warehousing. *Datenbanksysteme in Buro , Technik und Wissenschaft,* Berlin, Germany, 61-82.

Chapter XI

Toward a Model for Investigating Non-Decision Making in ERP Communities

David Sammon
University College Cork, Ireland

Frédéric Adam
University College Cork, Ireland

ABSTRACT

This chapter proposes to reframe current research on decision making process in the area of ERP selection and implementation and to study ERP communities, defined here as triadic groups composed of (1) an ERP vendor, (2) an ERP implementer and (3) an implementing organisation. In this novel perspective, the core contribution of this chapter is to introduce and apply the concept of Non-Decision Making (NDM) in its two basic forms—explicit and implicit—to the area of IS in general and more specifically to ERP research. As far as the authors are aware, this chapter is the first to examine the ERP decision making process under this light.

The researchers' objective is to structure their ideas in the shape of a model of ERP decision making, incorporating both the community dimension of ERP decision making and the ideas borrowed from the NDM literature, that can inform both the practice and investigation of ERP implementation and lead to higher success rates in ERP projects.

INTRODUCTION

Little attention has been devoted to NDM processes — the process of not deciding — even though it may be viewed as the prime mode of "response to crisis" of many human undertakings, as illustrated by many ongoing conflicts in the international community (Judge, 1997; Atlee, 2000). According to Judge (1997), parents make extensive use of NDM processes in persuading children to act, or not act, in particular ways, while sales personnel make use of these skills in dealing with customers or in handling product complaints — as do confidence tricksters. Physicians also use such skills in providing, or withholding, information to patients or their relatives; and couples use them in navigating their relationships. Atlee (2000) proposed five requirements for powerful NDM, for discovering "big obvious truths": diversity, passion, motivation, deep dialogue, and enough time. He stated: "Once the obvious truth has been found, there is no need for a decision. Such truth not only sets people free — it allows a group or community to self-organize."

In this chapter, we argue that *"midwifing the emergence of the obvious truth"* and the way that this can sometimes guide managerial decision making are key areas of research for understanding current developments in the off-the-shelf software market (e.g., the ERP market). In particular, this may be used to explain why some organizations are successful in deploying enterprise-wide solutions, and particularly Enterprise Resource Planning (ERP) systems. Thus, Donovan (2001) claimed that as many as nine out of 10 organizations do not get ERP right the first time around and experience the same kinds of difficulties that they faced with each new wave of IT since mainframe systems were first introduced (Markus & Tanis, 2000). Westrup and Knight (2000) made similar comments when they considered ERP systems in relation to previous approaches to deploying IS in organizations. Doyle and Adam (1996) described the slow and painful decision-making process followed by an organization trying to convince its parent company to let them invest significant funds in a much needed ERP, as the legacy systems of the company were slowly falling apart (see Chapter 3).

The malaise surrounding ERP seems to grow hand in hand with the astonishing escalation of its implementation market (Caldas & Wood, 1998). The observations made by many analysts lead us to believe that the ERP movement is one of the most sustained and long lasting in the IT area since companies began investing substantial amounts of money in package software. The pace of implementations has been such that SAP alone now have in excess of 19,000 customers in more than 120 countries, adding up to a user population of 12 million across 64,500 installations. Numerous reports on the state of the market for ERP packages are continuously published by research groups, speculating and forecasting on the future growth and adoption rates of ERP. However, it remains that the ERP project implementation failure rate is approximately 50% (Stefanou, 2000), along with an estimated 90% of ERP implementations failing to fulfill the promise of significant return on investment (Donovan, 1998). This highlights the fact that adopting organizations are not learning from, or are only paying "lip service" (Caldas & Wood, 1998) to the lessons learned, even during the MRP/MRPII era (Donovan, 1998). Furthermore, Donovan (2001) pointed out that organizations spent fortunes on ERP software and implementation only to discover that business performance did not improve. He, nevertheless, believes that ERP systems implementation disasters are avoidable. To receive benefit from implementing ERP, there must be no misunderstanding of what it is about, or underestimation of what is involved in implementing it effectively, and even more important, organizational decision makers must have the background and temperament for this type of decision making (Donovan, 2001).

This chapter offers an alternative perspective on the ERP phenomenon, illustrating the importance of the *ERP community* defined as a triadic group composed of an *ERP vendor*, an *ERP consultant*, and an implementing *organization*, sometimes further split between headquarters and a number of subsidiary organizations, and the need for research into the forms of decision making practiced by these actors, including the relationships and interdependencies that exist between them. The chapter proposes that decision making in the area of ERP is characterized by various forms of NDM and puts forward a model that illustrates the pervasiveness of NDM in ERP communities. The chapter concludes by tentatively validating this model in the light of previous empirical studies carried out in the ERP area and highlighting its usefulness in explaining observed patterns of managerial and corporate behavior in the ERP market.

ERP DECISION-MAKING AND
SOFTWARE SELECTION PROCESSES

Research was conducted to help gain a better understanding of the ERP decision-making process (Shakir, 2000) and to assist managers considering their ERP projects, by highlighting the critical issues involved in the selection process of ERP systems (Stefanou, 2000). However, there still remains an important managerial concern relating to the appropriateness of ERP software to meet an organization's needs. Paradoxically, even though the organization may not know what it is buying, there seems to be no alternative to the ERP trend (Caldas & Wood, 1998) sweeping across organizations at a "dizzy pace" (Donovan, 1998). Donovan (2001) further reiterated this point by stating that management all too often "plunge" into ERP less than fully informed, with limited knowledge of what to expect.

From a review of research on the subject of ERP software selection and the decision-making process associated, researchers commented on the confusing nature of many recorded instances of ERP decision making (Sammon & Adam, 2000; Sammon & Lawlor, 2001) and the presence of political decision making (Shakir, 2000; Sammon & Lawlor, 2001). This idea of confusion in organizational decision making is not new: March and Olsen (1976) talked of "reducing the confusion slightly" in their approach to organizational decision making. Furthermore, March (1987) and Adam (1996) pointed out that organizational decision processes and the resultant outcomes can appear difficult to understand and follow for an outside observer. Accountability for ERP software selection and implementation lies to varying degrees with organizational (internal) decision makers and external consultants (Donovan, 2001). All too often, ERP vendors are the easy targets for blame when anticipated benefits do not materializes; however, Donovan (2001) also highlighted that certain vendor practices add confusion to the software selection process, especially for the uninitiated. Therefore, can we as researchers be so naïve as to believe that the decision to select one ERP offering over another is subject to a totally rational and open-minded behavior on the part of the implementing organization?

Evaluating and selecting an ERP offering, although a complex process, should be a fact-based process that brings the organization to the point where comfortable, well-informed decisions can be made (Donovan, 2001). It was noticed that the preferences of managers are often vague and contradictory (March & Olsen, 1986), but in relation to ERP, it is not certain whether this is a result of poor ERP literacy on the part of the organization's decision makers or a direct result of the influential directions of both the ERP vendor and the ERP consultant. Carlton Collins (2000) stated that an implementing organization may save a great deal of time and money and arrive at a better decision by performing the needs analysis internally, however, the *system*, i.e., the ERP market, does not work that way. Caldas and Wood (1998) highlighted the existence of a central problem in relation to the decisions regarding the implementation of ERP systems. Caldas and Wood (1998) cited Lampel (1995) proposed that these decisions were made:

> ...[in an] atmosphere of great urgency, created by both the promotional strength of vendors, and the political agenda of executives within organisations. Options end up limited to the leading software vendors, on the one hand, and to the largest consulting firms, on the other. (p. 4)

This describes the *system* (Carlton Collins, 2000) that exists in relation to ERP software selection.

Software vendors often encourage organizations to jump right into looking at software functions and features because they want to move along quickly in the sales cycle and get an organization closer to licensing their products (Donovan, 2001). In an effort to facilitate this, ERP vendors sought to enter into partnerships with other firms to assist in ERP implementation (Westrup & Knight, 2000). According to Carlton Collins (2000), when a potential ERP implementing organization requires "independent assistance" in selecting an appropriate enterprise solution, the consulting company sends out a team of consultants, depending on the industry sector and consultant availability. However, 10 times out of 10, the ERP consultant will recommend the product they consult on, for example, SAP consultants will always recommend SAP and JD Edwards consultants, for the same consulting firm, will always recommend JD Edwards (Carlton Collins, 2000). Statistics reported by Caldas and Wood (1998) and Rutherford (2001) illustrate that more than 90% of companies use consultants throughout their implementation process. Accordingly, this highlights the frequency with which this type of vendor/consultant relationship (or collusion?) materializes. Furthermore, the "system" that Carlton Collins (2000) refers to can be illustrated as follows:

> *Often the vendors won't provide [the implementing organisation] with the information [they] need to properly evaluate the product and the high-priced consultants won't*

provide this information either without the "big-bucks".
Amazingly, some of the enterprise vendors have a built-in
incentive not to share this information, for example — in JD
Edwards' case, they pocket 15% of the consulting fees collected
by all of their approved JD Edwards consultants. (p. 1)

This approach can be seen as seeking to construct (and maintain) a network of actors, as illustrated in Figure 1, which can be controlled, at least in part, by the vendor (Westrup & Knight, 2000), while at the same time greatly enhancing their market reach.

Thus, regardless of which implementation approach is adopted, ERP implementation projects are always characterized by a set of relationships established between the implementing organization, the ERP vendor (or a local distributor of the software in question), and the ERP consultant. For the purpose of this chapter, we define these three entities and the relationships between them collectively as the *ERP community*. In some cases, the implementing organization is a multinational company with headquarters and a number of subsidiaries that may be instructed to implement ERP software packages by the parent company. This scenario is common and presents

Figure 1. Extended ERP Community Actors and Relationships/
Dependencies

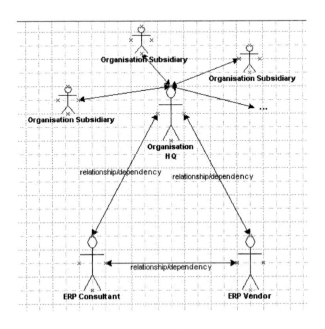

significant specificities that must also be addressed in our examination of ERP communities. The three entities that comprise our model of ERP community are the *de facto* actors that play a role on the ERP market. The implementing organization is dependent on the offerings of the ERP vendor and the ERP consultant within the ERP community, as we commented earlier. This may not be by choice of the implementing organization, but few, if any organizations can rely exclusively on internal resources to undertake an ERP implementation. Therefore, they are subject to the *system* (Carlton Collins, 2000) and the dependent actor in the ERP community. Markus and Tanis (2000) also believe that due to the all-encompassing nature of all ERP offerings, a level of dependence is created that "far surpasses the dependence associated with prior technological regimes" (p. 203). They further pose the following questions: "Does this dependence have negative effects on organizations?" "How do the effects manifest themselves?" "How do organizations cope?" and "What are the costs of picking the wrong vendor?" (pp. 203-204). However, they also question how adopting organizations "influence the strategic plans (behaviours) of vendors?" (p. 204). In the following sections of this chapter, we propose a way to address the issues raised by these questions by examining the relationships between the three core entities in the ERP community and proposing a model of ERP decision making based on currently accepted theories of managerial decision making (e.g., Mintzberg et al., 1976; Langley et al., 1995) and on the concept of NDM.

THE CONCEPT OF ERP COMMUNITY

To date, little attention has been focused on the influence of the ERP vendor and the ERP consultant over the organization implementing or deciding to implement ERP. When an organization adopts an ERP, there are obvious relationships forged between the implementing organization, the ERP consultant, and the ERP vendor. The ERP consultant may be introduced into the ERP project at an early stage, performing the role of a business analyst, or may be introduced as an implementation partner to the selected ERP vendor whose ERP offering is being implemented. According to Westrup and Knight (2000):

...the deployment of ERP systems takes place in a marketplace of ERP vendors generally mediated by ERP consultants. Their aims, though never publicly formulated, are to sell ERP systems and consultancy services respectively. (p. 641)

Ideally, all ERP projects should begin with a thorough examination of what problems exist and how to tackle them. However, too many ERP projects begin with a headlong rush to buy software without any preparation. Thus, it is our contention that the ERP vendor and the ERP consultant, through the direct and indirect relationships that exist between them and the implementing organization, actively demonstrate the techniques of what is termed *category manipulation* — the hidden art of NDM (Judge, 1997).

In the case of multinational organizations, it is also interesting to reflect on the relationship between the headquarters and the subsidiary or financial-dependent companies. In this scenario, it is typically the case that HQ would initiate the ERP project and impose a roll-out implementation of the software in all the sites within a timeframe of a few years. Based on our observations, this type of decision making can become extremely political, because there may be substantial objections to the choices made centrally, and some coercion may have to be used by managers in HQ. We visited sites where local managers admitted to having spent the last five years implementing three different ERP packages under instruction from three different owners. We were told of implementation schedules unilaterally decided upon centrally, and on a world-wide scale, and of implementation budgets that were so tight that it was obvious before the beginning of the ERP project that there would be a significant overrun (which was then borne by the local sites). We also heard of a small production unit with 50 staff members located on an island in the Caribbean being forced to implement a full version of the SAP software. It is difficult to view this type of implementation of ERP software as anything but misguided, but in fact, the standardization goal pursued by these multinationals is the dominant factor in the project, and these companies are willing to spend vast sums of money and tolerate high levels of disruption (not on their own doorstep) in order to achieve their targets. So strong is the wish to strengthen control on decentralized facilities and to standardize reporting practices across the board that the economic rationale one would expect to see for projects of such size and cost is largely ignored. This illustrates a fundamental clash between two schools of thought in the origins of ERP software: one route to ERP came from the engineering background of MRP/MRPII software and brought with it the idea that ERP is about optimizing operations and reducing costs; the other route to ERP came from financial consolidation systems and brought with it the idea that ERP packages are best viewed as instruments of control and standardization. These two visions are currently clashing at the core of ERP communities inside the organizations involved as well as in the relationships between them.

CRITICAL FACTORS IN
ERP DECISION MAKING

Decision making, as described in the previous section, where companies decide to adopt software in a manner that seems haphazard, not economically sound, and inefficient, indicates that our current thinking in relation to ERP decision-making scenarios may be incomplete. Caldas and Wood (1998) pointed out:

> *The benefit from the utilization of a broader (alternative) perspective to its (ERP implementation) comprehension, one that would challenge the reductionism and Information Technology biases that have characterised the prevailing approach to the subject. (p. 5)*

The proposed perspective, on the "phenomenon of ERP systems diffusion," arises from the confluence of three sets of factors: *substantive, institutional*, and *political*. All of these factors interact with each other, creating a complex dynamic process. And, they influence the *adoption*, the *implementation approach*, and the *assessment* of ERP systems in organizations (Caldas & Wood, 1998).

For the purpose of this study, we use the explanations provided by Caldas and Wood (1998) for each of the three factors (*substantive, institutional, and political*). These factors are closely connected and directly influence each other, as illustrated in Table 1.

One of the main arguments stated by Caldas and Wood (1998) is the following:

> *...the current reductionist discourse on ERP systems at the core of ERP communities concentrates solely on substantive factors, [even though] the ERP phenomenon can only be fully understood if it is also perceived in terms of the institutional and political factors which concur to define it, within and around the organization.*

Therefore, we pose the question: *How can such a complete understanding be achieved?* Then, we lay the foundations of the model that puts forward the issue of NDM within the ERP community as the key explanatory factor in ERP decision making.

Table 1. Substantive, Institutional, and Political Factor Influences

Substantive factors are generally influenced by contextual conditions, and they influence both *institutional* and *political* factors. On one hand, they generate the demand for solutions (production of innovations), activating institutional factors, and on the other, they provide the concrete arguments to validate internal justification (political factors) within organizations.
Institutional factors also influence political and substantive factors. Such influence occurs, first, because institutional factors provide legitimized vehicles to justify political factors, granting interest groups with a management technique they can take advantage of in their own benefit; and second, because institutional factors end up reinforcing most substantive factors, by giving them an image of particular urgency and relevance.
Political factors also influence substantive and institutional factors. They influence all substantive factors by giving them a sense of propriety and sufficiency, which was attributed to ERP by internal groups on their own behalf. They also reinforce institutional factors, by nurturing diffusion agents that will serve the purposes of power groups within the organization, and by reinforcing the idea of inevitability of the ERP adoption trend.

Source: Caldas & Wood (1998)

Concept of NDM — Application to ERP

We present the foundations of a model representing the two key aspects of NDM, both the clearly visible (which has been observed in a large number of cases of decision making in all areas of management and social communities), and the more-challenging and less visible aspects of NDM that are difficult to detect, comprehend, and communicate to others (Judge, 1997). The various forms of category manipulation, illustrated in Table 2, can be described and understood when applied to and analyzed in the context of the various relationships that exist between the implementing organization and the ERP vendor and the ERP consultant. The latter two actors in what we term the ERP community are the dominant actors in influencing the implementing organization's decision-making process through their practice of NDM processes. We believe that the accumulated evidence in the current ERP research illustrates that the various documented forms of NDM were already noted (though not identified as evidence of NDM) by many researchers, and this serves as initial validation for our model (until specific empirical data can be gathered to validate in a more formal sense).

Although each form of category manipulation must be examined in detail, there is prime facia evidence in research in the area of ERP software selection to support the hypothesis that this *art form* (Judge, 1997) not only exists, but is used as a vehicle for selling ERP. To illustrate these documented forms of category manipulation, we supply a small sample of references of other documented research illustrating the existence of NDM processes within the

Table 2. Descriptions of the Various Forms of Category Manipulation

Category Manipulation	Description
Definitional games	Whether deliberately or inadvertently, this is the process of defining categories in one way in one document or organizational unit, and then defining them in another way elsewhere or at some later time. The art is to use this approach to obscure opportunities or to selectively advance particular strategies. At the same time, competing definitions may be used to justify apparently incompatible strategies. In a sense, a new language is developed through which to perceive the environment. Typically, this process involves some degree of dissociation from conventional language.
Oversimplification	This technique is typical of those forcing through an agenda, where it is convenient to exclude categories and especially the relationships between them. This is commonly justified by the necessity to render the text simple enough to be communicable to the media and to various constituencies. Unfortunately, the process of simplification seldom ensures the memorability of the text and tends to guarantee limited life for initiatives based on such oversimplifications.
Overcomplexification	This technique is widely practiced by experts to limit access to their field of knowledge. It becomes a means of requiring that the expert be personally consulted in order to convey the insights in practice.
Narrowing the timeframe	This technique consists of elaborating initiatives without any reference to historical precedents from which insights might be usefully obtained to ensure the viability of the new initiative. By encouraging ignorance of the past, in pursuit of the current initiative, there is every probability that the new one will remain equally unmemorable. Similarly, by avoiding sensitivity to more than the short-term future, factors in the medium and longer term (that will probably counteract the initiative) can be ignored. Effective NDM can be achieved by benign positive focus on action in the immediate present.
Favoring the fashionable	At any one time, there are fashionable conceptual approaches to issues, and consultants "on the circuit" who enthusiastically promote their use. Institutions can be successfully panicked into exploring the latest intellectual fad for fear of offering a competitive advantage to their competitors through inaction. Because an approach is fashionable, "nobody gets fired" for adopting it. By encouraging institutions to take up a succession of particular fads, a broader view of the range of possible initiatives is inhibited. No sense of the strengths, limitations, and complementarities of the fads emerges.
Exertion of pressure	This is one of the most developed techniques. It can be effectively used in any peer group simply by implying that failure to act in a particular way will cast an unfavorable light, prejudicing career advancement, funding, honors, etc. ("the stick"). Pressure can be increased by offering rewards, career advancement, or promises of honors ("the carrot"). There is suspicion that attribution of a number of major prizes is occasionally affected by this process. Pressure can be further increased by unadulterated bribery and intimidation.

Source: Extracted from Judge (1997)

ERP community. This is illustrated in Table 3. In the next stages of this research project, we propose to include more supporting references in this table and to add our own empirical work to further support our ideas.

To date, no published research focused on the practice of NDM in the ERP community. Therefore, addressing the recommendations made by Caldas and Wood (1998), we propose the need for the examination of the interactions among the implementing organization, the ERP vendor, and the ERP consultant.

TOWARD A MODEL OF ERP DECISION MAKING

In creating our model, we propose to map the factors put forward by Caldas and Wood (1998) onto our model of the ERP community and to extend current thinking through the introduction of the concept of NDM, as illustrated in Figure 2.

The *political* factors (Caldas & Wood, 1998) "reflect the interests of power groups and coalitions inside the organisation. They relate to those organizational needs for which ERP systems do not pose direct solutions, but for which ERP systems are ideal means to obtain a solution, or yet its associated outcome." The most significant *political* factors are *"centralization interests," "standardization and concentration interests," "interest of power groups and coalitions,"* and *"IT departments quest to regain power"* (Caldas & Wood, 1998). If we examine the implementing organization and its

Table 3. The Existence of Category Manipulation in ERP Communities

Category Manipulation	Evidence in ERP Literature
Definitional games	Adam & O'Doherty, 2000a; Sammon et al., 2001a; Sammon & Adam, 2000; Saint-Leger & Savall, 2001
Oversimplification	Caldas & Wood, 1998; Sammon & Lawlor, 2001; Donovan, 2001
Overcomplexification	Markus & Tanis, 2000; Westrup & Knight, 2000; Carlton Collins, 2000
Narrowing the timeframe	Caldas & Wood, 1998; Markus & Tanis, 2000; Donovan, 2001
Favoring the fashionable	Caldas & Wood, 1998; Sammon & Adam, 2000; Sammon et al., 2001a
Exertion of pressure	Adam & O'Doherty, 2000b; Shakir, 2000; Sammon et al., 2001b; Sammon & Lawlor, 2001

subsidiaries (if it has any) and characterize this entity from the point of view of its actors' understanding of the organizational requirements to be fulfilled with the adoption of an ERP offering, it appears that while decisions are often political, rationales also appear weak and not well informed. The fact that resistance to change and failures are also commonplace illustrates the strong possibility of the existence of facets of a NDM process through the form of the *exertion of pressure*, for example. Thus, many SMEs end up implementing ERP for no other reason than because they are told to, and workers cope with ERP (not always very well based on our observations) because they are threatened rather than convinced.

The institutional factors, according to Caldas and Wood (1998), "comprise all external forces existing in the organizational environment, which

Figure 2. The Existence of NDM in an ERP Community

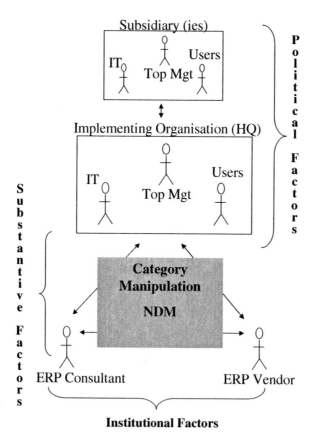

pressure the adoption of ERP systems," and the most significant institutional factors can be divided into *"interests of primary diffusion agents"* and *"interests of secondary diffusion agents"* (Caldas & Wood, 1998). For example, Caldas and Wood (1998) emphasized that the influence of the two types of diffusion agents "generates a strong isomorphic pressure, that pushes each organization to comply to institutionalized (i.e., socially legitimized) management practices." It is our contention that this influence is structured and imposed upon the implementing organization through executing the techniques of category manipulation and popularizing these forms of NDM within ERP communities. Thus, organizations may feel to be under strong pressure to become implementing organizations in order to meet certain expected standards of corporate behavior widely publicized by auditors, consultants, magazines, and peers working in other organizations who already invested large sums of money in ERP. The propagation of the ERP concept is, therefore, self-accelerating, as more managers become party to the process of social legitimization of ERP. This process, whereby managers' commitment to an idea increases radically once they are locked into their choices, was already observed and reported (Knox & Inkster, 1968).

According to Caldas and Wood (1998), the substantive factors "compromise all real imperatives, problems or opportunities that organizations face and for which ERP systems are an adequate and effective response." They are generally mentioned in vendor/consultant literature and include *drivers* and *enablers*. We propose that the substantive factors exist in what can be termed a *grey area*, and that gaining an understanding of these factors is complicated due to the existence and practice of category manipulation by both the ERP vendor and the ERP consultant, and by the dependent actor, the implementing organization, as illustrated in Figure 2. This makes it difficult for managers interested in ERP to gain an *a priori* understanding of what ERP packages are about and what potential they offer in the case of their organizations.

Therefore, to understand the relationships that exist within an ERP community and further understand the influences that these factors (substantive, institutional, and political) have on each other, we structure the relationships and influences within the model by projecting the various forms of category manipulation on the areas where they are most likely to be used. Therefore, the institutional factors (those that are circulated by the primary diffusion agents, namely, ERP vendors and consultants) influence and shape[2] the political factors (those that emerge in the implementing organization) by encouraging the emergence of the substantive factors (the accepted and publicized drivers and enablers of the ERP concept) using the forms of category manipulation already observed by Judge (1997) in international communities.

An example of this influence relationship can be taken from Carlton Collins (2000), where primary diffusion agents (institutional factors) pursue their commercial interest by practicing overcomplexification in their discussions with potential implementing organizations and in their day-to-day interactions with existing customers. Therefore, the drivers/enablers (substantive factors) for selecting one ERP offering over another, generating the demand for a solution, and providing arguments to validate internal justification, are designed by the primary diffusion agents and are presented to the implementing organization (political factors). However, as noted by Carlton Collins (2000):

> *Consultants will not recommend the product right away — they will first undergo a six month to 18 month evaluation of your needs in which they assemble committees, ask questions, and document various processes for a billing rate of approximately $365 per hour. The recommendation you receive is not delivered to you until $750,000 to $3,000,000 in fees have been churned in Work In Progress. And then they recommend the same solution that everybody knew — wink, wink — that they were going to deliver all along. (p. 1)*

This is an example of overcomplexification, introducing complexity into the selection process with the inclusion of possibly unnecessary actors (ERP consultants) and at enormous expense to the implementing organization.

ERP and the Paradigm Shift Toward Competitive Parity

The danger inherent in ERP implementations is illustrated in Figure 3, where a comparison between the perception of the organization's business requirements before and after the implementation of ERP is shown. It shows that the ERP package and the business activity of aspiring implementing firms are not aligned, and that the application of the business model underlying the package will necessarily result in a shift of priorities in the business away from current practices and toward a standardized way of doing business that may become pervasive in an industry if all players are equipped with the same package. It is usually necessary for an organization to redefine its business processes to fit the best practices built into the software (Bourdeau & Robey, 1999). This reiterates the argument presented by Sammon et al. (2001b):

It is difficult to see how an organization can derive any kind of sustainable advantage without a serious analysis of how the package bought will complement its unique assets or processes. Some degree of competitive parity is very likely to occur in many industries where the rate of ERP uptake is quite high.

Figure 3 also illustrates how the implementation of the ERP may lead to a loss of knowledge and processes for the organization, as requirements not catered for in the ERP packages are either accommodated by additional (costly) modifications or are discarded by the firm. Thus, the implementation of an ERP package may lead to the elimination of wasteful and inefficient resources and replacement by best practice processes. Alternatively, it may lead to the elimination of core competencies that distinguish a firm from its competitors. Thus, this indicates that organizations adopt ERP as a basis for a radical change rather than as a tool to protect and optimize their current competitive advantage (Sammon et al., 2001b). One area of the firm that was put forward as a potential victim of the "ERP steamroller" is procurement. Certain firms' procurement strategies rest on their ability to use multiple

Figure 3. Actual and Perceived Business Requirements Before and After Acquiring ERP

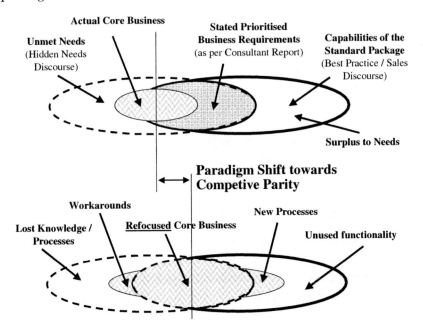

suppliers for some of their most-needed resources (and for those which costs fluctuate most substantially). This multiplicity of active contacts may be a firm's significant asset, if it leads to reduced materials costs. The implementation of ERP in the procurement function is likely to lead to a rationalization of the suppliers' accounts and purchasing patterns of the firm and the elimination of many "redundant" suppliers, the organization losing its ability to vary the origins of its supply in the process. In theory, the loss of such business advantages in ERP implementations is not a fatality and can be managed in the shape of a workaround (as shown in Figure 3). Our fear is that too many organizations do not analyze their needs prior to ERP implementations and rush into a sample implementation that flattens the very features that made the organization different. As highlighted by a survey conducted by Sammon et al. (2001b), organizations do not seem to be overly worried that they run the risk of sacrificing unique competitive advantage by implementing ERP packages, with 80% of managers not considering any alternative to an ERP package. Managers seem to be certain that acquiring and implementing a complete business solution and applying it to their companies is the main source of advantage in an ERP project.

CONCLUSION

In the face of a market where managers seek in ERP packages the solutions to a wide range of acute organizational problems — integration, standardization, reengineered business processes, or an aggressive search for competitive advantage — ERP vendors and ERP consultants must be wondering how to best market their products and services. This highlights the existence of the *sales* discourse and *selling the dream* as opposed to *selling the reality* (Carlton Collins, 2000). To our way of thinking though, the real benefits that can be obtained from enterprise-wide software (Davenport, 1998) will only come to those who perform a rigorous analysis of their needs and attempt to build upon the specificities of their companies with ERP functionalities, rather than merely apply a cookbook approach (Lee & Adams, 1990) to ERP implementations.

Currently, the ERP vendor and ERP consultant (Humphreys, 1998) have the power to "influence the nature of the planning which is accepted as the basis for the decision in such a way as to promote their own control over the choice" and thus get the decision implemented in the way they would wish. This reiterates the need highlighted by Southwick and Sawyer (1999) for an understanding of ERP implementation that accounts for the "subjective, interpretive mental processes of the managers' in *implementing organizations*—processes apparently constrained by diverse interests", those of the ERP vendor and ERP consultant. Therefore, the implementing organization needs to be empowered and made aware of the complexities of the ERP market and needs to internally assess, if not their readiness for ERP, their ability to manage the external parties (the ERP consultant and the ERP vendor) within the ERP community in which they are about to engulf themselves voluntarily.

Although it is clear that more research will be needed to fully validate and refine the framework proposed in this chapter, we believe that the explanations provided in the previous section illustrate the usefulness of the framework in explaining the key factors that frame managerial decision making on the ERP market. Decision making in this domain is often characterized by weak rationales, limited understanding of key concepts, and a high failure rate, and we think that the concepts that form the phenomenon described under the general heading of NDM will durably influence the investigation of the ERP movement.

In particular, an analysis of the ERP market based on the perspective of a network of actors with different interests, different techniques, and different modes of interaction will foster novel ideas for improved pre-ERP preparation and analysis, improved ERP selection processes, and easier and more successful implementations of ERP packages.

REFERENCES

Adam, F. (1996). Experimentation with Organization Analyser, a tool for the study of decision making networks in organizations. In P. Humphreys, L. Bannon, A. McCosh, P. Migliarese, & J. C. Pomeral (Eds.), *Implementing Systems for Supporting Management Decisions* (pp. 1-20). Boca Raton, FL: Chapman & Hall.

Adam, F., & O'Doherty, P. (2000a). Lessons from enterprise resource planning implementations in Ireland—Towards smaller and shorter ERP projects. *Journal of Information Technology, 15*(4), Special issue on ERP, 305-320.

Adam, F., & O'Doherty, P. (2000b). Do ERP implementations have to be lengthy? Lessons from Irish SMEs. Presented at *Conference de l'Association Information et Management*, (November). Montpelier, France.

Atlee, T. (2000). How to make a decision without making a decision. *Communities Magazine*, (Winter). Retrieved October 24, 2001 from the World Wide Web: www.co-intelligence.org/I-decisionmaking without.html.

Boudreau, M. -C., & Robey, D. (1999). Organizational transition to enterprise resource planning systems: Theoretical choices for process research. In *Proceedings of the 20th International Conference on Information Systems* (December 13-15, pp. 291-299). Charlotte, NC.

Burt, R. (1982). *Towards a Structural Theory of Action*. New York: Academic Press.

Burt, R., & Minor, M. (1983). *Applied Network Analysis: A Methodological Introduction*. Thousand Oaks, CA: Sage Publications.

Caldas, M., & Wood, T. (1998). *How consultants can help organizations survive the ERP frenzy*. Retrieved March 28, 2000 from the World Wide Web: http://www.gv.br/prof_alunos/thomaz/ingles/paper6.htm.

Carlton Collins, J. (2000). Opinion — Be wary of enterprise consultants. *Accounting Software News*. Retrieved December 13, 2001 from the World Wide Web: www.accountingsoftwarenews.com/charts/warning.htm.

Chang, S. -I., & Gable, G. (2001). A Delphi examination of public sector ERP lifecycle implementation, management and support issues. *Journal of Decision Systems*, *10*(1), 29-48.

Davenport, T. (1998). Putting the enterprise into the enterprise system. *Harvard Business Review*, (July/August), 121-131.

De, R. (2001). ERP is back with a bang. *Express Computer*, (October). Retrieved February 28, 2002 from the World Wide Web: http://209.61.143.1/credentialscenter1.htm.

Donovan, M. (1998). There is no magic in ERP software: It's in preparation of the process and people. *Midrange ERP*, (September, 8).

Donovan, M. (2001). *Successful ERP implementation the first time*. Retrieved July 25, 2001 from the World Wide Web: www.mdonovan.com/pdf/perfor8.pdf.

Estevez, J., & Pastor, J. (2001). Enterprise resources planning systems research: An annotated bibliography. *Communication of the Association for Information Systems*, *7*(8), 1-52.

Galaskiewicz, J., & Wasserman, S. (1994). *Advances in Social Network Analysis*. Thousand Oaks, CA: Sage Publications.

Hossain, L., & Shakir, M. (2001). Stakeholder involvement framework for understanding the decision making process of ERP selection in New Zealand. *Journal of Decision Systems, 10*(1), 11-27.

Humphreys, P. (1998). Discourses underpinning decision support. In D. Berkeley, G. Widmeyer, P. Brezillion, & V. Rajkovic (Eds.), *Context Sensitive Decision Support Systems* (pp. 1-23). Boca Raton, FL: Chapman & Hall.

Jones, T. C., & Dugdale, D. (2002). The ABC bandwagon and the juggernaut of modernity. *Accounting, Organizations and Society, 27*, 121-163.

Judge, A. (1997). *The art of non-decision making and the manipulation of categories.* Retrieved October 24, 2001 from the World Wide Web: www.uia.org/uiadocs/nondec.htm.

Knoke, D., & Kuklinski, J. (1982). *Network Analysis.* Thousand Oaks, CA: Sage Publications.

Knox, R. E., & Inkster, J. A. (1968). Post decision dissonance at post time. *Journal of Personality and Social Psychology, 8*, 319-323.

Lampel, J. (1995), as cited in Caldas, M. & Wood, T. (1998). How consultants can help organizations survive the ERP frenzy. Retrieved March 28, 2000 from the World Wide Web: http://www.gv.br/prof_alunos/thomaz/ingles/paper6.htm.

Langley, A., Mintzberg, H., Pitcher, P., Posada, E., & Saint-Macary, J. (1995). Opening up decision making: The view from the black stool. *Organization Science, 6*(3), 190-205.

Lee, M., & Adams, D. (1990). A manager's guide to the strategic potential of information systems. *Information and Management, 19*, 105-114.

March, J., & Olsen, J. (1976). *Ambiguity and Choice in Organizations.* Bergen, Norway: Universitetsforlaget.

March, J., & Olsen, J. (1986). Garbage can models of decision making in organizations. In J. March, & R. Weissinger-Baylon (Eds.), *Ambiguity and Command: Organizational Perspectives on Military Decision Making* (pp. 11-35). Cambridge, MA: Ballinger.

March, J. P. (1987). Ambiguity and accounting: The elusive link between information and decision making. *Accounting, Organizations and Society, 12*(2), 153-168.

Markus, M. L., & Tanis, C. (2000). *The Enterprise Systems Experience — From Adoption to Success.* Claremont, CA: Claremont Graduate University.

Mintzberg, H., Raisinghani, D., & Theoret, A. (1976). The structure of "unstructured" decision processes. *Administrative Science Quarterly*, *21*, 246-275.

Rebstock, M., & Sellig, J. (2000). Development and implementations strategies for international ERP software projects. Presented at the *Eighth European Conference on Information Systems*. Vienna, Austria.

Robson, W. (1997). *Strategic Management and Information Systems*. London: Pitman Publishing.

Rowe, F. (1999). Cohérence, intégration informationnelle et changement: Esquisse d'un programme de recherche à partir des Progiciels Intégrés de Gestion. *Systèmes d'Information et Management*, *4*(4), 3-20.

Rutherford, E. (2001). ERP's ends justify its means. *CIO Online Quick Poll Report*. Retrieved July 18, 2001 from the World Wide Web: http://www.cio.com/poll/042401_erp.html.

Saint-Leger, G., & Savall, H. (2001). L'apres projet ERP: Retour d'experience sur un changement qui n'a pas eu lieu (Post-ERP phase: Feedback from experience regarding a change which did not occur). Presented at the *Conference de l'Association Information et Management*. Nantes, Italy.

Sammon, D., & Adam, F. (2000). Towards a model of ERP software selection — Widening the debate. In *Proceedings of the 10th Annual BIT Conference*, (November 1-2). Manchester, UK.

Sammon, D., & Lawlor, D. (2001). An examination of an ERP software selection process: An Irish case study. In *Proceedings of the 11th Annual BIT Conference*, (October 30-31). Manchester, UK.

Sammon, D., Adam, F., & Elichirigoity, F. (2001a). ERP dreams and sound business rationale. Presented at the *AMCIS Conference*, (August). Boston, MA.

Sammon, D., Adam, F., & Higgins, K. (2001b). Preparing for ERP—Generic recipes will not be enough. In *Proceedings of the 11th Annual BIT Conference*, (October 30–31). Manchester, UK.

Shakir, M. (2000). Decision making in the evaluation, selection and implementation of ERP systems. In *Proceedings of the Sixth Americas Conference on Information Systems* (August 10-13, pp. 1033-1038). Long Beach, CA.

Shanks, G., Parre, E., Hu, B., Corbitt, B., Thanasankit, T., & Seddon, P. (2000). Differences in critical success factors in ERP systems implementations in Australia and China: A cultural analysis. Presented at the *Eighth European Conference on Information Systems*. Vienna, Austria.

Stefanou, C. (2000). The selection process of enterprise resource planning, ERP, systems. In *Proceedings of the Sixth Americas Conference on Information Systems* (August 10-13, pp. 988-991). Long Beach, CA.

Wasserman, S., & Faust, K. (1994). *Social Network Analysis: Methods and Applications*. Cambridge, UK: Cambridge University Press.

Westrup, C., & Knight, F. (2000). Consultants and enterprise resource planning (ERP) systems. In *Proceedings of the European Conference on Information Systems* (pp. 637-644). Vienna, Austria.

Chapter XII

Re-Examining the ERP Concept: Toward an Agenda for Reducing the Unbalance Between the Push and Pull Sides on the ERP Market

David Sammon
University College Cork, Ireland

Frédéric Adam
University College Cork, Ireland

ABSTRACT

In this chapter we use the concept of discourse to provide an insight into the current structure of the ERP market, from the perspective of an organisation adopting ERP. We propose that the ERP market is characterised by a subtle but pervasive conflict between two fundamental orientations: the arguments, methodologies and software products put forward by ERP vendors on the push side and the perceptions and goals of managers in the organisations implementing ERP on the pull side. We content that there is a mismatch between the rationale emphasised by the vendors and the goals pursued by managers and that the push side has been overly dominating the ERP agenda. This unbalance needs to be addressed, in part, through an analysis of the discourses that characterise the ERP Community. As far as the authors are aware, we are the first to approach the study of the ERP market from this perspective, attempting to facilitate the empowerment and enlightenment of the managers in charge of the organisations implementing these systems. This chapter reports on one element of a larger ongoing research study, the objective being to lay the foundations for a new research agenda in the area of ERP adoption.

INTRODUCTION TO A COMPLEX PHENOMENON

Although there is no agreed-upon definition for ERP systems, their characteristics position these systems as integrated, all-encompassing (Markus & Tanis, 2000), complex megapackages (Gable et al., 1997) designed to support the key functional areas of an organization. The American Production and Inventory Control Society (APICS) defined ERP as follows:

> *An accounting-oriented information system for identifying and planning the enterprise-wide resources needed to take, make, ship, and account for customer orders.*

Therefore, by definition, ERP is an operational-level system. Also, borrowing from the insights of Wood and Caldas (2001), ERP can be described as follows:

> *...a comprehensive Information Technology package built on the promise that all critical information should be totally integrated in one single information database. (p. 387)*

In examining the theoretical underpinning of the ERP concept, it is useful to go back to the first classification of systems and the most referenced framework for the implementation of management information systems, that of Gorry and Scott Morton (1971, 1989). In their seminal 1971 article, they developed a framework that has become the foundation for much of the research work in Decision Support Systems (Hamilton et al., 1982; Kirs et al., 1989). The framework allows an organization to gain a perspective on the field of information systems and focuses on understanding the "evolution of MIS activities within organizations," and recognizes some of the potential problems and benefits resulting from "new technology." This framework was criticized, most notably by Keen (1987) and Alter (1992), but it remains (Kirs et al., 1989) that "The Gorry and Scott Morton framework is perhaps the best known, most durable and most frequently cited in the IS field" (p. 184).

Gorry and Scott Morton (1971) report on their general observations about the different categories of management activity (strategic planning, management control, operational control) and also highlight differences in the information requirements to support these activities.

This suggests the reason why many organizations found it increasingly difficult to realize some of their long-range plans for information systems. Many of these plans are based on the "total systems approach." Some of the proponents of this approach advocate that systems throughout the organization be tightly linked, with the output of one becoming the direct input of another, and that the whole structure be built on the detailed data used for controlling operations. In doing so, they are suggesting an approach to systems design that is, at best, uneconomic and, at worst, based on a serious misconception. To say that management information systems activity must wait "until we get our operational control systems in hand," is to say that efforts to assist management with systems support will be deferred indefinitely.

On further examining the implications of the framework to system design differences, Gorry and Scott Morton (1971) noted that because the information requirements differ sharply among the three areas of managerial activity, there are "few occasions in which it makes sense to connect systems directly across boundaries." Therefore, as an implication of the decision classification (structured, semistructured, unstructured) of the framework, Gorry and Scott Morton (1971) stated the following:

> ...totally-integrated-management-information-systems ideas so popular in the literature are a poor design concept. More particularly, the integrated or company-wide database is a misleading 'notion,' and even if it could be achieved would be exorbitantly expensive.

However, this old notion is, in fact, a new reality for all organizations experiencing ERP systems implementations. An ERP system is built on an enterprise data model, and the ERP systems are expensive. Another old notion, which is, in fact, a further new reality, is that expressed by Dearden (1972), who stated:

> *The notion that a company can and ought to have an expert (or a group of experts) create for it a single, completely integrated supersystem — an MIS — to help it govern every aspect of its activity is absurd.*

Furthermore, if we consider the way in which ERP systems are introduced into organizations, we can observe, according to Westrup and Knight (2000):

> *...the deployment of ERP systems takes place in a marketplace of ERP vendors generally mediated by ERP consultants. Their aims, though never publicly formulated, are to sell ERP systems and consultancy services respectively. (p. 641)*

Overall, despite the strong push toward ERP in the wider organizational community, there is, in relation to ERP implementations, a lack of understanding of the difficulties that can arise when the business models used by organizations clash with the business models underlying the ERP packages implemented by these organizations. There seems to be a subtle but profound danger that the logic of the software package supplants the organizing logic of the corporation as a whole. There is also significant evidence that the disruptions to everyday business while ERP systems are implemented are putting undue pressure on organizations, regardless of their sizes and financial means.

Thus, Wood and Caldas (2001) commented that, in practice, the reality of ERP implementation for many organizations implementing this type of software is one in which "a golden dream has turned into a nightmare." The important question, of course, is where did this golden dream come from? The answer, as we see it when talking to managers in organizations where ERP is being implemented or debated, is that it comes from business media, software vendors, consulting firms, academics, and their collective discourses. This highlights the existence of the sales discourse, on the push side of the ERP market, which *sells the dream* as opposed to *selling the reality* (Carlton Collins, 2000). Facing this overpowering push, we contend that the pull side of the ERP market has not developed, which puts organizations at risk of spending large resources to acquire applications that do not truly serve their needs.

To date, researchers looked at the ERP market as the place where organizational needs, in terms of integrated enterprise-wide systems, were met by the packages proposed by ERP vendors. We contend that the ERP market is characterized by a strong vendor and consultant push, whereby organizations appear to have little choice but to jump on the bandwagon. In previous chapters, we proposed the concept of the ERP community (see Figure 1) as a research model more likely to allow research to account for the complex network of influence in which organizations find themselves when purchasing ERP packages.

The ERP community is defined as a triadic group composed of an implementing organization, an ERP vendor, and an ERP consultant. These three actors are the de facto participants in the ERP community. The implementing organization is dependent on the offerings of the ERP vendor and the services of the ERP consultant within the ERP community. In particular, the overriding arguments put forward by the ERP vendor and the ERP consultant, that ERP systems represent best practice, proved extremely difficult to avoid for many managers, who find themselves foolish to object to introducing packages that come so highly recommended, especially when their head offices

Figure 1. ERP Community Actors and Relationships

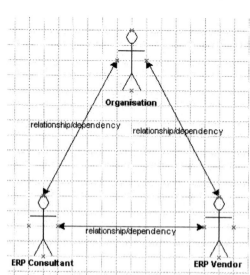

make the recommendations. Thus, the ERP market is characterized by a complex network of influence, both internal and external to organizations, targeted mostly at managers. As argued by the proponents of the network perspective to organizational analysis, (e.g., Knoke & Kuklinski, 1982), individuals and organizations are equally characterized by their specific attributes (which are commonly selected as objects of study) and by their relationships with one another. This observation clearly applies to organizations in the ERP market, and we argue that it is now impossible to study the ERP phenomenon at the level of a single organization, implementing or having implemented ERP, in isolation from its relationship with other actors in the ERP community.

UNDERSTANDING THE
DIMENSIONS OF DISCOURSE

The terms *discourse* and *discourse theory* have become common currency in a variety of disciplines and play an increasing significant role in many branches of the human and social sciences (Howarth, 2000; Mills, 1997; Van Dijk, 1997), so much so that it is frequently left undefined, as if its usage were simply common knowledge (Mills, 1997). In our efforts to understand the concept of discourse for the purpose of this study, we incorporate the three main dimensions of the concept, as identified by Van Dijk (1997) (illustrated in Table 1).

Van Dijk (1997) proposed that it is useful to include *written* along with *spoken* dimensions in the concept of discourse. Furthermore, Van Dijk (1997) emphasized that in theory, the study of discourse "should deal both with the properties of *text* and *talk* and with what is usually called the *context*, that is, the other characteristics of the social situation or the communicative event that may systematically influence *text* or *talk*" (p. 3). This is particularly useful in considering the sources and the situations where arguments for ERP implementations may originate and the pressures on managers to comply. Instructions from auditors and corporate headquarters and coordinated vendor/consultant briefings may be viewed in such a light.

Although there was widespread deployment of the concept of discourse in the human and social sciences, there is some "scepticism about the precise epistemological status and methodological suitability of discourse theory in the social sciences" (Howarth, 2000, p. 2). However, the lack of "purely algorith-

Table 1. Three Dimensions of Discourse

Dimension of Discourse	Description	Application to the ERP Market
Language use	Spoken or written	Media articles and reports, vendors and consultants documentation
Communication	Embodies some of the functional aspects of discourse in that people use language in order to communicate ideas or beliefs (cognition or to express emotions), and they do so as part of more complex social events	Seminars on IT deployment and management; technical briefings
Interaction	Whatever else may happen in sometimes complex communicative events (social situations), participants are doing something, that is, something else beyond just using language or communicating ideas or beliefs: they interact	Meetings with colleagues and consultants in various settings; informal communication in front of the water dispenser and other chance meetings

mic" methods and procedures of social science investigation for discourse theory "does not mean, however, that discourse theory promotes a kind of 'methodological anarchism' or 'epistemological irrationalism'" (Howarth, 2000), and researchers must show how the concepts attached to discourse analysis can be "operationalized" in meaningful ways for the purpose of their own studies. Howarth (2000) concluded that "the ultimate criterion for judging the adequacy of the discourse approach as a whole is pragmatic; it can be evaluated by the degree to which it makes possible new and meaningful interpretations of social and political phenomena it investigates. Our empirical observations of the ERP market indicate that it is an arena characterized by such complex influences that analyzing discourse is meaningful.

Furthermore, Howarth (2000) observed that discourse theory:

> *...does seek to provide novel interpretations of events and practices by elucidating their meaning (...) by analysing the way in which political forces and social actors construct meanings within incomplete and undecidable social structures [and] the particular structures within which social agents take decisions and articulate hegemonic projects and discursive formations.*

Based on this theory, we conclude that discourse theory is particularly suited and useful to our examination of how the ERP community operates, in that actors are engaged in the creation of complex discourses, as illustrated in Figure 1. Analyzing the ERP market/phenomenon as a network of actors with different interests, different techniques, and different modes of interaction, will foster novel ideas for improved pre-ERP preparation and analysis, and improved ERP selection processes. A reduction of what we perceive as an excessive dominance of the push side of the ERP market may result from a better understanding of the hidden influences it includes and from a strengthening of the client's needs and wants and the mechanisms whereby these are expressed (the pull side), either at a general market level or at the level of specific negotiations between vendors/consultants and their clients.

UNDERSTANDING THE DISCURSIVE ELEMENTS OF THE ERP COMMUNITY

Thus, a discursive perspective on the ERP market, focusing on both the actions of actors involved and the relationships between them, may enable researchers to transcend the problems identified by previous researchers of organizational decision making. These problems are that some organizational processes sometimes appear to be without order (March & Olsen, 1986), and that the preferences of managers are often vague and contradictory, even when there is agreement on the overall objectives of the firm (March, 1987) — for instance, let's acquire an ERP package, but let's not include manufacturing and sales, because we are doing things our own way (Saint-Leger & Savall, 2001).

While undertaking research in the area of ERP and in particular the decision-making process associated with selection and implementation, we observed that it would be naïve to think that a "holistic decision making" (Larichev, 1984) approach can be undertaken by managers involved in ERP software decisions. In the holistic decision-making situation (Humphreys, 1998), "there is little *discourse* underpinning the action (apart from internalised discourse) as there is no need to discuss with others in planning the decision, making the choice, or implementing the decision." As a result, we observe that with the introduction of ERP into an organization, the organizational decision makers often lack (Humphreys, 1998) the "expertise of information for exploring, estimating and constructing potential solutions in planning the decision." As a result, other (mostly external) participants occupy key subject

positions (Humphreys, 1998) in the decision-making process and the implementation of its prescriptions. With the introduction of external participants
occupying these subject positions in decision-making situations come interactions and communication that can be said to constitute the *discourse of
participants* (Humphreys, 1998). When combined with discourse analysis,
the concept of the ERP community is a good vehicle with which to focus on the
arguments employed in guiding the decision-making processes of managers by
those parties who participate in the making and implementing of decisions,
considering the decision-making process as a whole, as proposed by Humphreys
(1998). Our use of discourses follows that of Humphreys (1998), where we
"identify the kind of discourse employed in negotiating and constructing
decision problem representations." Furthermore, within the context of the ERP
community, the *discourse of truth* will be interpreted and structured differently
by each actor based on their subject positions and motivations in the decision-
making process, as illustrated in Table 2.

Over time, a variety of management and IT methodologies and associated
discourse emerged, and their rise and fall seem to follow the model of fads and
fashion (Humphreys, 1998). Management fads tend to generate cycles of
"management panaceas" (Caldas & Wood, 1998), and ERP can be perceived
as a successor of other universal remedies, such as TQM, downsizing, and
business reengineering (Caldas & Wood, 1998). Humphreys (1998) stated
that the "principal value that the fads offer to organizational decision makers is
the provision of *'expert discourse'* as a (fashionable) discourse of truth which
increases their own power and prestige in their organization." This is also
reminiscent of Feldman and March's (1981) ideas on the use of information as
signal and symbol, where they describe managers as collecting data or adopting
the arguments of dominant coalitions as insurance against being wrong at a later
stage and to be seen as good managers. Furthermore, Kieser (1997) pointed
out:

Table 2. ERP Community Discourse

Actor/Subject Position	Actor Position	Discourse	Strength of Discourse
Implementing organization	Dependent	Needs	Weak
ERP vendor	Dominant	Sales	Strong
ERP consultant	Independent	Expert/sales*	Very strong

* When consultant works exclusively with one software vendor.

...a management fashion is conceptualised as forming an arena in which different groups of participants bustle about....The participants can achieve their individual goals of highest possible profit, public image, power or career by widening the arena through luring further participants into it. For this purpose they play principally co-operative games. Rhetoric is the main input currency in this game. (p. 57)

Within the ERP community, the implementing organization and the organizational decision makers, are "clients of the *consultants*" (Humphreys, 1998), who introduce a variety of *"expert discourses"* (Humphreys, 1998; Wood & Caldas, 2001). According to Humphreys (1998), these expert discourses were introduced with the emergence of the structural approach to management theory. Humphreys (1998) cited Eccles et al. (1992), and stated:

...managers are eager to accept these [expert discourses] to incorporate the rhetoric of management fads and fashions in their own discourse and use such labels and concepts as they see fit as part of their ongoing use of language to coax, inspire, demand or, otherwise produce action in their organizations. (p. 10)

Toward a New Agenda for Research on ERP

In the face of a market where managers seek in ERP packages solutions to a wide range of acute organizational problems, such as integration, standardization, reengineered business processes, or an aggressive search for competitive advantage, ERP vendors must be wondering how to best market their products. This type of research must take place so that ERP packages stay at the leading edge of managerial thinking and technological development. However, Sammon et al. (2001) proposed that, from the point of view of managers in client organizations:

The dialogue in relation to ERP must take place at a fundamentally different level, more concerned with the philosophical implications of the concept of ERP and less concerned with the benefits in principle of ERP packages. Also, the ERP market is not well served by the futuristic marketing visions put forward by vendors and far remote from the reality of what ERP systems are being used for in organizations.

To conclude, we regret that, within the ERP community, the selection and implementation of an ERP are ultimately outsourced to the ERP consultant and the ERP vendor, by nature partisans and actors of the push side, rather than prepared and planned from the pull side. The implementing organization is pressured to conform to the decision-making processes and discourses designed and managed by the external parties (the ERP consultant and the ERP vendor). These external parties are recognized as being the experts in the area and, as a result, are used by the implementing organization. However, the discourses of these external parties emerge through understanding their ultimate importance and necessity for the selection and implementation of an ERP. As a result, they have the power to "influence the nature of the planning which is accepted as the basis for the decision in such a way as to promote their own control over the choice" and thus get the decision implemented in the way they would wish (Humphreys, 1998).

Therefore, it seems that there is an inherent danger in the way ERP packages are currently being adopted by organizations. As ERPs are being introduced, the specific needs of these organizations and the special features and assets that make them different may be lost or eroded in a way that is not controlled or understood by managers, as proposed by Sammon and Adam (2002). We illustrate this reality in Figure 2, where we use Robson's (1997) map of discrepancies resulting from the purchase of off-the-shelf (OTS) IS to represent what happens in the context of ERP. It shows how the needs discourse, *de facto*, needs to be flexible to meet a match on the ERP market, sometimes to the detriment of the firm.

Thus, implementing organizations need to be empowered and made aware of the complexities of the ERP market and need to internally assess whether ERP is right for them and what they seek through the implementation of such costly solutions. They also need to analyze, if not their readiness for ERP, at least their ability to manage the external parties (the ERP consultant and the ERP vendor) within the ERP community in which they are about to engulf themselves voluntarily. This requires that they adopt a more personal approach to ERP and, by doing so, strengthen the voice of their discourse within the community.

When this extra awareness is gained and shared among managers, the concerted needs discourse will gain added power and may enable organiza-

Figure 2. The ERP Market "Discourse Gap"

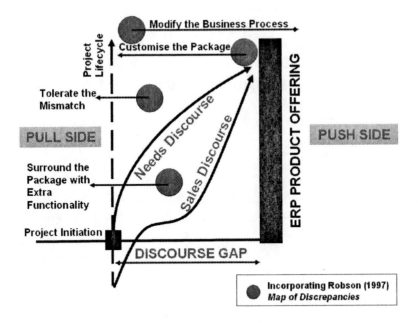

tions to dictate the ERP agenda to a much greater extent, thereby reducing their dependency on vendors and consultants and fostering the development of more flexible packages for a better fit to their own needs. The development of an ERP solution in the Application Service Provider (ASP) market may go some way toward a greater attention to the specific needs of certain categories of organizations (e.g., SMEs or public-sector companies). In the meantime, such evolution of the ERP market will require a greater understanding of the notion of "fit" (which in the perspective of the zero modification currently ruling the ERP market, means that the organization adapts its needs to fit an existing software product, never that the vendor changes its design to fit the specific needs of one organization). It will also require a different set of relationships between actors in the ERP community, both at a global level and at the level of individual firms in their negotiations with their vendors. When this is achieved, the pull and push sides of the ERP market may become more balanced, and the situation in Figure 2 may become one where the sales discourse becomes as flexible as the needs discourse has had to be. Academic research, because it is independent and bias-free (at least it should be), has a crucial role to play in this evolution.

REFERENCES

Alter, S. (1992). Why persist with DSS when the real issue is improving decision making? In Jelassi (Ed.), *Decision Support Systems: Experiences and Expectations*. New York: North Holland.

Caldas, M., & Wood, T. (1998). *How consultants can help organizations survive the ERP frenzy*. Retrieved March 28, 2000 from the World Wide Web: http://www.gv.br/prof_alunos/thomaz/ingles/paper6.htm.

Carlton Collins, J. (2000). Opinion — Be wary of enterprise consultants. *Accounting Software News*. Retrieved December 13, 2001 from the World Wide Web: www.accountingsoftwarenews.com/charts/warning.htm.

Dearden (1972), as cited in Markus, M. L., & Tanis, C. (2000). The enterprise systems experience — From adoption to success. In R. W. Zmud (Ed.), *Framing the Domains of IT Management: Projecting the Future Through the Past*. Retrieved October 9, 2001 from the World Wide Web: Pinnaflex.com.

Eccles, R., Nohria, N., & Berkley, J. D. (1992). *Beyond the Hype: Rediscovering the Essence of Management*. Boston, MA: Harvard Business School Press.

Feldman M., & March J. (1981). Information in organizations as signal and symbol. *Administrative Science Quarterly*, *26*, 171-186.

Gable, G., van den Heever, R., Scott, J., & Erlank, S. (1997). Large packaged software: The need for research. In *Proceedings of the Third Pacific Asia Conference on Information Systems (PACIS)*.

Gorry, A., & Scott Morton, M. (1989). Retrospective commentary on the Gorry and Scott Morton framework. *Harvard Business Review*, (Spring), 58-60.

Gorry, G. A., & Scott Morton, M. S. (1971). A framework for management information systems. *Sloan Management Review*, (Fall).

Hamilton, S., & Ives, B. (1982). Knowledge utilization amongst IS researchers. *MIS Quarterly*, (December), 61-77.

Howarth, D. (2000). *Discourse*. London: Open University Press.

Humphreys, P. (1998). Discourses underpinning decision support. In D. Berkeley, G. Widmeyer, P. Brezillion, & V. Rajkovic (Eds.), *Context Sensitive Decision Support Systems* (pp. 1-23). Boca Raton, FL: Chapman & Hall.

Keen, P. (1987). Decision support systems: The next decade. *Decision Support Systems*, *3*, 253-265.

Kieser, A. (1997). Rhetoric and myth in management fashion. *Organization*, *4*, 49-74.

Kirs, P. J., Sanders, G. L., Cerveny, R., & Robey, P. (1989). An experimentation of the Gorry and Scott Morton framework. *Management Information Systems Quarterly*, *13*, 183-197.

Knoke, D., & Kuklinski, J. (1982). *Network Analysis*. Thousand Oaks, CA: Sage Publications.

Larichev, O. I. (1984). Psychological validation of decision methods. *Journal of Applied Systems Analysis*, *11*, 37-46.

March, J., & Olsen, J. (1986). Garbage can models of decision making in organizations. In J. March, & R. Weissinger-Baylon (Eds.), *Ambiguity and Command: Organizational Perspectives on Military Decision Making* (pp. 11-35). Cambridge, MA: Ballinger.

March, J. P. (1987). Ambiguity and accounting: The elusive link between information and decision making. *Accounting, Organizations and Society*, *12*(2), 153-168.

Markus, M. L., & Tanis, C. (2000). The enterprise systems experience — From adoption to success. In R. W. Zmud (Ed.), *Framing the Domains of IT Management: Projecting the Future Through the Past*. Retrieved October 9, 2001 from the World Wide Web: Pinnaflex.com.

Mills, S. (1997). *Discourse*. London: Routledge.

Robson, W. (1997). *Strategic Management and Information Systems*. London: Pitman Publishing.

Saint-Leger, G., & Savall, H. (2001). L'apres projet ERP: Retour d'experience sur un changement qui n'a pas eu lieu (Post-ERP phase: Feedback from experience regarding a change which did not occur). Presented at the *Conference de l'Association Information et Management*. Nantes, Italy.

Sammon, D., & Adam, F. (2002). Needs discourse and sales discourse in the ERP market. In *Proceedings of the 12th Annual BIT Conference*, (November). Manchester, UK.

Sammon, D., Adam, F., & Elichirigoity, F. (2001). ERP dreams and sound business rationale. Presented at the *AMCIS Conference*, (August). Boston, MA.

Van Dijk, T. A. (1997). The study of discourse. In T. A. Van Dijk (Ed.), *Discourse as Structure and Process*. Thousand Oaks, CA: Sage.

Westrup, C., & Knight, F. (2000). Consultants and ERP systems. In *Proceedings of the Eighth European Conference on Information Systems* (pp. 637-644). Vienna, Austria.

Wood, T., & Caldas, M. (2001). Reductionism and complex thinking during ERP implementations. *Business Process Management Journal, 7*(5), 387-393.

Chapter XIII

From ERP Systems to Enterprise Portals

Sven A. Carlsson
Lund University, Sweden

Jonas Hedman
Lund University, Sweden

ABSTRACT

This chapter describes the development of Enterprise Resource Planning (ERP) systems toward Enterprise Portals (EPs). Enterprise Portals aim at creating a single entry point for its users to all internal and external applications, information, and services necessary for performing their jobs. EPs can be personalized to users depending on the roles they perform. There is a growing interest in EPs, but EP-research is scarce. Using a content analysis, we evaluate one specific EP—SAP AG's Enterprise Portal my SAP Workplace. The evaluation had an overall effectiveness approach. The evaluation suggests some of the strengths of current EPs, for example, their internal and control focuses, and some of their weaknesses, for example, lack of external focus and lack of support for top-managers.

INTRODUCTION

The purpose of this chapter is fourfold. First, to present and discuss some of the developments and changes of Enterprise Resource Planning (ERP) systems and the development of Enterprise Portals (EPs). Second, to present EPs and exemplify with a leading EP product: mySAP Enterprise Portals from SAP Portals.[1] Third, to evaluate SAP's EP solution using a content analysis. Fourth, based on the evaluation, discuss the future of EPs.

ERP systems, such as SAP R/3, Oracle Applications, PeopleSoft, and Movex, were criticized for being costly, being difficult to implement and change, being overly rigid and hierarchical, and using antiquated technology (Markus & Tanis, 2000; Davenport, 2000). There is a body of literature related to ERP systems addressing technical, organizational, strategic, economic, educational, evaluation, and implementation issues (Markus & Tanis, 2000; Ross & Vitale, 2000; Davenport, 2000; Shanks et al., 2002; O'Leary, 2000; Holland & Light, 1999) and product specific implementation issues (Curran & Ladd, 2000; Bancroft et al., 1998). In addition, there is also empirical research on different aspects of ERP development, implementation, use, and impact (Kalling, 1999; Adam & O'Doherty, 2000; Davenport, 2000; Shanks et al., 2002), which have applied different theoretical frameworks to analyze the ERP systems phenomenon.[2] The ERP literature suggests and shows that implementation and use of ERP systems is problematic and can lead to a number of drawbacks, for example:

- High and increased costs for running business information applications
- Difficult and time-consuming implementations
- Need for enterprise process reengineering due to standardized "best practice" processes embedded in the ERP systems — the "one-size-fits-all" fallacy
- Difficult and costly to fulfill specific requirements due to inflexibility in ERP systems
- Need for large allocation of internal resources (e.g., money, personnel, and time)
- Technical problems due to lack of technical skills and support by the ERP system vendors
- Cultural clashes due to that ERP systems force organizations to standardize business processes across intra- and interorganizational boundaries and that ERP systems require organizations to use unequivocal data definitions

- Monolithic and closed systems made it hard to transfer data and to integrate an ERP system with other systems and businesses
- Centralization of control and shifts in power structures
- Making organizations less flexible
- Long-term dependency on ERP vendors and consultancies

One explanation for "failures" and drawbacks is that many organizations did not choose ERP systems primarily as solutions to business problems. In the 1990s, ERP systems were, in many cases, chosen because they solved the Y2K problem. Another explanation for failures, even if the system is the "right" solution to business problems, is that ERP systems are extremely complex information systems and are, thereby, difficult to implement and use. At the same time, it should be recognized that ERP systems also benefited organizations, in both tangible and intangible ways, and made organizations more efficient, effective, and competitive. Much of these benefits were not predicted when organizations decided to implement the systems. ERP systems created an infrastructure useful for organizations when they grow or make changes. Implementations of ERP systems created common data definitions leading to higher transparencies and standardized business processes, leading to more effective and efficient business processes. The systems also made it possible for organizations to deploy new information and communication technologies (ICTs) faster and in a more flexible way. Many of the problems and benefits from ERP systems stem from the fact that they are internally oriented systems with rigid structures.

In order to overcome some of the problems with ERP systems, e.g., internal-oriented and monolithic, a growing number of organizations are turning to EPs. EPs are introduced and sold, by the vendors, as the next generation of business technology and a new type of information systems solution. The technology is marked as a solution to many ERP-related problems, yet it keeps and continuously builds on the strong parts of previous business technology. An EP is designed as a single access point to an organization's external and internal ICTs. The EP makes it possible for a user, e.g., a sales manager, to access internal and external applications and information needed through a single access and authorization point. The idea is to provide employees, business partners, customers, suppliers, and other stakeholders with one suitable info-media (Delphi Group, 2001). EPs are one technical solution to new business requirements, e.g., business process reengineering, customer relationship and Supply Chain Management efforts, electronic commerce, B2B trading, global presence, and "one-face-to-the-customer," as well as the result of technological development, from mainframe to client-server, and Web services. Although there is a growing commercial interest in EPs, there is a lack of research on EPs.

The remainder of this chapter is organized as follows: the following section presents and discusses some recent ERP systems developments; then, we present EPs. This is followed by an evaluation of SAP's EP. The final section presents conclusions, suggests further research, and discusses future EP developments.

FROM ENTERPRISE RESOURCE PLANNING SYSTEMS TO ENTERPRISE PORTALS

The development of corporate information systems, like ERPs, went through a number of developments and changes, technological as well as functional. Regarding technology, we can identify at least three major techno-logical "paradigms": mainframe computing, client-server technology, and Web technology. Each technology provided solutions to some time-specific prob-lems and requirements. As time goes by, new problems and demands arise, and new solutions are developed, or vice versa, i.e., new solutions are offered to meet emerging problems. At the same time, the applications or functionality of corporate information systems evolved. Initially, all applications were internally oriented, such as accounting, production planning, and payroll. Today, many applications include functionalities supporting collaboration and cooperation between organizations.

We illustrate the evolution of corporate information systems using the largest ERP firm's different architectural platforms — the firm is SAP AG. The main reasons for choosing SAP were that their systems are well-documented in research and trade literature, a lot of material related to SAP is publicly available, and SAP has consistently developed its products to compete with emerging products in new and "hot" areas, like supply chain, e-business, customer relationship, and data warehouse.

Mainframe Computing and Client-Server Architectures

SAP was one of the first ERP vendors to recognize that "true" integrated client–server technologies were likely to replace the historical mainframe and unintegrated stand-alone client-server architectures. The strength of mainframe computing — housing all memory, storage, and information-processing capac-ity — comes from its reliability and information-processing power, i.e., strength in transactional processing. A problem with old mainframe computing was that it was inflexible, e.g., hard-wired to dumb terminals. Mainframe systems are monolithic—indivisible into components—and closed and incompatible with products from other IT vendors. The unintegrated client-server solutions organizations did not turn out to be the "silver bullet." Unintegrated client-server solutions were prone to degenerate into an incoherent collection of disparate subsystems for different organizational functions or hierarchical levels. Not only are these inefficient from an organizational information-processing perspective, they are also expensive and difficult to administer and maintain.

With the release of the first three-tier client–server-based ERP system (R/3 system), in 1992, SAP set the standard for corporate information systems. Two main ideas were implemented through this solution: modular systems and open standards. The ideas addressed the monolithic and closed issues of mainframe computing and some of the problems with unintegrated client–server solutions, while keeping the strength of mainframe computing. The introduction of R/3 was at the hype of business process reengineering (Davenport & Short, 1990; Hamer & Champy, 1992), and the focus of the first integrated ERP systems was to integrate organizations internally through their information flows and business processes. However, many configurations[3] and implementation issues and problems remained after the first client-server ERP generation. In 1995, SAP released R/3 version 3.0, with features intended to make the system and its data more accessible for other R/3 systems and third-party software products. The extensions included the following:

- ALE (Application Link Enabling), which is a messaging technology that allows coupling of physically separate R/3 systems and information transfer between R/3 and other applications
- Business Objects, which are representations of R/3 transactions, events, and information in object-oriented programming terms; definition of these objects allowed for the possibility of communicating with these objects using object-oriented techniques
- BAPIs (business application programming interfaces), which are pre-defined methods by which other applications can communicate with R/3's business objects

These extensions made the system more flexible in a technical sense, but most of the previous organizational implementation problems remained.

Web-Enabled and Portal Technologies

Client-server technology and the new extensions made R/3 more open and less monolithic. This trend continued, and in version 3.1, released in 1996, other features made R/3 open to the Internet. The new features included: Internet Transaction Server (ITS); JAVA-based GUI (Graphical User Interface); Remote Function Calls (RFC), permitting the call of application functions from other computers and screen interface protocols; and new communication interfaces based on other technologies, such as HTTP, JAVA, COM/DCOM, CORBA, and IDOC (SAP's proprietary EDI standard). These features and enhancements solved many of the technological problems as well as met new business demands. They were used to extend and develop SAP's offerings, making R/3 a Web-enabled ERP system. From a technological point of view, this was achieved by adding a tier to allow browser access to the system. SAP also enhanced its offerings by releasing complementary products, such as Business Information Warehouse, Advanced Planning Optimizer, Strategic Enterprise Management, and linking back-end and front-end organizational processes by integrating the system with Supply Chain Systems and Customer Relationship Management Systems. These products were marked and sold under the concept of mySAP.com. Furthermore, the human resource module was packaged as a separate product and could be installed as a stand-alone application. The aim of these new technologies was to enhance and enable cooperation among business parties along extended value chains.

The next generation of SAP's ERP system, R/3 version 4.6, can be characterized as Web-centric (browser/server) using portal technology. SAP extended their offerings with business portals (e.g., market portals) with different focuses to enable collaboration among different business partners. By adding tiers, SAP enabled R/3 to be more adaptable to e-business demands, but the system is still based on a client-server solution, with enhanced communication technologies. In 2002, SAP announced that SAP R/3 Enterprise will replace R/3 4.6.[2] SAP R/3 Enterprise has, basically, the same functionality as the previous version, with a new technological platform. In the new R/3 architecture, functionality and technology are separated to enable different release strategies for different parts of the system. The technology in SAP R/3 Enterprise is based on SAP WEB Application Server, which has been in place for different mySAP.com components, such as the mySAP Business Information Warehouse (SAP's data warehouse). The major implication of this change is that new releases can either be of a technical or a functional nature, and each will have its own release strategy. Furthermore, the functionality, which is represented in the reference model, is divided into Enterprise Core and Enterprise Extensions processes. The first type of process is internally oriented and contains the same functionality as version 4.6, but the process model was optimized and can be separately upgraded. For example, fixed asset accounting and payroll processing are two such Enterprise Core processes that are bounded to a firm, both from practical and legal perspectives. Enterprise Extensions processes include new functionalities, e.g., electronic bank account statements were added to the financial model, and the human resource model was enhanced by mobile time management. The separation of Core and Extensions processes makes it easier for a customer to upgrade those parts of the system that are considered essential.[4] The offerings based on portal technologies have internal and external views and have extended reference models (e.g., e-business process models).

ENTERPRISE PORTALS

Portal-based technologies, such as EPs, are said to reshape the future of information services and information sharing (Wilder et al., 1999). Portals started as Web-based applications providing a single point of access to distributed online information, such as documents resulting from a search, news channels, and links to specialized web sites. Examples of business portals include e-business portals (including consumer, community, and market portals), information portals, knowledge management portals, enterprise portals (EPs), and business intelligence portals — there are no accepted names for the different types of portals. Hence, there are several types of portals with different scopes and focuses. One type is oriented toward information and knowledge management. Another type has its roots in ERP systems. This type builds on the "underlying" ERP system functionality and features and uses the transactional power of the ERP system (Carlsson & Hedman, 2001). The early portal market (1998-2000) was dominated by portal application start-ups and the offerings of portal access to specific ERP applications — the latter described as Web-enabling ERP (Delphi Group, 2001). Beginning in 2000, ERP systems providers, like SAP, PeopleSoft, and Intentia, and other software providers, like IBM, Oracle, and SUN, came on stream. The providers offer platforms targeting portal requirements of e-business firms. The providers' move signals a broad acceptance of portal computing as the next model for enterprise knowledge and information work.

The Core Ideas of Portals

What makes a system a portal and not just another corporate information system? Three capabilities differentiate portals from other corporate information systems: single access point, self-employee service, and personalization (Kotorov & Hsu, 2001; Kim et al., 2000, Hansen & Deimler, 2001; Mack et al., 2001; Markus, 2000; Carlsson & Hedman, 2001; Wilder et al., 1999; Kim et al., 2002).[5]

Single access and authorization point means access, through one access point (i.e., the portal), to the following:

1.   All internal and external applications, e.g., ERP system, CRM system, e-commerce tools, SCM system, e-mail, calendar, and legacy systems
2.   Information, e.g., company newsletters, financial statements, product shipments, document repositories
3.   Internal portals, such as knowledge management portals

The EP keeps track of who is authorized to do what; the EP presents to each user only those resources the user is allowed to see and use. For instance, a customer service representative might have access to certain sales-side e-commerce tools, self-service human resources services, and perhaps, with very low spending limits, to the "company store" for purchasing office supplies. An accounting manager might have access to financial systems, data, and decision support tools, to the store, to the administrative applications, and to communication and personal productivity software.

Self-employee service or B2E (business-to-employee) consists of three parts: online business processes, online people management, and online services to the workplace community. The portal's role is to provide an employee with one place to get not only information but also services. Online business is motivated by reduction of interaction efforts, for example, online scheduling compared with phone or fax, and knowledge repositories with data and information concerning the core business processes of a firm. People management supports the individual worker by providing online training and career development. Furthermore, the portal allows employees to update their personal data, e.g., a new address, which will increase the flexibility for the individual as well as save money for the employer. The third part of self-employee is to bundle work and life, which allows an employee to take care of personal business during working hours, for instance, paying their bills.

Personalization means adapting the portal to individual needs by adding or deleting functionality (Markus, 2000). This is a critical capability of portals.

SAP introduced the concept of roles to support implementation of the portal (PeopleSoft also uses the concept of roles). Initially, it was used as an authorization and administration tool, but has continuously been developed and is today a core design and configuration concept. The roles determine the information, application, and services individuals can access to support them in carrying out their tasks and activities. A role defines an activity set that a portal user, internal or external person or application, undertakes in order to achieve a desired business objective. Roles, rather than persons or functional position, define how a work-task should be performed. Each role can only access information and applications that are included in that specific role. For instance, an internal sales person having the role "sales assistant" can only access the applications and information associated with that role. What information and application requirements a role can have is up to the subjective judgment of the vendor. However, each role can be modified by adding or deleting applications or information. A role in SAP's portal is defined as follows:

> *...a collection of activities that an employee carries out in one or more business scenarios of an organization. Users access the transactions, reports and Web-based applications in a role via a series of menus. Roles are specific to individual employees and match their specific tasks and service/information needs.*

SAP provides some 300+ role templates. These templates are divided into different functional and hierarchical categories (such as accounting, procurement, and management) and different industry solutions (such as automotive and banking). A firm-specific EP can be designed and built using templates, or the roles can be designed and built from scratch without using the templates. A user firm does not have to use the concept of roles; they can choose to label a role as a function. In any case, firm-specific roles are unique because they can be configured by adding or deleting functionality, for example, information reports, access to other applications, or even adding other roles into the role. A role can thereby be developed to reflect changes in a particular task. For instance, if the sales people have to make deeper analysis, e.g., credit rating prior to accepting an order, can this functionality be included into a role? Employees have several roles within a firm — a person might work both as a sales assistant and as an accountant. The solution to this is to allow users (people) to have several roles, e.g., sales assistant and accountant. The benefits of linking information and applications to roles are severalfold:

- Easier administration of users
- Better control of who has access to information and applications
- More convenient log-in procedure for users

However, there can also be drawbacks, such as centralized control of people.

PORTAL TECHNOLOGY

Portal technology or portal architecture is not one technology. It is a number of open technologies or standards bundled together. The IS problem that portals attempts to provide a solution to is the heterogeneity in corporate IS environments. We will illustrate portal technology through SAP's Portal solution.

mySAP Enterprise Portal

SAP AG released several products during the past years in response to demands for e-business solutions. One of their products is mySAP Enterprise Portal, which is, in part, SAP's answer to the growing market for EPs — it is also a new graphical user interface to SAP's other products (e.g., R/3 and CRM solution).

The technologies embedded in mySAP Enterprise Portal are designed from an enterprise information perspective and are structured around four different but complementary sources of enterprise information. The first source is transactional data and legacy systems. This source contains data and information-processing functionality, traditionally found in ERP systems and different databases. Incoming orders, accounts receivable, order status, inventory, billing, production schedules, invoices, etc., are typical data items found here. Furthermore, legacy systems are also included, with firm- or industry-specific data. The second source of information is aggregated data and information (business intelligence in SAP's terminology) that provides a broader perspective on business activities, such as monthly sales reports. This source contains online transaction-processing capabilities, extensions to marketplaces, and data warehouses. The third source of information is unstructured data and information, sometimes referred to as knowledge management systems. Finally, the last source is the external environment, i.e., the Internet. Based on these four information sources, SAP provides a technical architecture enabling users to access all information sources and the required applications to process the information. The technical infrastructure is shown in Figure 1.

The Portal architecture consists of a presentation or user layer, an infrastructure layer (middle part of Figure 1), and the information and the application layers. The presentation layer is where the end-users interact with the portal through requests for information and application functionality in some underlying systems. The underlying systems can be ERP systems, data ware-house systems, Knowledge Management Systems, legacy systems, or third-party systems. The users can be employees, customers, suppliers, or partners of the firm. Which information or applications a user is able to interact with is governed by the user's "role(s)." Role descriptions are found in the portal content directory. End-users may use a variety of devices, such as mobile phones, pocket PCs, and laptops. The bottom layer in Figure 1 illustrates the different sources of data and information and the different applications a user may need to fulfill his or her work-tasks. The portal infrastructure layer functions as a broker between the presentation layer and the information and

Figure 1. Portal Infrastructure (SAP References, 2001-2002)

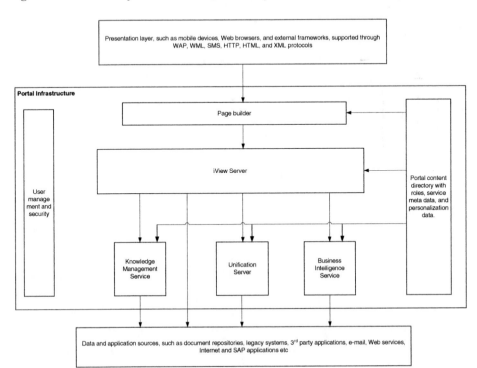

application layers. It consists of page builder, user management and security, portal content directory, iViewServer, knowledge management service, unification server, and business intelligence service. The page builder is used to design user interfaces. User management and security is the administrative part of the portal, where user data repositories are stored, and it is based on LDAP (Lightweight Directory Access Protocol). The iViewServer functions as a connector to the different information and applications sources. It has a repository of predefined connectors, but a firm may develop new connectors. Connectors can be built into most programming languages and will give a consistent XML-based output. Business Intelligence Service contains analysis and reporting, OLAP functionality, and data warehouse capabilities. Knowledge Management Service manages unstructured data and information and functions as a content management system. Finally, the Unification Server manages the integration of data and information from disparate systems.

A CONTENT ANALYSIS OF
AN ENTERPRISE PORTAL

SAP Portals deliver a variety of EPs: Enterprise Information Portal, Enterprise Collaboration Portal, and Enterprise Unification Portal. In addition, SAP Portals offer business intelligence in the form of a toolset for data warehousing, data analysis, and knowledge management, all through SAP's role-based concept. Because the role-based concept is the basis of SAP Portals, we decided to focus our evaluation on the formal roles provided in SAP Portals. Having decided to focus on roles, the evaluation of SAP Portals still presented several difficulties, e.g., the complexity and comprehensiveness of the system, the lack of portal implementations, and the lack of empirical research on portals.

Based on our literature review, we found few academic papers addressing portals. Except for Carlsson and Hedman (2001), they focus on Information and Knowledge Portals, not on EPs. The distinction is that EPs also include transactional data and systems. Three papers are worth mentioning. Kim et al. (2002), using an activity theory perspective, presented and discussed how one commercial portal supports knowledge management activities. Mack et al. (2001) described a knowledge portal developed at IBM. It is a technical description, but it also describes are how work processes are affected by the use of the knowledge portal. Kotorov and Hsu (2001) proposed a management model for portals analogous to the management model for newspaper production, and they argued that the model provides the adequate organizational structure for portals. In searching the literature, we found numerous whitepapers from consulting and portal vendor firms promoting and selling the idea behind portals. For example, Roberts-Witt (1999) presented a list of 50 portals and coined some portal products' concepts, and Vering et al. (2001) described SAP's portal technology.

IS evaluation research has focused on artifacts (like ERP systems) from primarily a positivistic perspective. Hirschheim and Smithson (1999, p. 402) denote this as a *"technical interpretation of evaluation"* since there is a widespread view that information systems are fundamentally technical systems. Following Hirschheim and Smithson (1999), we decided to use an interpretive approach and, specifically, to use a content analysis. In general, content analysis concerns the analysis of texts for occurrences of specific categories or constructs (Miles & Huberman, 1994; Bryman, 2001). Quantitative content analysis is a method of categorizing subjective/qualitative information based on frequency of occurrence. It uses predetermined categories to count the content of sources, like documents, archival records, and articles. It is a method where a researcher "goes by numbers." Using a qualitative content analysis (also referred to as ethnographic content analysis), a researcher "goes by feel and intuition." Through the analysis, categories emerge from the data — the categories are grounded in the data. We decided to do a quantitative content analysis. This will allow researchers to compare different EPs using the model we propose. In order to make the analysis of EP, we had to choose an evaluation model, decide what constructs and categories to use, and develop an analysis procedure. We chose Robert Quinn and associates' competing values model (CVM) (Quinn & Rohrbaugh, 1981, 1983). There were three main reasons for using the CVM. First, it is a well-established framework, and it has been developed and empirically tested in organizational, management, and IS research over a number of years. Second, it has been developed into a model of managerial roles. Third, it is related to the critical construct of individual and organizational effectiveness.

THE COMPETING VALUES MODEL

The Competing Values Model (CVM) is a framework of organizational effectiveness and includes some theoretical underpinnings of organizations (Quinn & Rohrbaugh, 1983). First, CVM views organizations as purposeful systems that exist to achieve certain goals or ends (Scott, 1992). Second,

CVM acknowledges the existence of conflicting goals, which an organization must attain simultaneously time in order to be effective and efficient (Hart & Quinn, 1993). Furthermore, CVM is based on the hypothesis that there is tension between existing underlying value dimensions in organizations (Quinn & Rohrbaugh, 1983). The first value dimension is focus; internal focus puts emphasis on well being in the organization, while external focus addresses the environment. Structure is the second value dimension; stability refers to the need of top management to control, and flexibility refers to adaptation and change (Quinn & Rohrbaugh, 1981, 1983). Using the two value dimensions, four organizational models emerge: human relations model (HR), open systems model (OS), internal process model (IP), and rational goal model (RG) (Figure 2). Quinn (1988) translated the construct of effectiveness into managerial roles — two for each of the four organizational models.

The *IP model* is characterized by a focus on internal stability, and it uses information management, information processing, and communication to develop stability and control. This includes information processing, ensuring that standards, goals, and rules are met, maintaining organizational structure and

Figure 2. Competing Values Model

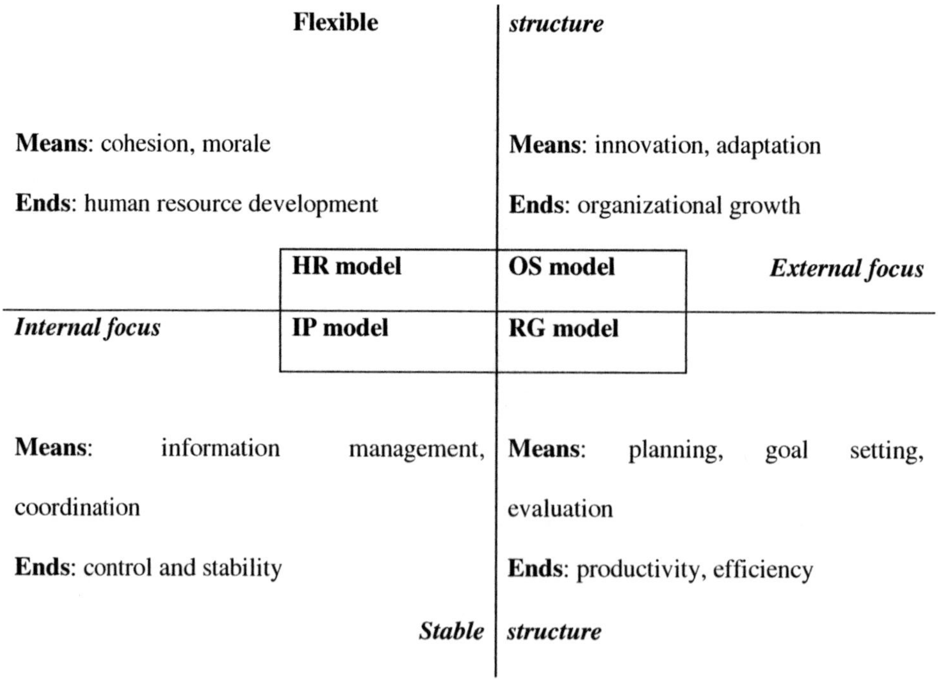

	Flexible	**structure**	
	Means: cohesion, morale	**Means**: innovation, adaptation	
	Ends: human resource development	**Ends**: organizational growth	
	HR model	**OS model**	*External focus*
Internal focus	**IP model**	**RG model**	
	Means: information management, coordination	**Means**: planning, goal setting, evaluation	
	Ends: control and stability	**Ends**: productivity, efficiency	
	Stable	*structure*	

Source: Adapted from Quinn & Rohrbaugh (1981, 1983)

workflow, coordinating activities, as well as collecting and distributing information internally. In the *monitor role*, a manager collects and distributes information (mainly internal and quantitative information), checks performance using traditional measures, and provides a sense of stability and continuity. In the *coordinator role*, a manager maintains structure and flow of the systems; schedules, organizes, and coordinates activities (logistic issues); solves housekeeping issues; and sees that standards, goals and objectives, and rules are met (Quinn, 1988).

The *RG model* is characterized by a focus on external control and relies on planning and goal setting to gain productivity. This includes clarification of expectations, goals and purposes; development of rules and polices; evaluation of performance; decision support; quality control; motivation of organizational members to enhance productivity; sales support; and profit maximization. In the *director role*, a manager clarifies expectations, goals, and purposes through planning and goal setting; defines problems; establishes goals; generates and evaluates alternatives; generates rules and policies; and evaluates performance. In the *producer role*, a manager emphasizes performance, motivates members to accomplish stated goals, gives feedback to members, and is engaged in and supports the action phase of decision making (Quinn, 1988).

The *OS model* is characterized by a focus on external flexibility and relies on readiness and flexibility to achieve growth. Important issues are acquisition of scarce resources, interaction with the external environment, business intelligence, research and development, and maintaining external legitimacy through a network of external contacts. In the *innovator role*, a manager interacts with the environment, monitors the external environment (environmental scanning), identifies important trends, is engaged in business and competitive intelligence, develops mental models, convinces others about what is necessary and desirable, facilitates change, and shares "image and mental models." In the *broker role*, a manager obtains external resources; is engaged in external communications; tries to influence the environment; and maintains the unit's external legitimacy through the development, scanning, and maintenance of a network of external contacts (Quinn, 1988).

The *HR model* is characterized by a focus on internal flexibility to develop employee cohesion and morale. It stresses human resource development, empowerment, team building, internal communications, development of individual plans, feedback to individuals and groups, and development of management skills. In the *facilitator role*, a manager fosters collective efforts, tries to build cohesion and teamwork — building the "trustful organization," facilitates participation and group problem solving and decision making, pursues "moral" commitment, and is engaged in conflict management. In the *mentor role*, a manager is engaged in the development of employees by listening and being supportive, is engaged in the development of individual plans, and gives feedback for individual and team development (Quinn, 1988).

Content Analysis of the Role-Based Concept

We evaluated the whole package of roles provided in mySAP Portals. We used SAP's Web pages to find the role descriptions. We found 433 individually labeled roles. From the 433 roles, we excluded all roles associated with the industry solution of SAP Healthcare and were left with 359 roles. Then we took away duplicates and nonclassifiable roles and ended up with 329 roles. The evaluation of the remaining 329 roles was done in a four-step process, i.e.:

1.   We listed the 329 individual roles found.
2.   Each role was categorized along the value dimensions — internal versus external and stable versus flexible. An example of a role is billing clerk. The tasks a billing clerk moderates are:

> *"the entire procedure for billing document processing, that is, the processing of invoices, credit memos, debit memos and cancellation documents. He is responsible for insuring that the invoices are correct and complete. The billing clerk carries out the following tasks:*
>
> *Entering and processing of invoices, credit memos and debit memos Invoice verification*
> *Creation of invoice lists, lists for credit memos and rebate agreements*
> *Creation of lists for sales orders blocked for billing*
> *Release of sales orders blocked for billing*
> *Settlement of rebate agreements."*

3.   Each role was mapped into the CVM with regard to the value dimensions, i.e., into the four organizational models. The billing clerk role was classified as belonging to the IP model, because the tasks are measured mostly with internal effectiveness measures.
4.   In addition, each role was evaluated regarding its hierarchical level using the following five levels: top-management, middle, operative and support

personnel, experts and specialists, and outsiders (the levels are based on Mintzberg, 1979).

Both authors conducted the evaluation and classification independently of each other (working through Steps 2 through 4 independently). The two outcomes were compared. There was more than an 80% agreement between the two evaluations (some roles were question-marked in the evaluations), which is an acceptable level of intercoder reliability. Where nonagreement remained, the authors evaluated the role again, and a final decision was made.

RESULTS

The evaluation shows that most of the EP roles map to the internal process (IP) model and the rational goal (RG) model, with more roles mapped to the IP model. A summary of the evaluation is depicted in Table 1.

Accordingly, most of the EP roles support IP and RG associated organizational goals. Hence, the EP roles primarily support roles related to efficiency and productivity, and means such as coordination and planning. The hierarchical evaluation showed that primarily operative and middle management roles are supported. This finding is reasonable, because they are likely to support the same goals as the roles associated with the IP- and the RG- models. The strong support of IP is natural because the foundation of this EP is an ERP system, which is largely an internal-oriented system. However, the lack of support for the human relations and the open systems models was a surprise.

Table 1. Evaluation of the Role-Based Concept

CVM	Top	Middle	Operative	Experts	External	Total
Internal process	3	77	83	21	0	**184**
Rational goal	4	33	46	23	8	**114**
Human relations	1	2	2	2	0	**7**
Open systems	5	8	2	9	0	**24**
Total	**13**	**120**	**133**	**55**	**8**	**329**

DISCUSSION

Theoretically, the development of SAP R/3 (its different versions and the launching of SAP R/3 Enterprise) and SAP Portals signals a move away from "strategic leaps" implementation toward more of "continuous improvement." The latter, a path-based approach to IT implementation and improvement, is advocated for today's ERP-enabled organizations (Upton & McAffe, 2000). SAP's development of its products addresses two aspects of how IT can facilitate continuous improvement: *modularity*, to facilitate changes in the system after installation without changing the whole system; and *accessibility*, to provide for easy change of parameters in a system. A third way to facilitate continuous improvement is *inclusiveness*, i.e., to decrease the likelihood that a system is perceived as a black box by its users (Upton & McAffe, 2000) is still not well addressed. Even if the users are trained to use the system (EP) and are involved in the implementation, use of best practice roles might lead to less inclusiveness than if the roles are developed from scratch. At the same time, research suggests that the use of best practice can improve effectiveness and efficiency. The development of a Web-based access technology, i.e., a portal solution, can also be interpreted as a natural development of the graphical user interface of an ERP system.

Our evaluation suggests what organizational models, with their associated roles, are supported by mySAP Portals. The evaluation suggests that the CVM roles associated with the IP and RG models are the roles primarily supported by mySAP Portals. It would be tempting to suggest that the EP is weak, because it seems that there exists an unbalanced support of the CVM roles. Such a suggestion would be based on the fact that a well-balanced support is good. However, such a suggestion misses an important aspect: the context of where the EP is to be used. Studies, based on the CVM, suggest that all organizational effectiveness measures are not equally important and critical all the time. There are changes in the importance of the organizational effectiveness measures in relation to hierarchical levels and what evolutionary stage a firm is in. Quinn and Cameron (1983) found, in relation to the CVM, four different states a firm can be in, namely, entrepreneurial, collectivity, formalization and control, and elaboration of structure state. In the entrepreneurial state, the organizational effectiveness measures in the OS model are critical, and in the collectivity state, the organizational effectiveness measures in the HR model are critical. In the formalization and control state, the measures in the IP and RG models are critical. The elaboration state has a more balanced emphasis of the measures.

Based on Quinn and Cameron's findings, we can argue that the evaluated EP will be more effective in firms in the two latter states and less effective for firms in the entrepreneurial and the collectivity states. In another study it was found there is also a difference in the importance of effectiveness measures in relation to hierarchical levels (Quinn, 1988). Two major findings in the study were that there equal emphases exist for IP model and RG model effectiveness measures, and the importance of the OS model effectiveness measures increase as we move up the hierarchical levels. In relation to our classification, the first finding suggests that although the EP seems to support the IP and RG roles, it does so better for middle- and lower-level managers than for top managers. The second finding in our classification suggests that an important improvement of the EP for top managers would be to better support the roles associated with the OS model. Another improvement, important to all levels, would be to enhance the EP in its support of the roles associated with the HR model.

CONCLUSION AND FURTHER RESEARCH

This chapter, based on an accepted framework of organizational effectiveness, presents a content analysis of the Enterprise Portal mySAP Portal. The evaluation suggests that mySAP Portal's strengths are its strong internal and control focus, and its weaknesses are its lack of external focus and lack of support for top managers. The results challenge the myth and sales arguments made by vendors and consulting firms that the technology (EP) is the silver bullet to all ERP-related problems.

Our evaluation suggests areas where mySAP Portals could be enhanced — primarily in the HR model and in support for top managers. The former is supported by Hansen and Deimler's (2002) discussion on how portals can support business-to-employees (B2E).

Our model for evaluating EPs can be used as a tool for supporting implementation by enhancing or enabling better communication between designers and users. This is achieved by using the evaluation for discussing organizational requirements of EPs and related improvements.

Important limitations of the model are that the following aspects are not taken into account. First, the value of role-support in context is not addressed. The model does not evaluate the value or perceived value of the support given by the different EPs roles. Second, the impact of the environment and technology of the user is not taken into account — some roles are more important than other roles, depending on the environment and technology of a specific organization. Third, the number of each roles in an organization can be problematic — it is likely that some roles will have several users.

EPs is another new IT artefact that will draw much research attention during the coming years. Based on this work, we see two lines of further research: one is related the phenomenon of EPs as such, and one is related to evaluation of ICTs (like EPs).

Research on actual EPs implementation, use, and impact is critically needed. It is important that this research applies a variety of different conceptual and theoretical frameworks and models, such as TAM (Technology Adoption Model), Perceived Characteristics of Innovation (PCI), and Innovation, Diffusion, and Adoption frameworks. This research would be especially interesting if it were possible to compare EPs and ERP systems implementations. Following this, it would be interesting to focus on decision and selection processes, especially if an EP replaces an ERP system. For example, a question worthy of investigation would be, what are the mechanisms that make an organization terminate a US$500 million investment?

Furthermore, research on EP software design processes, focusing on what guides EP design and what the design rationales are, would be of interest. The available information does not indicate how the roles were selected or designed. It is reasonable to assume that the role-based concept is based on a best practice idea (as are the processes in R/3). How does this differentiate from traditional systems development? Are new skills needed, such as cognitive abilities compared to business skills? Studies can also further explore the concept of roles, for example, by using Katz and Kahn's (1978) view of the organization as a system of roles. This might be a fruitful way to explore the role concept using a different theoretical base and might enable a better theoretical consideration of the ICT artifact. EPs can also be studied from an attention-based view of the firm. The main argument of the attention-based view of the firm is that firm behavior is the result of how firms channel and distribute the attention of their decision makers (Ocasio, 1997). It can be argued that portals are a means for firms to channel and distribute the attention of organizational members (Carlsson, 2002). Enterprise portals' possibility to support users' mobility can also be addressed. In this case, mobility will include technical mobility (to different places) and social mobility (in and out of different roles and contexts). For example, Hansen and Deimler (2002) suggested that enterprise portals should also support personal businesses, like paying phone bills, and that this could increase the likelihood that employees would use portals in their jobs.

The other line of research concerns evaluation of ICT. The introduction or diffusion of EPs is related to the research on selection and ex-ante evaluation of ICT. The challenging question is whether content analysis can form a basis for ex-ante evaluation. If so, the approach has to be more rigorously tested and applied in different settings and contexts. Other related questions are what frameworks to apply and what levels of analysis are feasible. Related approaches to this are artifact evaluations (Järvinen, 2000; March & Smith, 1995; Lee, 2000), which could be used as reference procedures. The overall research question this research has to proceed along is: how effective and efficient is the EP artefact and what impact will it have on organizations?

REFERENCES

Adam, F., & O'Doherty, P. (2000). Lessons from enterprise resource planning implementation in Ireland — Towards smaller and shorter ERP projects. *Journal of Information Technology, 15*(4), 305-316.

Agassi, S. (2002). We wanted to be in a position where we could say we're a number one player. *Community Spotlight.* Retrieved July 26, 2002 from the World Wide Web: http://www.sap.com/community/entries/enterpriseportals/spotlight.asp.

Bancroft, N. H., Seip, H., & Sprengel, A. (1998). *Implementing SAP R/3: How to Introduce a Large System into a Large Organization.* Greenwich, CT: Manning.

Carlsson, S. A. (2002). Designing DSS based on an attention-based view of the firm. In F. Adam, P. Brézillon, P. Humphreys, & J. -C. Pomerol (Eds.), *Decision Making and Decision Support in the Internet Age* (pp. 635-646). Cork, Ireland: Oak Tree Press.

Carlsson, S. A. & Hedman, J. (2001). An artefact evaluation of the role concept in SAP's enterprise portal. *Proceedings of the Sixth INFORMS Conference on Information Systems & Technology.* Miami Beach, Florida.

Curran, T. & Ladd, A. (2000). *SAP R/3 Business Blueprint: Understanding the Business Process Reference Model (2nd ed.).* Upper Saddle River, NJ: Prentice Hall.

Davenport, T. & Short, J.E. (1990). The new industrial engineering: Information Technology and Business Process Redesign. *MIT Sloan Management Review,* Summer, 11-27.

Davenport, T. H. (2000a). *Mission Critical: Realizing the Promise of Enterprise Systems*. Boston, MA: Harvard Business School Press.

Davenport, T. H. (2000b). The future of enterprise system-enabled organizations. *Information Systems Frontier, 2*(2), 163-180.

Delphi Group. (2001). *Business portals: The new media for e-business interchange,* White Paper. Boston, MA: The Delphi Group.

El Sawy, O. A. (2001). *Redesigning Enterprise Processes for E-business*. New York: McGraw-Hill.

Esteves, J., & Pastor, J. (2001). Enterprise resource planning systems research: An annotated bibliography. *Communications of the Association for Information Systems, 7*(8).

Hansen, M. & Champy, J. (1993). *Reengineering the Corporation: A Manifesto for Business Revolution*. New York: Harper Business.

Hansen, M.T. & Deimler, M.S. (2001). MCutting costs while improving morale with B2E Management. *MIT Sloan Management Review,* Fall, 96-100.

Hart, S. L., & Quinn, R. E. (1993). Roles executives play: CEOs, behavioral complexity, and firm performance. *Human Relations, 46,* 543-574.

Hirschheim, R., & Smithson, S. (1999). Evaluation of information systems: A critical assessment. In L. Willcocks, & S. Lester (Eds.), *Beyond the IT Productivity Paradox* (pp. 381-409). Chichester, UK: John Wiley & Sons.

Holland, C. & Light, B. (1999). A critical success factors model for ERP implementation. *IEEE Software,* May/June, 30-36.

Jarvinen, P.H. (2000). Research questions guiding selection of an appropriate research method. *Proceedings of the Eighth European Conference on Information Systems,* Vienna.

Kalling, T. (1999). Gaining competitive advantage through Information Technology. A resource based approach to the creation and employment of strategic IT resources. Doctoral dissertation, Lund University. Lund: Lund Business Press.

Katz, D., & Kahn, R. L. (1978). *The Social Psychology of Organizations* (2nd ed.). New York: John Wiley & Sons.

Kim, Y.J., Chaudhury, A., & Rao, H. R. (2002). A knowledge management perspective to evaluation of enterprise information portals. *Knowledge and Process Management, 7*(2), 57-71.

Kotorov, R., & Hsu, E. (2001). A model for enterprise portal management. *Journal of Knowledge Management, 5*(1), 86-93.

Lee, A. S. (2000). Editor's comments: The social and political context of doing relevant research. *MIS Quarterly, 24*(3), v-vii.

Mack, R., Ravin, Y., & Byrd, R. J. (2001). Knowledge portals and the emerging digital workplace. *IBM Systems Journal, 40*(4), 925-955.

March, S. T., & Smith, G. F. (1995). Design and natural science research on information technology. *Decision Support Systems, 15,* 251-266.

Markus, M. L. (2000). Paradigm shifts — E-business and business/systems integration. *Communications of the Association for Information Systems, 4*(10).

Markus, M. L., & Tanis, C. (2000). The enterprise systems experience — From adoption to success. In R. W. Zmud (Ed.), *Framing the Domains of IT Management: Projecting the Future Through the Past* (pp. 173-207). Cincinnati, OH: Pinnaflex.

Miles, M. B., & Huberman, A. M. (1994). *Qualitative Data Analysis* (2nd ed.). Thousand Oaks, CA: Sage.

Mintzberg, H. (1979). *The Structuring of Organizations: A Synthesis of the Research.* Englewood Cliffs, NJ: Prentice Hall.

O'Leary, D. (2000). *Enterprise Resource Planning Systems.* Cambridge, UK: Cambridge University Press.

Ocasio, W. (1997). Towards an attention-based view of the firm. *Strategic Management Journal, 18,* Summer Special Issue, 187-206.

Quinn, R. E. (1988). *Beyond Rational Management: Mastering the Paradoxes and Competing Demands of High Performance.* San Francisco, CA: Jossey-Bass.

Quinn, R. E., & Cameron, K. S. (1983). Organizational life cycles and shifting criteria and effectiveness. *Management Science, 9*(1), 33-51.

Quinn, R. E., & Rohrbaugh, J. (1981). A competing values approach to organizational effectiveness. *Public Productivity Review, 5*(2), 122-140.

Quinn, R. E., & Rohrbaugh, J. (1983). A spatial model of effectiveness criteria: Towards a competing values approach to organizational analysis. *Management Science, 29*(3), 363-377.

Roberts-Witt, S. (1999). Making sense of portal pandemonium. *Knowledge Management,* (July), 37-48.

Ross, J. W., & Vitale, M. R. (2000). The ERP revolution: Surviving vs. thriving. *Information Systems Frontier, 2*(2), 233-241.

Scott, W. R. (1992). *Organizations: Rational, Natural, and Open Systems* (3rd ed.). Englewood Cliffs, NJ: Prentice Hall.

Shanks, G., Seddon, P., & Willcocks, L. (eds.). (2003). *Second-wave Enterprise Resource Planning Systems*. Cambridge, UK: Cambridge University Press.

Tsui, E. (2002). Knowledge portal technologies. In C. W. Holsapple (Ed.), *Handbook on Knowledge Management 2: Knowledge Directions*. Heidelberg: Springer-Verlag.

Upton, D. M., & McAffe, A. P. (2000). A path-based approach to information technology in manufacturing. *International Journal of Technology Management*, 20(3/4), 354-372.

Vering, M., Norris, G., Barth, P., Hurley, J. R., MacKay, B., & Duray, D. J. (2001). *The E-business Workplace*. New York: John Wiley & Sons.

Wilder, C., Davis, B., & Dalton, G. (1999). Data gateway. *Information Week*, 720(February), 18-22.

SAP REFERENCES

SAP. (2000) mySAP technology — Business technology solution map. Solution Brief No. 50044172s, SAP AG.

SAP. (2001a). mySAP technology for open e-business integration — Overview. White Paper No. 50050876, SAP AG.

SAP. (2001b). Portal infrastructure: People-centric collaboration. White Paper No. 50050879, SAP AG.

SAP. (2002a). mySAP technology — Overview. Brochure No. 50047444, SAP AG.

SAP. (2002b). mySAP enterprise portals — Overview. Brochure No. 50056866s, SAP AG.

SAP. (2002c). Managing business heterogeneity. Solution Brief No. 5056681, SAP AG.

SAP. (2002d). SAP R/3 Enterprise. White Paper No. 50056097, SAP AG.

SAP. (2002e). SAP Web application server: Building reliable business applications. White Paper No. 50052038, SAP AG.

SAP. (2002f). Web Dynpro: Professional Web-based user interfaces. White Paper No. 50057743, SAP AG.

SAP. (2002g). Exchange infrastructure: Process-centric collaboration. White Paper No. 50052041, SAP AG.

SAP. (2002h). Security: Secure business in open environments. White Paper No. 50052040, SAP AG.

SAP. (2002i). Globalization: Meeting local and global requirements. White Paper No. 5057742, SAP AG.

ENDNOTES

[1]   mySAP Enterprise Portals is developed and market by SAP Portal Inc., which is a wholly owned subsidiary of SAP AG. The firm was developed through a merger between TopTier (acquired by SAP AG in March 30, 2001), eSAP Gmbh (a German subsidiary focusing on professional services related to enterprise portals and e-business projects), and two of SAP AG's divisions (mySAP Business Intelligence and mySAP Work-place), according to SAP Portals' CEO Shai Agassi, SAP INFO, July 2000.

[2]   For a review of ERP research, see Esteves and Pastor (2001).

[3]   Note: Terms are contantly changing, but to our knowledge correct in the summer of 2003.

[4]   See http://service.sap.com/enterprise, the SAP Service electronic mar-ketplace, for details on SAP R/3 Enterprise.

[5]   Although, the technologies applied by portals do not comprise the factor that differentiates portals from other systems, we still provide an overview of the portal technology in the next section on Portal Technology.

Chapter XIV

Looking to the Future of Enterprise-Wide Systems

Frédéric Adam
University College Cork, Ireland

David Sammon
University College Cork, Ireland

Many readers of this book may come to the conclusion that the collection of chapters presented here yields more questions than answers. This may well be true, but it is more a reflection of the difficulty and enormity of the problems raised by enterprise-wide systems than a failure on our part, and the part of the authors of the different chapters. We are believers that the concept of a unified system serving the needs of the whole corporation is a suitable and exciting target for researchers and IS managers. We are, however, also convinced that it is less straightforward a target to achieve than many software vendors and consultants would like managers to believe.

As early as 1972, Dearden declared his belief that:

> *The notion that a company can and ought to have an expert (or a group of experts) create for it a single, completely integrated super-system — an MIS — to help it govern every aspect of its activity is absurd.*

This statement indicates that, on the one hand, IS specialists have been trying to develop such systems as ERP systems since the beginning of IS times. It also indicates, on the other hand, that it is probably only now that we have the technology and the platforms necessary to achieve such an ambitious objective. This will not happen without extensive research into the design of ERP systems and the *correct approach* to their implementation; or the problems raised by *organisational fit* may persist in keeping failure rates with ERP type systems unacceptably high.

FROM MRP TO ERPII

One key point about the dilemma faced by managers in relation to enterprise-wide systems is whether the different versions of these systems, as they evolved over time, reflect significant progress in our understanding of business processes, and how to support them with large applications, or whether they merely reflect the changing marketing orientations of their vendors.

Looking back over the last 20 years of integrated software packages, firms that have implemented MRP, MRPII, ERP, SCM and CRM systems will be wondering whether this long road was worth travelling or whether key managerial attention and company resources were wasted on pursuing the dreams sold by management gurus and software vendors. For example, a recent 'bizarre trend' (Hayler, 2003) is emerging in the enterprise-wide systems market: the re-implementation and extension of ERP, under the new name of ERP II (Humphries & Jimenez, 2003; Hayler, 2003). As a result, nowadays, in the enterprise-wide systems market, managers, for the most part, want "assurances that the system will deliver the performance and business benefits that were promised when they agreed to sign on the dotted line." That is because they know from bitter experience that "keeping such promises is easier said that done" (Pallatto, 2002). For example, ERP vendors and ERP consultants now talk about collaborative, component-based systems for specific vertical rather than all-encompassing generic ERP; opening and maintaining full communication channels with implementation partners to avoid disputes over business objectives, deadlines, project scope and system design, which were common in ERP implementations; shorter implementation projects; quicker actual Return on Investment (ROI) and benefits realisation; systems implementation knowledge transfer and dedicated system experts for implementation. It is worth questioning whether this ERP market admittance of past problems signals a failure in addressing the critical issues of organisations in terms of previous ERP implementations or are truly aimed at future evolutions of the enterprise-wide systems market addressing ERP post-implementation concerns and emerging organisational requirements?

This question is not merely an intellectual quest by isolated academic researchers to find the truth about enterprise-wide systems, rather, it is a burning issue for managers who now face a fresh vendor push towards a new generation of systems, labelled ERPII or XRP (for eXtended Resource Planning systems). Figure 1 illustrates what vendors seem to be saying ERPII is going to be about. Looking at some of the novelties that are promised to managers, we are led to conclude that ERPII may be more about correcting the errors of previous ERP systems rather than radically reforming any aspect of an organisation. Enterprise-wide systems are supposed to be about integrating key aspects of organisations. Managers may legitimately be wondering just how much integration they have yet to accomplish before they can rest assured that their IT infrastructure has reached maturity. We would also argue, that this blind reliance on the integration paradigm as the driving force in developing enterprise-wide systems can be damaging for the ability of the firm to respond to change and to customer needs. These points have been illustrated in a number of chapters in this book.

It also worth noting that some managers working in organisations with leading edge IT 'know-how', have taken such doubts on board and followed a *best of breed* approach, rather than buying into the ERP market, which enabled them to pick and choose which targets they wanted to pursue and which ones they were not interested in. Such an approach also frees managers from the generic cycles of the ERP software market, whereby additional modules in their software suit become available at regular intervals and must be acquired and implemented even when it does not suit the timing of the company strategy. Best of breed strategies for Information Systems infrastructure building are also a very promising topic, but would warrant another book by themselves.

TOWARD AN AGENDA FOR FURTHER RESEARCH IN ENTERPRISE-WIDE SYSTEMS

In this concluding chapter, we put forward an agenda for further research. Figure 2 uses the most famous normative model of decision making in the IS area, that of Herbert Simon (1977) to illustrate how complex the process of

Figure 1. Enterprise-Wide Systems Evolutions

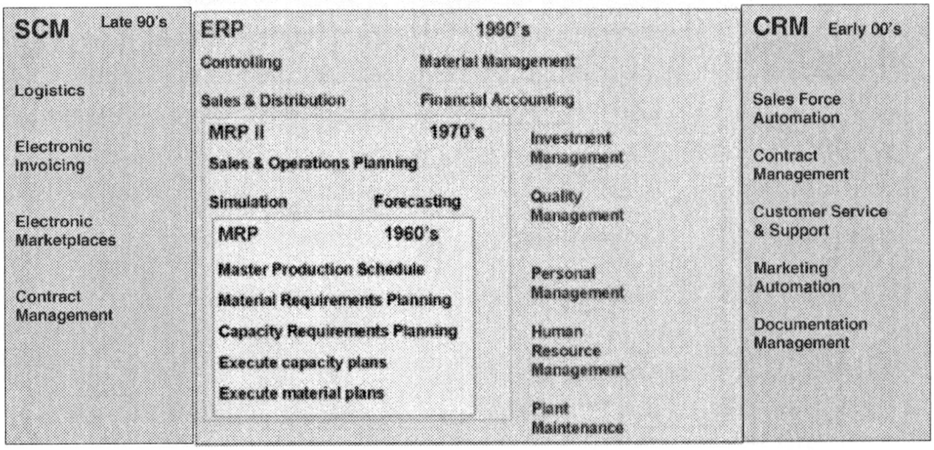

SCM Late 90's	ERP 1990's	CRM Early 00's
Logistics	Controlling Material Management	Sales Force Automation
	Sales & Distribution Financial Accounting	
Electronic Invoicing	**MRP II** 1970's Investment Management	Contract Management
	Sales & Operations Planning	
Electronic Marketplaces	Simulation Forecasting Quality Management	Customer Service & Support
	MRP 1960's	
	Master Production Schedule Personal Management	Marketing Automation
Contract Management	Material Requirements Planning	
	Capacity Requirements Planning Human Resource Management	Documentation Management
	Execute capacity plans	
	Execute material plans Plant Maintenance	

selection and implementation of ERP can be from a research point of view. It shows the different avenues for further research that we see as important for the future of the ERP market.

In an attempt to illustrate the importance of the 'Intelligence' phase of a decision making process and the activities to be conducted to facilitate its completion, the researchers propose a model of 'Organisational Prerequisites'. Organisational Prerequisites are defined as:

> *necessary elements existing within the organization, which are examinable [internally] by the implementing organization, prior to the organization undertaking the initiation of an ERP project.*

Therefore, an organization should be empowered to assess its readiness/ preparedness for the successful implementation of an ERP system prior to project initiation, in a vendor/consultant independent, methodology independent, and pre-implementation thought process.

The objective of the literature-based model, illustrated in Figure 2, which integrally covers the phases which organisations go through when purchasing ERP packages from the identification of the problems facing them to the review of the outcomes of the ERP projects, is to capture their learning experiences. This represents a departure from current ERP literature, which has often focused on the software selection phase as if it were the key to organisational success. It draws on the increasing volume of organisational ERP literature now

Figure 2. Key Areas of Concern for Further Research in Enterprise-Wide Systems

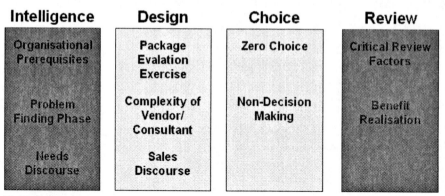

Intelligence	Design	Choice	Review
Organisational Prerequisites	Package Evalation Exercise	Zero Choice	Critical Review Factors
Problem Finding Phase	Complexity of Vendor/ Consultant	Non-Decision Making	Benefit Realisation
Needs Discourse	Sales Discourse		

Vendor-Independent,
Methodology-Independent and
Pre-Implementation thought
process

being published, but also attempts to draw lessons from the traditional research on decision making processes carried out over the last 30 years.

Therefore, as researchers and practitioners we need to keep the following harsh realities in mind and ensure that history does not repeat itself throughout future evolutions of the enterprise-wide systems market. In 1996, FoxMeyer Drug, a $5 billion drug distributor declared bankruptcy after failing to implement an ERP system over a three year period. FoxMeyer sued SAP, the worlds leading supplier of ERP software for $500 million stating that its system was a "significant factor" which brought about the company's financial ruin, this despite the fact that FoxMeyer only spent $30 million dollars on the ERP project (Davenport, 1998). Mobil Europe invested many millions of dollars in an ERP system only to abandon it as a result of objections by its merging partner (Davenport, 1998). Unisource Worldwide Inc. wrote off $168 million in costs when it abandoned its pan-American implementation of SAP software (Bingi et al., 1999). Dell Computers, after months of delay and cost over-runs, abandoned their ERP project because they found that the new system was not appropriate for its decentralised management model (Stefanou, 2000). More recently, Goodyear Tire & Rubber Co. announced that it plans to restate earnings by up to US$100 million for financial periods going back as far as 1998, primarily due to the 'faulty' implementation of SAP in 1999 and 'malfunctions' in inter-company billing systems (Songini, 2003). Hershey's

Food Corporation, Whirlpool, Dow Chemical, Boeing, Apple Computers, Applied Materials have all experienced disasters of varying proportions as a result of ERP implementation projects.

In the recent past, vendors and consultants have tented to discard these stories as mistakes from the beginnings of the ERP market, or at least as not representative of the reality of the ERP market. We do not regard these stories as evidence of the failure of ERP systems either, but we refuse to discard them for they are key symptoms of important problems with off-the-shelf packages that must be solved so that the full potential of enterprise wide systems can be unleashed.

REFERENCES

Bingi, P., Sharma, M., & Godla, J. (1999). Critical issues affecting an ERP implementation. *Information Systems Management*, (Summer), 7-14.

Davenport, T. (1998). Putting the enterprise into the enterprise system. *Harvard Business Review*, (July/August), 131-131.

Dearden (1972). MIS is a mirage. *Harvard Business Review*, (January/ February).

Hayler, A. (2003). ERP II — Déjà vu? *IT Toolbox — ERP Knowledge Base*. Online at: http://erp.ittoolbox.com/documents/document.asp?i=2515 (28/ 10/2003).

Humphries, T. & Jimenez, M. (2003). ERP scenario. In *Proceedings of Software Infrastructure Track at Gartner Symposium ITXPO*, Florence, Italy (March 10-12).

Songini, M.L. (2003). Goodyear Hits $100M Bump with ERP System. Online at computerworld.com: http://www.computerworld.com/industrytopics/ manufacturing/story/0,10801,86744,00.html?from=imutopicheads (1/12/ 2003).

Stefanou, C. (2000). The selection process of enterprise resource planning, ERP, systems. *Proceedings of the 6th Americas Conference on Information Systems*, Long Beach, California (August 10-13, pp. 988-991).

About the Authors

Frédéric Adam is a senior lecturer in the Business Information Systems Group at University College Cork (Ireland) and a senior researcher with the Executive Systems Research Centre (ESRC). He holds a PhD from the National University of Ireland and Université Paris VI (France). His research has been published in the *Journal of Strategic Information Systems*, *Decision Support Systems*, *Journal of Information Technology*, *Systèmes d'Information et Management* and *Journal of Decision Systems* for which he is now editor-in-chief. He is the co-author of the *Manager's Guide to Current Issues in IT* and *Postgraduate Research* (Blackhall Publishing, Dublin, Ireland).

David Sammon is a lecturer in Business Information Systems at University College Cork, Ireland. David holds a BA in Economics and an MSc in Management Information Systems from University College Cork. His current research interests focus on decision making and organisational experiences around data warehousing, enterprise resource planning systems implementation, and ASP adoption. He has presented his research at major international conferences in Europe and in the U.S. and has published in top ranking international journals including *Information Systems Journal* and *DATABASE*.

*   *   *   *   *

Tom Butler is a college lecturer in Information Systems at University College Cork, Ireland. Before joining academia, Tom had an extensive career in the telecommunications industry, chiefly in the development and operation of ICT infrastructures. His research is primarily qualitative, interpretive and case-based in nature and focuses on the development and implementation of IT architectures in organizations. Other research interests include hermeneutics, knowledge management, e-learning, educational informatics, IT education and the digital divide. Tom received his PhD from the National University of Ireland at UCC, where his doctoral research examined the role of IT competencies in building firm-specific IT resources in knowledge-intensive organizations. To contact: tbutler@afis.ucc.ie.

Sven A. Carlsson is a professor of Informatics at School of Economics and Management, Lund University, Sweden. His current research interests include the use of ICT to support management processes, knowledge management, enterprise systems, the use of ICT in electronic value networks, and the use of critical realism in IS research. He has been a visiting scholar at University of Arizona, Tucson; National University of Singapore; and Marshall School of Business, University of Southern California. He is a regional editor for *Knowledge Management Research & Practice* and is on the editorial board of the *Journal of Decision Systems* and *Electronic Journal of Business Research Methods*. He has published in such journals as *Journal of Management Information Systems, Decision Sciences, Information & Management, Journal of Decision Systems, International Journal of Technology Management*, and *Knowledge and Process Management*. To contact: sven.carlsson@ics.lu.se.

Eleanor Doyle is a college lecturer in the Department of Economics at UCC. She completed her PhD in International Trade at the University of Birmingham and has lectured at UCC since 1993. She has actively developed the MBS in Business Economics and has been its academic director since its launch in 1996. She has experience of lecturing, consultancy, and executive development and has published in the areas of business economics and international economics. Her main research interests include the economics of firm strategy (organisational resources and competitive advantage), business macroeconomics, and international competition.

Jonas Hedman is a PhD candidate at the School of Economics and Management, Department of Informatics, Lund University, Sweden. He has been responsible for the development of their e-business management program and SAP university alliance program. He has been published in international conferences, published in the *European Journal of Information Systems*, and recently published a book entitled *IT and Business Models: Concepts and Theories*.

Kevin Higgins graduated from University College Cork (1999) with a Bachelor of Commerce before pursuing a two-year MBS programme in Managerial Accounting and Information Systems. After spending six months in Boston on internship with Fidelity Investment, he returned to write his research dissertation on ERP Systems and Competitive Advantage. He is currently studying toward his accounting professional exams and has recently joined the Group Finance Team in Ulster Bank, Ireland.

David Lawlor left University College Cork in 2001 with a BA in Economics and Computer Science and an MBS Masters in Managerial Accounting and Information Systems. He joined Kentech Engineering, a company involved in the construction of oil refineries all around the world, as a systems analyst. His main role involved setting up and implementing a database to keep track of materials and labour used as well as reporting progress on a number of projects. He then joined Stryker Instruments (a leading medical device provider) as a supply chain specialist in charge of planning/buying and logistics for one of the production cells. He is currently working on bringing in a new ERP system, JD Edwards, as the current PRMS system is out dated. Another project he is involved with will see the implementation of Lean Manufacturing at Stryker Instruments, Ireland.

Peter O'Doherty is a business analyst and project leader with Seabrook Research Limited, an Irish software company based in Cork and Dublin specializing in ERP software implementation. He has more than 15 years experience in the deployment of IT resources and has been helping companies carrying out successful ERP implementations for the last 10 years. He is also an associate researcher of the Executive Systems Research Centre (ESRC) at University College Cork, Ireland, and has special interest in developing project management methodologies better suited to ERP projects.

Bill O'Gorman is a lecturer in Management at University College Cork (UCC), Ireland, teaching Manufacturing Systems, Enterprise Management, Small Business Ventures, Organisation Development, and Quality Management; and is also director of the Diploma in Family Business Management. Prior to joining UCC, Bill, originally qualified as an engineer in industrial electronics, and accrued over 25 years of industrial experience working in several multinational corporations (MNCs) and as managing director of his own electronics sub-contract company. His breadth of experiences ranges from process engineering, through production management, manufacturing and engineering management to general management. As part of his role as academic mentor to the students' entrepreneurship society, E-Soc, he also supports the Technology Transfer Initiative (TTI) develop closer practical links between industry sectors and the university. Bill is a director of the South Eastern Business Innovation Centre (SEBIC), who is responsible for nurturing micro-industries and nascent entrepreneurs in the South East region of Ireland. He has also served as external examiner to the electronics and engineering departments of both Carlow and Waterford Institutes of Technology. His research is focused on examining the linkages between multinational corporations and indigenous companies.

Aidan Pyke is a lecturer in the Department of Adult & Continuing Education, Cork Institute of Technology, Ireland. Aidan has a lengthy career in materials and logistics for major manufacturers in Ireland. His research interests centre on the issues surrounding the implementation and use ERP systems in manufacturing organizations. To contact: aidanpyke@eircom.net.

Peter B. Seddon is an associate professor in the Department of Information Systems at the University of Melbourne, Australia. His teaching and research interests focus on helping people and organizations make more effective use of Information Technology. His particular research interests are (1) evaluation of information systems success, (2) packaged enterprise application software, and (3) IT outsourcing. Peter is on the editorial boards of a number of publications, and has recently completed a term as an associate editor for *Management Information Systems Quarterly*.

Graeme Shanks is professor in the School of Business Systems at Monash University, Australia. His teaching and research interests include implementation and impact of enterprise systems, information quality, conceptual modelling and decision support systems. Graeme has published the results of his research widely in journals and conferences and he is on the editorial board of the *Journal of Data Warehousing* and the *Journal of Knowledge Management Research and Practice*.

Lorraine Staehr is a lecturer in the Department of Information Technology at La Trobe University, Australia. Her research interests are in the business benefits of ERP systems, women in computing, and information systems education. She has published research papers in a number of international conference proceedings and journals.

Mark Synnott graduated from University College Cork (Ireland) with an MBS in Managerial Accounting and Information Systems in 2002. As part of his degree, he wrote a dissertation on ERP implementations in multi-national corporations. He now works for Intel in Ireland.

Index